# FAST CYCLE TIME

## *How to Align Purpose, Strategy, and Structure for Speed*



**Christopher Meyer**

Foreword by Peter M. Senge

THE FREE PRESS
*A Division of Macmillan, Inc.*
NEW YORK
Maxwell Macmillan Canada
TORONTO
Maxwell Macmillan International
NEW YORK OXFORD SINGAPORE SYDNEY

The Free Press
A Division of Macmillan, Inc.
866 Third Avenue, New York, N. Y. 10022

Maxwell Macmillan Canada, Inc.
1200 Eglinton Avenue East
Suite 200
Don Mills, Ontario M3C 3N1

Macmillan, Inc. is part of the Maxwell Communication Group of Companies.

Printed in the United States of America

printing number

4 5 6 7 8 9 10

**Library of Congress Cataloging-in-Publication Data**

Meyer, Christopher
Fast Cycle Time: how to align purpose, strategy, and structure for speed / Christopher Meyer.
p. cm.
Includes bibliographical references and index.
ISBN 13: 978-1-4165-7624-2 ISBN 10: 1-4165-7624-X
1. Industrial management. 2. Just-in-time systems. 3. New products—Management. 4. Manufacturing resource planning.
I. Title.
HD31.M417 1993
658.5'6—dc20 93-7306
CIP

*This book is dedicated to Nancy, Frank, and Breckin—*
*whose love is present all the time*

# *Contents*

# *Foreword*

Ever since I first heard the term I've had a sort of love-hate relationship with time-based competition—competing through shortening organizational cycle times. The basic logic is compelling. Long cycle times in distribution, order filling, new product development, and services of all types increase instability, create unnecessary costs, and frustrate customers. Conversely, shortening cycle times can be a high leverage approach to improving costs, innovativeness, and customer service.

What has concerned me is not the logic but the implementation of the logic. In particular, I believed American corporations, ever in search of the "quick fix," would see this as the ultimate bromide. By trying to "speed up," we would simply take one more step in a long-term trend of shortening time horizons, discounting the past, and living for the moment. Overstretched workers would be stretched a bit more. Managers distracted by crisis after crisis would find even less time for reflection and planning. "Do it faster" was not a message I welcomed.

Fortunately, Chris Meyer shows that becoming a "fast cycle time" competitor is not about running around even more like chickens with our heads cut off. It is not about "turning the crank faster—a sort of cardiac stress test for organizations." It is definitely not about simply setting more demanding cycle time targets and then driving everyone to meet those goals. As Meyer points out, "If people try to do more and more in the same amount of time, they will likely just end making more mistakes." In one study done at MIT, we found that focusing narrowly on cycle time targets can also invite game-playing. For example, in one case, management targets for dramatic reductions in new product development time led people to focus on the new products that were easiest to complete—leaving aside the riskiest and potentially most important new developments. Management's goals were met while the company's stock price steadily declined.*

Being a fast cycle time competitor *is* about carefully designing and developing multifunctional teams, and changing the larger organizational structures that thwart such teams from functioning. It is about redesigning work processes so that people can focus on value-added time and eliminate nonessential work. In sum, it is an integrated and methodical approach focused on purpose and strategy, process redesign, and learning how to work together across organizational "stovepipes" that have traditionally fragmented our efforts.

Meyer interrelates many pieces that we have all read about in different places into a coherent guide to making it happen. The emphasis is on implementation. Ironically, as Chris Meyer shows, implementing fast cycle time means almost the opposite of what most American managers are inclined to do. In a culture of instant gratification and a management system based on "results tomorrow," the hardest lessons may be learning that speeding up our organizational systems depends on fostering commitment, carefully analyzing underlying processes and systems, and building a foundation for ongoing learning—the very attributes of the Japanese and other Eastern cultures that have been winning at time-based competition.

Not too long ago my ten-year-old was playing a game to see how quickly he could add a column of numbers. After several trials he was unable to improve below 30 seconds. The more he tried to cut the time, the more he fidgeted, jumped around, and did everything he could to "speed himself up." But his time didn't improve. Finally, I suggested that the only way to improve further was actually to be more still, to eliminate wasted effort. By moving less, by trying less hard and relaxing, he could actually devote all of his energies to the task. His time improved to 20 seconds.

As time-based competition fast becomes a management buzzword for the 1990s, businesses of all types are realizing that time is both a competitive weapon and a meaningful organizational yardstick.

* F. Kofman, N. Repenning, and J. D. Sterman, "A System Dynamics Approach to TQM," Sloan School of Management Working Paper, Fall 1992.

The problem is is how to do it. Most of the available books describe the concept—but not the process of becoming a fast cycle time competitor. Many years of practical experience have shown Meyer and his colleagues the wisdom of a paradox, the very paradox my son encountered—that to speed up you often have to slow down.

PETER M. SENGE

Center for Organizational Learning
MIT
Cambridge, Mass.

# *Preface*

In 1989, Nick Nichols at the California Institute of Technology asked me to teach a course on fast cycle time for executives. Having forgone an academic career for the business world fifteen years earlier, my first temptation was to say no. Of all my concerns, I was most anxious knowing that no one ever changed a company's way of doing business in a classroom. Fast cycle time is a new way of managing that a student can only taste, and a teacher only simulate, in the classroom setting. At best, I could create a simulator that caused people to want to "fly" the real thing.

On the positive side, putting a course together would require all of us at the Strategic Alignment Group to review our implementation experience and to distill the common threads. Furthermore, explaining them to others would inevitably invite challenges that in turn would clarify and drive our thinking further. We realized that we would probably learn as much as, if not more than, the participants—and so I said yes.

During these sessions, participants ask for literary references on fast cycle time. Without exception, the available literature is slim: Most articles and books focus on why one should pursue cycle time reduction but say little about how to do it. The need for a book that detailed implementation became obvious. This book aims to fill that need.

In writing this book, I have blended twenty years of organization strategy and design know-how with my experience as an executive change agent. Fast cycle time will not be in place until people behave differently. It has to be packaged, presented, chewed on, and eventually swallowed before speed becomes a way of life. As difficult as organizational life may sometimes be, we must never forget that organizations are social systems. People make up organizations, and their behavior that must change if we are to improve performance.

*Fast Cycle Time* integrates all the key elements required for implementing fast cycle time. In doing so, I draw on the work and experience of those who have gone before me in the fields of cycle time reduction, strategic management, organizational design, system dynamics, and organizational change. My efforts have been to synthesize their contributions into an experienced-based, implementation framework that works; and not to create new theory.

Therefore several people who have guided my learning deserve acknowledgment, although not responsibility for the contents of this book. Herb Shepard and Neely Gardner taught me through love and humor that the human spirit is the primary source of all that happens within organizations. Jonno Hanafin daily redefines for me what support, insight, and friendship are all about. Just when I think I'm learning at top speed, Steve Pile's love of learning hits me in the rear and forces me to learn even faster. Rick Ross' indefatigable quest for how-tos that are "slam-dunk winners" always challenges me to clarify my thinking. Joyce Ross's value-based judgment and intellectual discipline make mistakes harder for me to make. My ability to understand and apply systems thinking to cycle time would not have been possible without the efforts and patience of Barry Richmond, Mark Paich, Mike Goodman, and Peter Senge.

Several people have contributed directly or as sounding boards during the development of this book. David Brown taught me that truth and common sense are the best tools for making rapid decisions and recovering from mistakes. John Walker helped me test these ideas in cultures other than my own. Bob Larson taught me about speed and balance. Michael Brown showed me how feedback and learning tie to action through his ability to do both in real time. Karen Stewart gave new meaning to "just do it." Steven Wheelright demonstrated that crisp thinking and good theory are good practice. Ken Lee, Pierre Patkay, and Joe Shepela all pushed back when it was needed. John Turner, Bill Westhaus, Dick Hartshorn, and Al Solvay each helped me refine what fast cycle time could mean to a large organization. Nick Nichols, Valerie Hood, and the rest of the staff at the Industrial Relations Center at the California Institute of Technology started this ball rolling and helped me to learn from every executive who attends the seminar by taking the work out of teaching. For everything I learned from each executive participant in the course, my thanks.

By its very nature, implementation pulls the best from several sources, many of which blur after years of work. My thinking has been directly influenced by the contribution of many professional colleagues. Although it is impossible to list all or define the order of importance, my thanks to Jim Swartz, Jack Sherwood, Ralph Gomery, George Stalk, Ed McCracken, Ken Coleman, Roselie and Andre Schwager, Don Reinertsen, Geary Rummler, Bill Moon, Chuck House, Charles Golden, Marvin Patterson, Carl Shelton, Denny Gallagher, Bill Pasmore, John Adams, Laura Susman, Randi Brenowitz, John Carter, Carolyn Luckensmeyer, Michael Doyle, Larry Wilson, Steve Berkley, Mark Wilson, Tom Fahey, Roger Harrison, Larry Greiner, Warren Bennis, Bernie Huth, Mark Jackson, Charlie Szuluk, Bud Marx, Ken Kohrs, Stephen Jenks, Jim Kouzes, Del Stover, Jon Younger, John Alden, Bill Lambert, Ted Pittiglio, Wolfgang Hausen, Bill Miller, and Max Hall.

The clients of the Strategic Alignment Group provide the laboratory for our work. Without their support, all of what follows would not be possible. In each and every case, they have joined in the hunt for fast cycle time with enthusiasm and persistence. It is not us but they who actually transform organizations into fast cycle time dynamos.

The thinking within this book is blessed by the testing and scrutiny given it by the staff of the Strategic Alignment Group. Jonno Hanafin, Steve Pile, Sarah Engel, and Tim Fredel have contributed by testing, applying, and refining these concepts daily. Rick Ross, Peter Senge, Dan Kim, and Steve Wheelwright all provided insightful comments that improved the final product. Marci Kahn keeps my life in order and tirelessly picks up each new challenge. Through her support, dictation tapes, handwritten scrawls, and weekend phone calls were transformed into this book.

This project would not have happened if Jim Levine had not guided and supported me during the entire period. Lisa Cuff and Bob Wallace provided encouragement, enthusiasm, and insightful suggestions that turned a good manuscript into a better one.

The most important of my thanks go to my family. Frank and Breckin were drafted (as children are) to follow my relocations from Los Angeles to Houston and back to the Bay Area. Their love, caring, and humor have always provided more nourishment and learning than they know. My wife, Nancy, is always a glowing spirit of light, silent editor, and the person who fuels my excitement for this work while reminding me of the other worlds and realities that really matter in life.

# PART ONE

## *FCT Introduction and Core Concepts*

# 1

# Implementing Fast Cycle Time

## *The Simultaneous Act of Letting Go and Adding On*

This book is a pragmatic guide for implementing a fast cycle time strategy (FCT). Authors such as Stalk and Hout[1] provide the basic rationale for a fast cycle time strategy and demonstrate the dimensions of success possible. Yet they say relatively little about how to put their ideas into practice. Regrettably, far too many implementation efforts begin and end with an externally driven, expert analysis that identifies cycle time barriers and bottlenecks. The experts identify the problems but don't specifically define how to design and implement changes that create lasting improvement.

To transform a traditional organization into a fast cycle time competitor requires a systemic organizational change strategy combined with cycle time reduction methods and tools. The strategy has to define what the organization has to let go of as well as what it must simultaneously add to reduce cycle time. When top management actively leads this change process from within, cycle time reductions as high as 100% are possible. This book presents an implementation blueprint based on twenty years of hands-on experience in organizational change and re-design combined with five years experience implementing fast cycle time strategies. By focusing on implementation, we hope to give life to the basic concepts underlying FCT.

Fast cycle time implementation transforms the entire organization. Implementation is complete only when all those in the organization change their behavior and treat time as a valuable resource just as they would capital, technology, or people. To do this, they must first understand the value of FCT. Then they must have the skills and the tools to identify and pursue cycle time opportunities. All of this must be blended into a clear and simple change strategy that facilitates the letting go process. This book shows how to do that by:

1. Demonstrating how to transmit a systemic focus for speed through strategic alignment
2. Illustrating the importance of increasing the speed of organizational learning through redefining core work processes and structures
3. Defining how to create effective multi-functional teams that cut through organization "silos" or "chimneys"
4. Detailing how to analyze and redesign work for speed that uses the redesign process itself to create immediate improvements
5. Providing specific tactics for implementing fast cycle time in product development—from product planning through the mass production ramp
6. Detailing the leadership behaviors necessary to implement FCT
7. Providing measurements that support and monitor fast cycle time implementation

This book also shows how to implement the "soft" elements of the fast cycle time strategy: strategy development, multi-function team effectiveness, process improvement, and empowerment. Although these issues may be less tangible, their impact is anything but soft. By using cycle time, which is considered "hard" by most managers, one can legitimately address the critical soft issues. As the reader will see, sustained cycle time improvement depends more on improving the firm's social architecture than its technological assets. This book provides tools for making these less tangible issues easier to address.

We will use product development as a focus because it and other forms of "knowledge work" have an enormous potential impact on profits and growth. Implementing fast cycle time in knowledge work has received significantly less attention by cycle time experts than the more tangible processes such as paper flow or manufacturing. Because the cycle time of knowledge work is often longer and the steps less tangible than manufacturing, it is harder to address. Our implementation framework for product development can be adapted to other forms of knowledge work, such as marketing. For those readers who need to reduce cycle time in downstream operations, all the techniques and models that apply to knowledge work can be applied with even greater ease to manufacturing, for example. It is much easier to transfer cycle time reduction processes designed for less tangible processes to those that are more tangible; however, the reverse is not true.

## How to Read This Book

This book is divided into two sections. The first section provides the conceptual foundation of the FCT strategy, and the second focuses on implementation. If this is your first contact with the FCT strategy, we suggest you begin at the front. If you have a basic understanding of the concept and are focused on implementation, then you will want to skim this section and concentrate on the second one. Others may read as we do and selectively choose chapters that fit their particular needs. To facilitate that, the list below captures the essence of the remaining chapters.

### *Part 1*

*Chapter 2—Be Fast or Be Last: The Competitive Mandate for Fast Cycle Time.* Why fast cycle time is a competitive requirement in the 1990s, how the rules have changed, and why moving FCT upstream into new product development provides a sustainable competitive advantage.

*Chapter 3—Fast Cycle Time: The Basics.* What fast cycle time is and is not, characteristics of world-class cycle time companies, and the internal and external benefits one can expect.

*Chapter 4—Systems and Organizational Learning: The Foundation for Fast Cycle Time.* Defines the paradigm shift required from traditional thinking and organizational models to support implementation.

### *Part 2*

*Chapter 5—Strategic Alignment: Moving Up and to the Left.* Details how to create strategic alignment between purpose, strategy, and structure to enable speed at the working level; explains the role of executive management.

*Chapter 6—Structuring for Speed: Designing and Implementing Multifunctional Teams.* Details how to architect and implement multifunctional Teams including structure, reward systems, team development, and relationship to the functional organization.

*Chapter 7—FCT Process Redesign.* Details how to define, analyze, redesign, and implement new processes to increase the value-added time and reduce the non-value-added time.

*Chapter 8—Tools and Tactics to Speed Product Development.* Details specific tools and tactics for new product development that increase value-added time and increase the speed of learning.

*Chapter 9—Implementation Dynamics and Measures.* Details the implementation process and measures used to make FCT the way you manage your business.

*Chapter 10—Leaders Pave the Road Ahead.* Details the change process dynamics and the leader's role during the change process, followed by a closing summary.

---

Throughout we will refer to a running case study of Core Products' experience defining and implementing FCT, as well as multiple other examples. Let's get started.

# 2

# Be Fast or Be Last

## *The Competitive Mandate for Fast Cycle Time*

### The Competitive Situation

The competitive position of U.S. industry is under serious and increasing challenge. Some simplify the problem by saying we've grown fat and lazy, while others point to the lack of cooperation between business, government, and labor. Some decry the lack of inexpensive capital or the ever-growing national deficit. The analysis and arguments are seemingly endless. On the one hand, there is no question that the decline in U.S. competitiveness results from a complex web of factors that require definition and thorough analysis prior to action. On the other hand, one is reminded of George Bernard Shaw's comment that put end to end, all the economists in the world couldn't reach a conclusion.

In an increasingly competitive environment, providing top value for a price is a rapidly moving target. To sustain growth, a firm has to refine current products continually as well as introduce new ones faster than its competitors. As the competition heats up, product life cycles shorten. Shorter life cycles mean that whoever gets there first garners the bulk of market share while the remainder are left to compete on price. Those who are late find that the product life cycle ends too soon after introduction, thus making the cost of each development quite expensive.[1]

Witness the trials of the U.S. auto industry. Sales incentives and rebates were originally designed to manage end-of-life product transitions;

they were a vehicle to stimulate sales and thus avoid large write-downs of outdated inventory. Over the years, rebates have been used earlier and earlier in a car's lifetime, to the point that some actually start with the introduction of the new model. What happened? As foreign competitors turned up the heat, U.S. models quickly lost their remaining competitive advantage, so that they were almost outdated at the time they were introduced. Once a product or service's perceived value is no longer inherently compelling, price becomes the primary basis for competing. One has only to look at the enormous losses in the auto industry to understand the futility of price only competition.[2]

The competitive pressure also propels greater product differentiation. Most markets have segmented into smaller markets, with the result that there are now more products than before *and less* revenue per product. If increased development speed is achieved solely by allocating more resources to each individual effort, then the firm must limit the number of new products it can afford to develop for the same cost. Without a significant improvement in development productivity, some markets must be abandoned to provide resources for the remaining ones.

The picture is not all doom and gloom. Several competitors have stepped up to this challenge successfully. Hewlett-Packard has continued to dominate the desktop computer printer market by regularly upgrading its product's price/performance ratio ahead of domestic and international competition. Quantum Corporation, a leading disk-drive manufacturer, has become a major turnaround story as it has added speed to already strong capabilities in product performance and quality. Federal Express and Cable News Network have created businesses that use speed as their primary operating premise. Each of these companies shares one thing in common: the ability to operate in *fast cycle time* (FCT).[3]

The basic premise of FCT is shortening the overall business cycle, which begins with the initial identification of a customer's need and concludes with the receipt of payment for the product shipped or service delivered. The overall cycle is composed of many subcycles (the new product development cycle, production cycle, sales cycle, hiring cycle, and so on) and repeats itself based on how well the product or service continues to meet customers' needs. The business expands or contracts based on how well it continues to satisfy their needs over time.[4]

Every time the business completes a full cycle, it accumulates raw data about the relationship between itself and its customers. How fast this data is transformed into learning determines the rate at which the organization can adapt and change. Cycle time advocates assert that learning is at the heart of a sustained competitive advantage. FCT competitors are fast not because they handle complexity any better than their competition, but because they consistently strive to eliminate complexity whenever possible. Complexity and speed do not mix. FCT is based on the premise that business is basically simple to understand; it's just extremely difficult to execute.

*Rule 1: The competitor who consistently, reliably, and profitably provides the greatest value to the customer first, wins.*

There are no other rules.

### *FCT and New Product Development*

To date, the majority of cycle time improvement efforts have been in downstream operations. Projects are easier to launch there, because the work itself is tangible. For example, there have been many successful applications of FCT to order-fulfillment processes and manufacturing.[5] An order can easily be tracked through the entire system until fulfillment; even when it gets lost in a bureaucratic quagmire, the order ticket itself provides a tangible target. The same occurs in manufacturing, where parts are tracked from the moment they land on the receiving dock to the time they reach the shipping dock in the form of a final product. Depending on the particular business, these may provide the highest leverage points for improvement. In those cases, these opportunities should be pursued.

In many businesses, however, this is not the case. For example, the manufacturing cycle time for a car is less than a day, whereas the development cycle time for a new automobile in the United States is approximately 48 months. By moving FCT upstream, one begins to achieve significant leverage. The root cause of major manufacturing cycle time improvements begins with product and process design. Design for manufacturability and design for assembly provide enormous leverage to reduce manufacturing cycle time.

Focusing on new product development extends FCT process improvement into knowledge work. Although many who have been successful with FCT in manufacturing suggest that the same methods can be used, experience suggests otherwise. The principles are valid, but knowledge work uses a fundamentally different process than manufacturing; hence it requires a different approach to cycle time improvement. For example, product development lacks the predefined statement of outcomes or established processes that manufacturing has. One knows what the car is supposed to look like and how it should be built before it starts down the assembly line, whereas no one knows what the design is supposed to look like in the styling studio. In contrast to the repetitive routine of production, knowledge work has a large, nonroutine component to it. This requires a modification in cycle time reduction methodology. This book will focus on how to achieve fast cycle time within new product development as a vehicle to extend its leverage upstream.[6]

For those readers whose interest is in downstream operations, this book will help you for several reasons. First, although the proportions are different, the amount of knowledge work in manufacturing is increasing daily. In several industries, manufacturing process development is more knowledge intensive than product development. Second, although FCT techniques that work well in downstream tangible processes do not translate well upstream, the reverse is not true. FCT techniques that work with intangible upstream processes provide a good starting point for downstream cycle time reduction. Third, major downstream cycle time problems often are caused upstream. By understanding the differences in implementation, one can exert greater influence.

One cannot expect current products to carry the burden of a company's growth indefinitely. New products and services become the seeds that fuel continued growth. As customer needs and technologies change, products and services that at one time created competitive advantages eventually become liabilities. To become a market leader over time, one has to increase the value delivered to the customer constantly by rapidly introducing new products and services that refresh current offerings and add to them.

The success of Japanese autos in the United States is tightly linked to the value built into new products such as the Lexus and Infinity models. These new product lines have helped Japan to displace Germany as the country's largest volume source of imported luxury cars. Citibank leapt to the top of U.S. mortgage lenders by introducing a mortgage program based on fifteen-minute approval cycles. Even the rapidly growing computer market has seen companies like Sun Microsystems join the Fortune 500 by offering the latest performance before such traditional competitors as IBM or Digital Equipment Corporation.

As suggested by Wheelwright & Clark, new product development reinvigorates an organization internally.[7] It is the channel through which new ideas are introduced to the enterprise that challenge existing assumptions about what customers value. The process energizes and changes us in the same way that young children do in our families and personal lives. Just as children moving on and being successful in the world creates proud parents, successful products bring attention and credit to the firm.

The value of an FCT product development strategy is beginning to be more and more accepted by business leaders. But there is little written that describes the path one takes to transform an organization from a slow, traditional, functionally based product developer to a fast, network-based development dynamo. Although our examples focus on new product development, the principles apply to service development and other value delivery process.

### *Why Has Speed Become a Competitive Requirement?*

Speed was not always a requirement. In fact, as long as every competitor marches to the same beat, speed isn't necessary. It becomes a competitive requirement when someone marches faster *and* they are rewarded for it. Such is the Federal Express story. As a graduate student, founder Fred Smith conceived the idea of overnight small-package delivery. At that time, no one was clamoring for such a service. In fact, existing air freight companies were astounded at the high rates Federal Express initially quoted. Using outdated pricing models based on weight and size, traditional air freight suppliers laughed at Smith's idea.

Herein lies the heart of why speed has become a competitive requirement. *As long as the global rate of change continues to accelerate, the competitor who not only recognizes the change but acts on it can achieve a competitive advantage.* To be sure, Smith's Memphis single-hub concept was daring *at that time.* Today, not only does Federal Express use a hub system, but so do most of the domestic passenger airlines.

There are four domains of change that drive the requirement for faster cycle times. The first is the dramatic increase in global competition. To underscore this, let's quickly roll back the clock to the 1950s. At that time, the United States dominated every global market it chose to play in, as well it should have. Germany and Japan were decimated by World War II, as was Europe at large. In addition, the cold war artificially divided Europe into east and west. And what we think of today as the Third World was what might well have been termed the Fourth World on a comparative basis; it was truly underdeveloped in economic and educational terms. In short, the United States was not a better global competitor—it was the *only* global competitor. Add the fuel of a huge, pent-up domestic demand, and one can readily imagine how these times gave birth to the long-running Broadway show *How to Succeed in Business Without Really Trying.*

Contrast those days with the 1990s. Japan is the acknowledged global economic powerhouse, Germany is reunited, and the European Economic Community is the largest single market in the world. The developing or Third World is truly that, and membership has rotated as such countries as Singapore, Taiwan, and Malaysia transform themselves into bustling economic centers. In short, the global economic environment is once again robust and vibrant. *When the competitive environment heats up, players seek any advantage they can.* Speed is one such advantage.

This can be readily seen in the personal computer (PC) industry. For example, during the 1980s, branded manufacturers such as IBM and Compaq dominated the PC market. As the 1990s began, the underlying technology and manufacturing processes became sufficiently stable that the established brands no longer justified the premium price they historically commanded relative to the "no-name" clones. The added value of buying IBM and Compaq was no longer a better deal than picking up a Taiwanese clone such as Acer. Almost overnight, customers' concern about buying clones disappeared. They voted with their dollars, and IBM and Compaq experienced major drops in revenues, market share, and stock price. Once established as legitimate providers of quality machines, the clone manufacturers continued to gain share by providing the latest features faster and cheaper than the majors. In the portable segment, Toshiba was the first to provide affordable color and a broad line of lightweight models in the market created by Compaq. Clone manufacturers now dominate the market for laptop and smaller personal computers.

This example is dramatic, but hardly unique. Global competition has turned the competitive standings in the auto industry upside down. Even where the United States still holds a dominant market share, as in the commercial aircraft industry, there are such significant competitors as the European consortium, Airbus Industries. In July 1992, United Airlines placed a multibillion dollar order with Airbus instead of Boeing, its historical supplier. Add to this the unrealized potential from the fall of state-controlled economies in Russia and Eastern Europe, and there is little question that competition will continue to increase.

The second change driving FCT is the accelerating pace of technology development. Technology enables us to make more intelligent products that require less space than ever before. Think about where color vacation pictures were developed twenty years ago. Many people sent them to Kodak's film processing laboratories using prepaid mailers. About ten years ago, Fotomat appeared, along with supermarket and drugstore photo finishing. Today, there are one-hour photo finishing outlets throughout the world, and the free-standing Fotomat store has nearly disappeared. What enabled this to happen? The equipment required to turn film into prints no longer fills a factory; it fits in the corner of a store and is almost totally automatic. Intelligence and miniaturization are being built into cameras, microwaves, cars, and even toilets now sold in Japan.

Note that these changes are driven not by breakthrough technologies but by the refinement of existing technologies. *The competitor who incorporates technology that makes its product or service more attractive first sets a new standard for others to follow.* This is what Sony did when it shrank the stereo tape recorder into a Walkman.

The third change driving FCT is the rapid growth of global educational parity. Be it through their attendance at U.S. universities or through the development of local universities, students around the world have ready access to technological advances. For those that have made it to the university, a Third World residence no longer dictates an inferior education. The differences that remain are often compensated for by electronic, real-time access to the latest journals and symposiums, regardless of locale.

The increased rates of technological change and educational parity feed on each other. As frequently described by futurists, the half-life of a college education shrinks inversely in relation to the discovery of new knowledge. Thus, a current computer science graduate student in New Delhi may have a better understanding of the methodology required to test object-oriented software than the thirty-five-year-old programmer sitting in Hewlett-Packard's Palo Alto facility.

The implication is serious. Adding value was historically a process of applying muscle to materials; today, it is one of using brains to produce new knowledge. And since this knowledge becomes widely available to everyone more quickly, catching up to or leapfrogging a competitor happens easiest where technology advances most rapidly.

The last and potentially most critical factor fueling speed as a competitive requirement is that major corporations have been successful using the fast cycle time strategy. Sun Microsystems now dominates a market created by others simply by introducing increasingly powerful workstations much faster than either of its competitors. Toyota, Nissan, Mazda, and Honda have all gained market share and reduced costs because of their ability to develop new cars faster than Detroit.

Although the impact of time to market is the lifeblood of high-technology companies, FCT success stories are not limited to these firms. The crux of the strategy rests on understanding how speed adds value for your customers. Dominos Pizza's success is driven by a conceptual breakthrough, not a technological one. It simply challenged the traditional thinking in its industry regarding the cost-benefit equation of fast delivery. The impact on competitors has been enormous: in the early 1990s, it is hard to find a pizza chain (such as Pizza Hut, Round Table, or Little Caesar's) that *does not* offer delivery.

The consequences of not being fast are also increasingly clear. New products and service create the next generation's revenues. Regardless of how successful your current portfolio of products and services is, your destiny is inextricably tied to what you have under development. Those who lag lose market share and profits. Most importantly, once behind, they have to scramble even faster than the fastest competitor in order to catch up.

For example, Lotus Development Corporation's 1–2–3 program literally owned the PC-compatible spreadsheet market. Its inability, however, to introduce rapidly an updated version with enhanced graphics enabled Borland's Quattro and Microsoft's Excel software to gain 52% of that market, representing $473 million[8] in sales in a little less than three years. The sluggishness of Lotus opened the door to credible competition in a market where there literally wasn't any. The same story holds true for the more mundane domestic soup market. A handful of Japanese and Korean companies (such as Nissin) stole $685 million of that $2.4 billion market from Campbell's by introducing their inexpensive dry soups, made using thin ramen noodles, before Campbell's or the U.S. dry soup leader, Lipton, could react.

One doesn't need to be a rocket scientist to see the trends forming. What may initially appear as a slight loss in market share can rapidly escalate to downsizing and layoffs. One only has to look at the number of Fortune 500 companies that have downsized over the last five years to confirm this. Is slow product development the exclusive cause of the U.S. competitive downfall? Certainly not, but this country's inability to develop and introduce new products rapidly rests within the "critical few" key problems and thus deserves our strategic attention.

#### *What Are the New Rules, and How Do We Change?*

Late in 1986, the Massachusetts Institute of Technology convened its first commission on a major national issue since World War II. The purpose was to address the decline in U.S. industrial performance, which threatened the nation's economic security. The summary of that report[9] cited six factors found in common among U.S. corporations that were successful global competitors:

1. Simultaneous improvement efforts in quality, cost, and speed
2. Closer ties to customers

3. Closer ties to suppliers
4. Integration of technology into manufacturing and marketing strategies, linked to organizational changes that promote teamwork, training, and continuous learning
5. Greater functional integration and less organizational stratification
6. Continual training

The list is not surprising, nor is it very controversial. What is missing from this list and most others like it is a clear strategy of how to lead one's company from today's behaviors to tomorrow's. That is the goal of this book.

# 3

# Fast Cycle Time

## *The Basics*

This chapter defines the fast cycle time strategy and details its key ingredients. The reader will learn about the core elements of the strategy and the characteristics world-class FCT leaders share in common. First, let's sharpen our understanding of what fast cycle time is.

*Fast cycle time is the ongoing ability to identify, satisfy, and be paid for meeting customer needs faster than anyone else.* There are several key words or phrases in this definition. The first is *ongoing ability.* Because the race for leadership is never over, single-shot cycle time reductions do not provide a sustainable competitive advantage. Instead, FCT must become a way of life. Competitors who continuously improve their cycle times will pass those who pause to relax.

Every employee has to be continuously involved to make FCT an ongoing ability. Involvement begins by managing time as we do other resources, such as capital and people. Although no one likes to waste time, it is rarely viewed or managed as a competitive resource. As a first step, time-based performance measures are required throughout the organization. Next, all employees should be trained how to analyze work processes to eliminate non-value-added work from their specific area. Using our product development focus, human resources might measure how long it takes to recruit and assimilate a new development engineer. It would then analyze the recruitment process and design improvements that would reduce the time it takes to recruit and assimilate technologists.

A central implication is that the time devoted to cycle time analysis and improvement has to be considered work just as much as the time spent designing the product itself. In product development, most people limit the definition of work to those tasks that produce drawings, prototypes, or the like. FCT organizations expand the scope of development work to include the analysis and redesign of the development process.

The next key word is *identify*. FCT is the responsibility of all organization functions from the start of the business cycle through the end. In fact, the cycle actually begins when the customer has an itch that goes unscratched. Organizations march to the pace of the company clock, whereas the market place marches to the market clock.[1] The market clock begins ticking whenever customers have needs that are not met, and the company clock starts when it takes the first action to meet those needs. FCT leaders try to eliminate any delay between the starting of those two clocks.

For example, in the nascent days of the personal computer, users did not cry out for an easy-to-use graphical interface. Xerox's Palo Alto Research Center created the first graphical user interface, which Apple later introduced in its Macintosh. Apple recognized the need *and* pursued introduction. After the Macintosh's success established the importance of the graphic interface, Microsoft began development of its PC-based Windows product. Apple's company clock ran closer to the market clock than those of any of its competitors. It responded to the customer's itch before it was a clearly articulated need. By definition, the market window for the graphical interface was already open, otherwise the Macintosh could not have been successful. The first successful product introduction confirms that the market exists; it doesn't create it.

Indications that the company clock has started ticking are typically symbolic, such as assigning a project code name, budget numbers, equipment, or personnel. The company clock dominates thinking inside the company and sets the pace of daily activities and due dates. Delays that are acceptable to the company clock, though, are rarely tested against the market clock. For example, a project review may be delayed because of travel schedules, or testing may take longer because the test chambers have to be shared with other projects. The market clock reappears when a competitor introduces a similar product before you do. Typically, a competitor's success tells when one has missed the market clock.

Sales and marketing departments are the champions of the market clock within the FCT organization. Although many might act as though cycle time improvement in product development is simply an issue for development engineering or manufacturing, this is simply not true. The organization's time to market is governed by the speed at which every function required for product development operates individually *and* together. The organization that identifies a customer's itch quicker than the competition does not need to change its development cycle in order to be first to market.

Sales and marketing are not the only players FCT companies expect to identify customer needs. When DuPont technicians visited their athletic shoe customer Reebok, they heard that Nike's "Air Cushion" heel pad was killing Reebok in the marketplace. Although the visit was for an entirely different purpose, the DuPont technicians suggested a competitive solution that embedded rubber tubes in the heel of the shoe. The solution was implemented and Reebok regained several share points, plus DuPont sold more product. Similarly, in technology-based businesses, technologists must often educate customers to the availability, potential applications, and drawbacks of new technologies. To accomplish this, technologists must meet face-to-face with their customers in order to learn and demonstrate how new technologies can be transformed into customer-defined solutions.

*Satisfy* means that one cannot use FCT as an excuse for inferior product performance or quality. The traditional rule of thumb that says rapid product development will cost more and degrade quality is long dead. World-class FCT competitors such as Toyota have clearly demonstrated that speed does not have to sacrifice quality or cost. As the reader will see, speed can create a focus that actually improves quality and reduces cost.

*Paid* has two dimensions. First, FCT companies focus on completing the entire business cycle quickly. Less outstanding receivables means more cash in hand to invest in future products and services. More importantly, *paid* certifies that the customer prefers your product over others. Customers vote with their wallets. Every time a customer chooses your product, he or she is effectively saying that you offer greater value than the competition. Conversely, when one selects a competitor's product, he or she is sending you a message that must be heeded. The best assessment of long-term customer satisfaction is sustained market share growth.

*Faster than anyone else* reflects the intensity and growth in global competition. If there is a foreign competitor who is faster, it is only a matter of time before that competitor enters one's local market and potentially dominates it. Detroit and the semiconductor industry have learned this lesson the hard way.

## Core Elements of the FCT Strategy

The FCT strategy is based on four fundamental principles. These principles are reflected in the daily practices of successful FCT competitors. Though on the surface they may appear obvious, the seriousness with which they are taken is absolutely central to a company's ability to operate in fast cycle time.[2]

### *Business Strategy and Organization Are Driven by What Adds Value to Revenue: Paying Customers*

The business of business is to provide customers the maximum value for a price. FCT organizations define their business strategy and structure their organization based on the processes that deliver value to their customers. We call these *value delivery processes.* They constantly work with their customers to hone and adjust their definition of value added as markets and technology change. As changes occur, they do not hesitate to adjust strategy or structure to be in alignment with the new definition.

This contrasts with traditional organizations, which start with the customer but muddle their strategy and operations by giving other stakeholders (such as employees or stockholders) equal weight. This is a trap that quickly turns the organization inward. Let's examine the employee element first.

When organizations are small it is easy to keep employees focused on the customer. As organization mass grows, the percentage of employees that have direct contact with customers grows increasingly smaller. Soon, the vast majority of employees spend most of their time *serving other employees.* The aggregate needs of employees increase to the point where they seemingly equal or surpass those of revenue-paying customers. In a relatively short time, the focus shifts from serving the customer to serving each other. Absurd as this sounds, it is a familiar phenomena that is in part reflected in the new language of "internal customers." Most internal customers generate cost; not revenue.

There is only one customer who defines value added, and that is a revenue-paying customer. Although internal transfer prices may make some internal customers into revenue-paying customers, be careful. Transfer price politics often becomes a game in itself and distracts one from the customer at the end of the value chain. Only customers outside the boundaries of the organization provide revenue that ultimately generates profits.

Stockholders benefit when a firm defines its strategy and structure based on adding value to its customers. Stockholders want a strong return on equity and consistent earnings per share growth; these two elements ultimately drive the value of stock upward. One is hard-pressed to find a more sustainable method of achieving this performance than by efficiently providing greater value to one's customers. The stockholder's long-term interest is met by being successful at the core business.

The FCT competitor concentrates on providing the most value in the shortest time for its revenue-paying customers by focusing on value delivery processes. In turn, this satisfies the long-term needs of investors and provides more opportunities for those who work within the enterprise. Subordinating end customer needs to those of stockholders or employees may quell an immediate problem, but it sets in place a cancer that eventually destroys the organization's ability to succeed.[3]

### *FCT Competitors Continuously Improve the Processes That Generate Results*

*Every* result a business achieves is the output of a process. Most of management's time is spent comparing actual outputs to desired or expected results. When a mismatch occurs, focusing people's attentions on the mismatch itself may be motivating, but it does not provide much insight into what caused the mismatch. *FCT organizations treat results that do not meet expectations as symptoms of process errors.*

Specific to new product development, FCT companies continually redefine the set of processes at play in the development process, from overall strategy definition to product specification and final execution. "What can we do to reduce the overall development cycle time *and* increase the time spent adding value?" is asked regularly. Time is the common denominator and helps illuminate quality and cost issues. For example, multiple rework and testing cycles take significant time, cost money and are symptomatic of a poorly understood technology development process.

Traditional organizations, when first undertaking process analysis, often mistakenly make it an end in itself rather than a means for cycle time improvement. For example, a major auto company recognized the need for process improvement and established an internal process improvement unit. The unit sought advice from process improvement experts worldwide and created its own process improvement methodology. Paradoxically, the process improvement process itself was thirty-two steps long! The average process improvement project took six months to complete and was quite painful for those involved.

In contrast , FCT firms limit the scope and complexity of each process analysis and increase the frequency. The more frequent, smaller process studies lend themselves to better implementation because the breadth of change recommended per study is manageable. Large studies produce so many recommendations that change implementation becomes overwhelming and is never satisfactorily completed. The smaller, simpler approach also facilitates keeping the ownership for process improvement within the line organization. This is particularly true in new product development, where the development process itself is much more intangible than production processes.

For example, a division of the same auto firm spent two days building a map of its current development process and a new map that defined the major changes required for 50% reduction in development time. The meeting involved more than 150 line managers from 13 development teams. Within the two days, the top issues were identified. Comparison between teams showed there was very little disagreement regarding the major opportunities. They developed improvement plans and implemented the first changes within sixty days. Cycle time improvements in specific subprocesses exceeded 50% within six months.

### *Fast Cycle Time Competitors Manage Their Business and Organization as an Interdependent System Using Cycle Time Measures*

FCT competitors focus their attention on understanding how their markets, strategy, and organization operate as a system of interdependent structures rather than as a collection of independent elements. Under most circumstances, rapid product development depends more on managing the connections between the involved functional disciplines than it does on increasing the capability of the individual functions.

By using cycle time as a central measure, FCT competitors highlight deficiencies that may be hidden between functions in a traditional organization. For example, let's say engineering reduces its cycle time for first prototypes from twelve weeks to six. If test engineering still requires sixteen weeks for test development, engineering itself may be off the critical path, but overall cycle time doesn't change. The goal is to reduce total system cycle time rather than changing the critical path of tasks. Fast cycle time development is always limited by the slowest element in the development process.

Likewise, the ability to bring leading-edge products to market is often more dependent on access to suppliers possessing advanced technologies than it is on internal development capabilities. When Toyota introduced FCT into manufacturing, it found that the barrier to further cycle time improvement was outside the traditional boundaries of the organization.

It worked with its supply base to improve the latter's development and manufacturing processes in order to continue forward. In contrast to American auto companies, Japanese companies are much smaller in size and rely heavily on the capabilities of their supply base.

Using cycle time measures also provides a quick and painless way to identify and measure defects. To achieve speed, one cannot repeat tasks two, three, or more times. First-time yield is essential for speed. Thus, whenever cycle times grow, one can be confident there is probably rework occurring due to mistakes or defects. By using cycle time as a lightning rod, one zeroes in on defects *as they occur.* This shortens the time to detect and facilitates defect definition because one is looking at a known problem instead of engaging in an intellectual discussion of what defines a defect in any particular process.

By managing through cycle time, process defects within and between functions are surfaced earlier. Because cycle time can be used as a common measure for every organizational process regardless of function or level, it serves to integrate the organization. Senior management can monitor its decision cycle time, just as line operators can measure their process cycle time. Using common measures such as cycle time and defects (as identified by cycle time delays) keeps the business management process simple. One only has to use two basic measures to ensure that work is done quickly and correctly.

### *FCT Competitors Deploy Their Ability to Learn and Change Quickly as a Competitive Advantage*

If there is a particularly unique element to FCT, it is the focus FCT competitors place on learning. Fast cycle time companies revere learning as the only truly inexhaustible source of competitive advantage. In Exhibit 3.1, *available knowledge* refers to the knowledge available inside the firm that can be used to meet domestic customer needs, including product development, manufacturing, distribution, and service. Throughout the 1960s and early 1970s, U.S. auto makers had more available knowledge about what it takes to satisfy domestic customers than their Japanese counterparts. Their dominant market share during this period reflected this. Since the 1970s, the Japanese have learned at a faster rate than U.S. manufacturers. Their ability to learn faster enabled them to become the market leader. In 1992, if one eliminates fleet sales, the Japanese collectively held the largest share of the U.S. auto market.

Even more critical are the requirements for U.S. manufacturers to catch up. The slope of each line shows the learning rate. Once the cross-

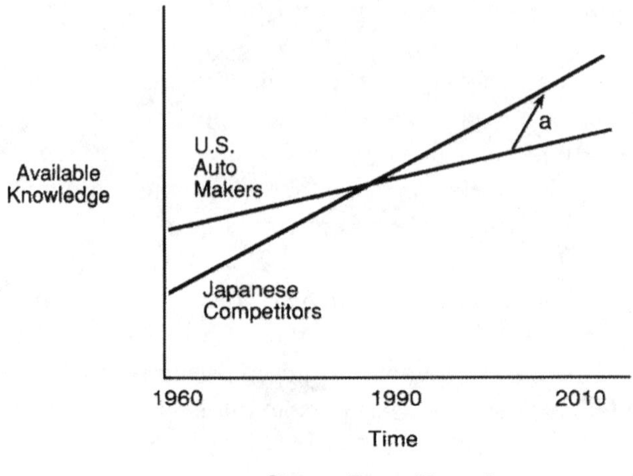


**EXHIBIT 3.1**

ing point is passed, the trailing competitor must increase its rate of learning to a rate *faster* than that of the leading competitor. This is illustrated by arrow (a).

Upstream cycle time reductions place the greatest importance on learning speed. For example, the development process creates new knowledge from raw data. The rate of knowledge production is limited by how fast the organization learns. Therefore, as one moves cycle time reduction upstream in the organization or business cycle, the importance of learning becomes even greater.

*A sustainable FCT capability can be achieved only by learning faster, not by working faster.* If one only doubles the speed of the current work process, the only guaranteed outcome is that there will be twice as many mistakes in the same time. FCT requires that one increase the rate of learning particularly on those processes that deliver value to revenue-paying customers. Although the focus here will be the product development process, the FCT concepts are applicable to any process.

FCT requires a fundamental reframing of the role of learning in business. For the most part, organizations do not discuss the learning process itself, nor is it a subject in our individual lives. Organizational and personal learning focus on the subject matter rather than the learning process that we use to ingest it. The focus on the learning process is a relatively new emphasis in organization strategy.

As long as changes in technology continue to fuel global competition, those competitors who learn how to operate in this new manner will have a significant competitive advantage. As we learn more about successful FCT implementation, it becomes clear that successful implementation of the FCT strategy requires a systemic integration of new values, processes, goals, and rewards into the core work processes in order to increase the rate and speed of organizational learning. The learning itself must be targeted to adding value, as defined by the end customers, and systematically improving the processes that deliver value.

## What Fast Cycle Time Is Not

Say "fast cycle time" to an engineer, and the default translation is "work faster." The typical mental image is a cardiac stress test: the organization treadmill increases in speed and elevation, while your manager assures you this is good for you and the company. The engineers' fears are not misplaced. Too often, management simply demands shorter development schedules. Everyone has been through the routine of generating bottom-up schedules only to have management say "not quick enough" and establish its own arbitrary completion dates. One has to educate people at all levels about what is required to become an FCT competitor.

FCT is not compressing today's activities into a shorter time frame. *The only way to increase product quality and reduce cost while concurrently improving product development speed is to fundamentally change the development process itself.* Compressing the same activities into a shorter time frame without question will increase errors, escalate costs, and degrade quality. Furthermore, time compression increases risk and reduces flexibility.

FCT is not achieved solely through the use of such new technologies as computer-aided design of manufacturing tools. Effective FCT competitors *precede* the installation of new tools with a thorough analysis of the current value delivery processes. After the process is redesigned to increase the throughput, support technologies are assessed and implemented that facilitate the new work flow. The different approaches taken by Honda at its Marysville, Ohio, Accord factory and by General Motors at the Saturn plant in Spring Hill, Tennessee, illustrate this point well:

> The original Marysville, Ohio plant started up in 1982 by building an existing model, the Accord. Automation was modest; some 35% of the welding was done manually. Honda developed its facilities in stages, adding capacity as demand required and more sophisticated automation as workers became more adept at using it.
>
> Saturn, in contrast, started out trying to design a facility so automated that much of it would run without human workers. But Saturn abandoned

> much of that goal, partly because other high-tech GM operations simply don't work.
>
> Moreover, Honda, once it got started, moved faster. GM took more than three years to decide that Saturn should have its own plant and should locate it in Tennessee. Meanwhile, Honda expanded the Marysville assembly plant and began building its Ohio engine factory. Then, in 1985, it launched an all-new Accord, whose development had started before the Saturn project was conceived.
>
> The result: for roughly what GM spent at Spring Hill, Honda got not one but two assembly plants with total annual capacity of 510,000 cars—more than double Saturn's. Honda also got a factory capable of building almost all the engines, transmissions, and related components needed by its auto assembly operations and its Ohio motorcycle plant.[4]

We have seen far too many examples, from the General Motors Vega plant forward, of how simply installing computer-aided design or robotics does not produce miracles.

FCT is not simply limiting the number of new product developments in order to increase the speed on the remaining ones. FCT requires both an increase and a sustained improvement in development productivity.

FCT is not the latest managerial fad. One cannot help but be concerned at American management's penchant for quick fixes. Financial quarters are not the best measure to assess the time it took Toyota to transform itself into a world-class quality leader and an FCT competitor. Properly implemented, FCT is a way of managing. Cycle time becomes the focal point of management attention; it serves as a vehicle that enables corporations to establish a clear simple measurement system that is focused on detecting and correcting problems earlier than traditional "results management" does. Every FCT success story is distinguished by a fundamental change in business strategy, structure, and management focus.

FCT is not a new name for quality. FCT helps identify quality improvement opportunities because defects and rework slow down cycle time. FCT goes hand in hand with quality programs that are focused on fixing root causes. As long as one's quality efforts are not trying to test or beat quality into the product through extensive monitoring, then FCT is fully compatible. As will be demonstrated later, FCT can accelerate quality program implementation.

## The External Benefits of FCT

The advantages that accrue to an FCT competitor are significant. As you read about the benefits, note how they reinforce each other.

### *Provides a Tough-to-Copy Organizational Capability*

A competitor may see that you are first to market and even understand the basics of the FCT strategy, but it cannot copy the processes that enable you to get there. This highlights the fundamental difference between the results and process orientations. For example, one can buy a Hewlett-Packard laser printer, plug it in, and use it immediately. At the same time, one cannot buy their capability to develop that printer in record time. Developing an FCT capability takes time; once you have it, it can not be copied, even if others know you have it. In contrast, a single hot product may give a one-time boost to a firm's profits, but its advantage fades as competitors respond with their own.

### *Yields Higher Margins/Profits*

Although it is always good to beat the competition, FCT does one better: it eliminates the competition. By definition, the first to market does not have any competition, and as a result it lies outside of competitive pricing pressures. This gives the firm greater leverage to set pricing that ensures sufficient profit. Apple Computer enjoyed this position until the public acceptance of Microsoft Windows. Pre-Windows margins at Apple were 54%, compared to 47% after acceptance of the competing product.

### *Increases Market Share*

Using the same logic, the first to market has the largest market share. Even more important is the sustainability of that market share. By being first, the FCT competitor gets earlier feedback from customers than its competitors. This enables it to develop a second-generation product based on feedback from the first. In the meantime, others are still working on their first product without any feedback. Chrysler introduced the first minivan and retains market share leadership for exactly these reasons.

### *Establishes Industry Standards*

The first competitor to market sets the standards that others will be judged against. For example, although there are several competitive operating systems to Microsoft's MS-DOS, each must demonstrate full compatibility with the Microsoft product. The success of the Ford Explorer was paradoxically demonstrated in the initial reviews of Chrysler's new Grand Cherokee Jeep, which constantly used the Explorer as a benchmark.

### *Locks Up Distribution Channels*

The first competitor to market locks up the best distribution channels. Any channel has a maximum capacity, and the first have the opportunity to lock up the most powerful ones. In the early days of the personal computer market, major dealers would only carry IBM, Apple, and Compaq. Competing brands were forced to use alternative channels (such as mail order) to establish themselves. Only when the technology matured to the point that price became a key buying factor did the clones push their way into dealer outlets.

### *Positions One as an Innovator*

The competitor who continually introduces products first becomes positioned as an innovator in the customer's mind. Toshiba's and Compaq's sustained prowess in the laptop computer market causes customers to investigate their products independently even when considering another brand.

### *Enables More Accurate Market Forecasts*

Because their development cycle is shorter, FCT competitors have more accurate demand forecasts. Forecasting is a process of predicting the future. If one has to predict what customers will need in only two years rather than in five, there is little question that the shorter-term forecasts can be more accurate. This is true whether one is forecasting demand or defining product requirements.

### *Incorporates the Latest Technology*

The FCT competitor can incorporate new technology more quickly than its competitors because shorter development cycles create more windows for incorporation. Although people express dislike of the "not invented here" attitude, it is perfectly appropriate to resist incorporating new technology during the last quartile of a development effort. In Exhibit 3.2, the firm with a twelve-month development cycle will be able to incorporate and introduce the new technology by month twenty-four, whereas the firm with the eighteen-month development cycle must wait until month thirty-six. Assuming the technology is available at month fifteen, the firm with the twelve-month development cycle can introduce the new technology 42% faster than the firm with the eighteen-month development cycle, even though the longer development cycle is only 30% greater.

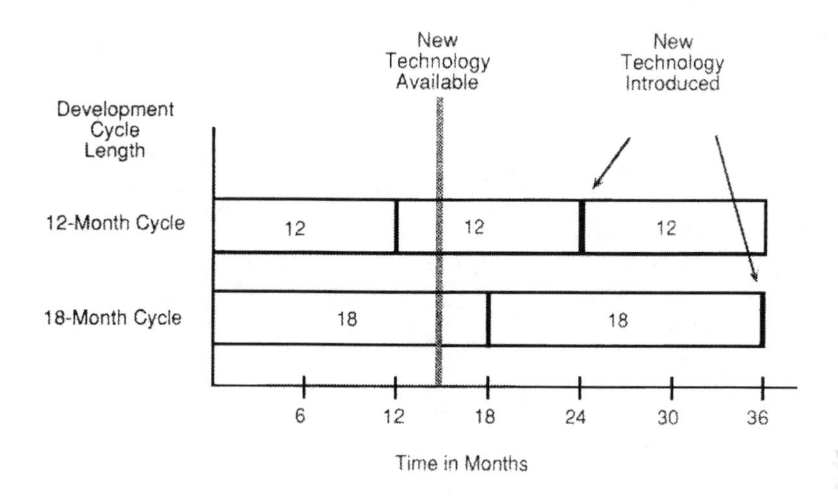


**EXHIBIT 3.2**

### *Increases Quality and Decreases Cost*

Experience shows that redesigning the development process to focus on the elements most valued by customers also increases product quality. This only occurs when the development process itself is redesigned; speed without process redesign will erode quality.

A major cost in product development is the human resources cost. Common sense suggests that if one can reduce the time it takes to develop a product using the same number of people, costs will drop dramatically.

### *Customer Responsiveness Increases/Lead Times Drop*

Becoming an FCT supplier demonstrates customer responsiveness because there is less delay between customer need and its fulfillment. For example, rather than telling customers that they have to wait three years before they can have the product they seek, it is now available in two years or less. Although not the focus of this work, the impact of reduced lead times is absolutely critical to manufacturing operations and inventory control. A short cycle producer can trim inventory by tailoring production mix to customer demand in real time.

## The Internal Benefits of FCT

The FCT strategy also provides many internal benefits. As was the case with the external benefits, the internal benefits feed on each other.

***Process Focus Reduces the Time to Detect and Correct Problems***

A results focus tells one when there is a problem, but it provides little insight into what caused it. FCT adds a *process orientation* that illuminates root causes of problems earlier and therefore enables one to attack them quicker. A central value of the process focus is that it reduces the time it takes for the organization and individuals to learn. The firm that learns faster than its competitors will be able to improve itself constantly and eventually to lead. The learning cycle (see Exhibit 3.3) has four major components: (1) time to detect, (2) time to correct, (3) time to verify, and (4) time to err.[5]

*Time to detect* is the time from an error's creation to its discovery. The longer the time to detect an error, the greater the amount and consequences of rework. A rule of thumb is a change made during design that costs $1,000 will cost $100,000 if made after design but before production, and $10,000,000 if made during production. *Time to correct* is the time required to correct known errors, and *time to verify* is the time it takes to confirm that the correction has fixed the problem. When using these measures, it's important to include the breadth of problems generated by the initial error.

*Time to err* is another way to think about total cycle time. The longer a project exists, the greater the exposure is for error creation. For example, inadvertent errors such as computer crashes have a greater probability of occurring when a project takes three years rather than one. A more subtle variant of time to err is "creeping elegance," which refers to misapplied creativity by developers. Developers thrive on enhancing and improving products. They will often make small improvements to their component without thinking about the systemic consequences these changes create for the overall product.

For example, during the development of a new printer, the team designing the electronics had to wait for a new motor to be qualified by the mechanical engineers. While they waited, they began to add an additional semicustomized chip that promised to increase product performance by 10%. They did not consider the chip vendor's reputation as an erratic supplier of production quantities. The team's efforts marginally increased

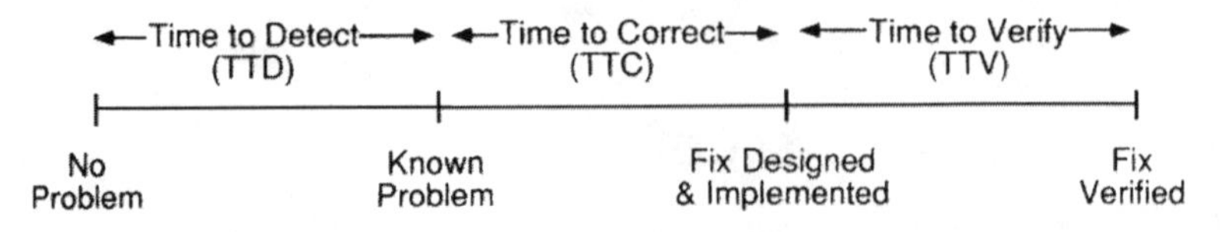


**EXHIBIT 3.3**

performance but severely degraded manufacturability. After the line was forced to shut down several times, the circuit was reengineered to its original specification, and the chip was removed.

### *More Complete Learning Loops*

The business cycle can be thought of as a learning cycle. Each time a firm defines, develops, and introduces a product, it completes the entire business cycle or *learning loop.* FCT companies learn faster than their competitors because they have more *complete* opportunities: Each time the total cycle is completed, one learns the consequences of decisions made earlier in the process. What appeared to have been a good decision during the product specification phase may not pan out that way.

The more learning loops one completes, the greater the potential for learning. For example, during the specification of a new medical product, several features were added that were thought to give the product a competitive advantage. Closer to introduction, the firm learned that the market's perception of a specific feature's importance was much less than it had initially perceived; also, the feature drove manufacturing costs significantly higher. Had the firm not completed the business cycle, this would never have been known.[6]

Learning loops also occur on an individual level. A firm with an average 5-year development cycle will provide a young engineer with two complete development opportunities in 10 years, whereas a company with a 2.5-year development cycle will provide five complete efforts. By completing more cycles, the entire organization learns more about the development process and implements more incremental improvements. Learning and speed feed on each other and become a development "breeder reactor." (A breeder reactor is a nuclear reactor that produces more fuel than it uses.)

### *Measures Are Easy to Use and Understand*

A major advantage of FCT is that cycle time is easy to measure and use throughout the organization. If you define the end points of a process and have a watch, you can measure cycle time. Because the measurement is that easy and can be done within any function, team, or level in an organization, people can use a common language to discuss business issues.

Cycle time also avoids many of the definitional issues that accompany measures such as quality. Whenever one tries to define what a defect is, particularly in upstream knowledge work, there's potential for debate.

Cycle time is much easier to understand, and cycle time delays illuminate defects.

***Reduces Overhead***

One cannot be fast and have a tall hierarchy that drives people to check before they act. The flat, multifunctional, team-based network organization reduces the need for management overhead by putting the right people in real-time contact so that coordination is not required. For example, memos, phone calls, and scheduling reduce dramatically when the right people to complete a process are co-located. Almost by definition, a fast organization must eliminate any extra overhead. This in turn, reduces non-value-added time and costs.

***Drives Information Flow Across and Within Functions***

Data are the raw material of product development. Development speed is paced by how fast one transforms data into knowledge in the form of a reproducible design. In a traditional organization, sluggish data flows or operating on a "need to know" basis are accepted. In an FCT organization, problems accessing information and knowledge are rapidly elevated. Speed requires rapid communication throughout the entire organization. Faster information flow also reduces the time between detection, correction, and verification of problems and therefore reduces rework.

***Empowers People and Builds Trust***

One cannot be fast without empowering people to take action based on their own judgment. Rather than preaching empowerment, FCT organizations demand speed, which in turn drives empowerment. FCT eliminates the philosophical debate and focuses empowerment on making processes move faster to achieve results quicker.

People are more prone to trust others who have similar backgrounds and work experience. In organizations, these people are usually found within the same functional discipline. Chemical engineers work with other chemical engineers, while marketers work with other marketers. One only has to listen to discussion of tossing products "over the wall" to verify this bias. Because FCT requires real-time, multifunctional input to speed products through development, people have more substantive contact with people from functional perspectives besides their own. Initially this is uncomfortable, but very quickly both parties find that their stereotypes of others are not completely true. Over time, the cross-functional interaction builds more trust and less defensiveness, which ultimately results in faster detection and correction of problems without blame. Increased trust and loyalty is a common outcome of working in Fast Cycle Time.

### *Increased Sense of Accomplishment*

People develop an increased sense of accomplishment in an FCT company because their efforts reach a tangible conclusion that is visible to colleagues and friends at release. FCT companies know that a decision to defer making a decision is by no means cost free. Once identified, issues are pushed quickly to resolution. As cycle time drops, people get to work on more new products, which generates its own excitement. The FCT environment is honest and down to earth because there is simply not time for politics.

Possibly the most important and least expected benefit of becoming an FCT competitor is that the firm's deficiencies are rapidly and continuously exposed. Increasing development speed has the same impact on an organization that stress testing does on a new product: it quickly illuminates problems that heretofore were buried under other problems. FCT will not cure all of your company's problems, but it will do an excellent job of exposing them.

### *Increases Quality Quickly*

Every process has three outputs that should concern management: how long the process takes to complete, whether it delivers the required quality, and how much it costs. Using continuous process improvement (CPI) methodology, total quality management (TQM) programs focus *on all three dimensions concurrently*. In contrast, FCT focuses on the time dimension and, through it, pulls cost and quality into line (Exhibit 3.4).

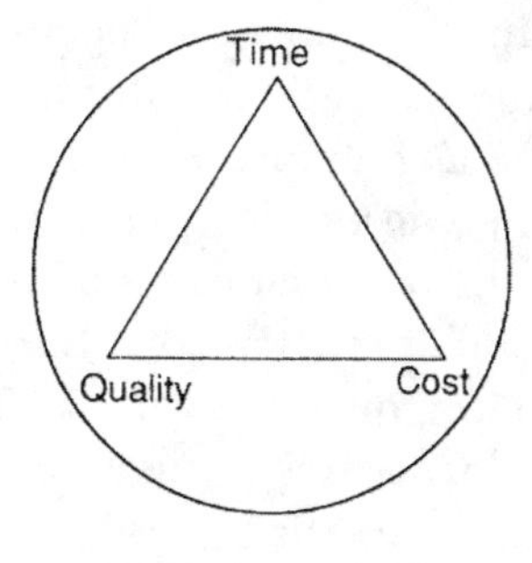


Traditional Continuous Process Improvement

FCT Focused Process Improvement

**EXHIBIT 3.4**

Quality improves because one cannot achieve short cycle times if large amounts of rework are required throughout the process. In the same vein, if a development program takes half the time using the same number of people, it costs significantly less.

FCT is a better strategic umbrella for improving cycle time *and* quality than total quality management. First, FCT provides a sharper focus that is easier to communicate and understand. The critical factor in this argument is that *reducing cycle time can never be used as an excuse to compromise meeting customer requirements.* Second, FCT is much easier to use in less tangible, upstream processes such as development. Third, FCT provides an ongoing competitive advantage, whereas quality eventually reaches a point where it is no longer a competitive differentiator. Let's explore this argument by first examining the fundamental cause of quality and cycle time problems.

The most difficult and costly quality and cycle time problems are cross-functional in nature. For example, poor product quality problems can not be fixed by manufacturing alone. If the product design or technology is inherently unstable, then the best manufacturing can do is screen parts or wait until engineering develops a long-term solution. Apple Computer was the first manufacturer to adopt active matrix displays for its portable computers. Initially, display manufacturing yields and fragility were quite high. The manufacturing operation instituted costly procedures to handle the part carefully, but the real leverage for yield and cost improvement was in redesigning the component itself. This was out of the hands of manufacturing.

Cross-functional problems are difficult to manage because most organizations are functionally structured. People have colorful language that describes the functional bias, such as "organizational chimneys" or "silos." The fundamental issue is that the chimney's needs take precedence. Cross-functional cooperation only occurs *after* functional needs are met. Therefore, a process improvement methodology that easily moves across functional boundaries has more power than one that doesn't.

The quality movement has enjoyed significant success in manufacturing. Based on this success and the fact that the root cause of most manufacturing problems was upstream, quality gurus saw that the only way to improve quality substantially was to move quality programs upstream. Using terminology such as *total* quality management, they tried to push the quality process into development and marketing.

Despite their efforts, quality does not migrate well. There is a visceral difference in the impact of quality in design or marketing relative to manufacturing. As the work process and outputs become less tangible, the traditional quality tools and techniques lose their punch. The common problem is that quality, or its absence, becomes very difficult to define upstream. Ask a group of engineers or marketers to agree to what defines a defect in the product definition process, and you're in for a long discussion. Attempts to do so are frustrating, and the conversations turn people off.

Imagine that your firm produces packages for processed food manufacturers. If you took a finished package off the assembly line and gave it to a multifunctional group including product designers, test engineers, and finance, marketing, and personnel people, they could quickly determine if the product met quality standards or not. The package itself could be passed around for each person to inspect.

But what if that same group had to reach a consensus on the styling quality of a new package design or its market introduction plan? It is reasonable to assume that the same group would find this task much more difficult. The tangibility and exactness of the definition of quality drops dramatically when one moves upstream into design and marketing. Reaching consensus on the criteria for a design that meets stylistic as well as functional needs is much more difficult.

In contrast, cycle time moves easily across organizational boundaries. In manufacturing, one can define production cycle time as the time from when the first component starts on the assembly line until the product is completed. One can also define the start and end points of the product development or market introduction process. The development effort may begin at product concept signoff and conclude with first revenue shipments; how long a market introduction plan takes to develop and execute is also easy to measure. In other words, cycle time can be defined and measured easily within each function. It does not lose its punch as one moves upstream, thereby allowing everyone to participate fully in cycle time reduction efforts.

Here is the punch line: to create sustainable quality *or* cycle time improvements, one must focus on cross-functional process improvement. The cycle time approach enables you to define measures for processes within and across functions much more easily than quality does. It avoids the endless subjective debates about what defines quality in engineering, marketing, styling, and so forth. Long cycle delays attract attention and become powerful catalysts for process improvement *across organizational* boundaries, where the greatest leverage is. Additionally, among the major causes of cycle time delays are defects. By using cycle time as the lens one looks through, one will find where defects are in the process. It is also easier to define a defect that already is a problem than to try and come up with a generic definition. Because of this, many firms have begun to use FCT as the umbrella strategy and then nest quality improvement within it.

Externally, quality is a differentiating factor for buyers as long as there are significant differences between competitors. As differences disappear, quality becomes a requirement, and only its absence is a negative differentiator. For example, although quality remains a substantial factor when choosing between a General Motors product and a Toyota, it is rarely a factor in considering whether to buy a Nissan or a Toyota. Typically the decision to buy either a Nissan or a Toyota will be based on factors other than quality, such as styling, performance, or cost. FCT, however, can provide an ongoing competitive advantage. For example, the Mazda Miata's success is due to its being the first low-priced sports convertible in approximately ten years. Modeled after the old MG and Austin-Healey Sprite, the Miata was first to market in a now-vacant segment.

A final note regarding FCT and quality. Total quality is essential; those who try to sneak by without it are committing suicide. The issue is how to achieve it throughout the *entire* organization. The FCT strategy simply greases the skids to move the basic process of quality improvement into knowledge work where it has not taken hold.

## Characteristics of World-Class FCT Companies

In 1989, the Strategic Alignment Group conducted an analysis of documented case studies to identify the common characteristics (Exhibit 3.5) of world-class FCT companies. The study results are divided into four categories: operating philosophy, organization architecture, leadership, and business strategy. The study provides a benchmark of best-in-class practices to assess your organization against.

### *Operating Philosophy*

#### *Crystal-Clear, Customer-Driven Context*

FCT competitors drive their decision-making processes based on external customer's needs. They use direct, real-time customer input whenever possible rather than depend on aggregated market research to increase the clarity of customer needs. This becomes increasingly difficult in areas such as consumer products, yet as companies such as Frito-Lay demonstrate, there is more opportunity than many take advantage of.

At the end of each workday, Frito-Lay's 10,000 salespeople plug their hand-held computers into minicomputers that zap a report of their day's efforts to the company's headquarters in Dallas. Frito-Lay executives get the data twenty-four hours later—crunched, sliced, and diced however

**Best-in-Class FCT Practices**

*Operating Philosophy*

Crystal-clear, customer-driven context
Every action tested by its value added
Open sharing of information
Make decisions locally in real time
Employees are considered appreciating resources

*Organization Architecture*

Dense, mission-focused structures emphasizing value added
Flat with blurred boundaries
Multifunctional and team based
Work design pecedes new work technologies
Partnerships are the norm

*Leadership*

Define purpose; mission and goals folded into an evocative vision
Initiate strategy and development and ensure execution
Secure and develop resources: people, financial, technology
Design the organization to be in alignment with purpose and strategy
Ensure that the organization develops as a learning system

*Business Strategy*

Bold cycle time reduction goals
Process development pursued jointly with product development
Trade cost for time
Time-sensitive performance metrics
Co-location

**EXHIBIT 3.5**

they'd like. In 1990, for example, Frito-Lay had a problem in San Antonio and Houston. Sales were slumping in the area's supermarkets. Executives called up the data for south Texas and quickly isolated the cause: a regional competitor had just introduced El Galindo, a white-corn tortilla chip. The chip, it turned out, was getting good word of mouth—and, as a result, more supermarket shelf space than Frito's traditional Tostitos tortilla chips. Within three months, Frito-Lay was producing a white-corn version of Tostitos that matched the competition and won back lost market share. Two years earlier, it might have taken Frito-Lay three months just to pinpoint the problem.[7]

Suppliers to original equipment manufacturers are increasingly targeting specific customers to sponsor products that they later offer to other customers. Quantum Corporation's successful ProDrive 240 was developed initially for Hewlett-Packard and later won major contracts with Digital Equipment Corporation, Compaq, and Apple Computer.

### *Every Action Tested by Its Value Added*

FCT competitors test proposed actions against their customer's definition of value added. The ultimate goal is to have every action within the company deliver value for its revenue-paying customers.

Organizations become defocused and bureaucratic when operations detach themselves from the customer. Defining customer value added becomes difficult the more one moves upstream or into staff organizations, but the discipline is still extremely important. One has to look through internal customers and assess the impact of a suggested action on end customers. If there is no value added, then that action may still be approved, but there will always be pressure over time to shorten or eliminate the need for it.

### *Open Sharing of Information*

Speed and a need-to-know mentality cannot coexist. In a need-to-know organization, information is hoarded to the benefit of some and the detriment of many. FCT firms know that a person without information cannot take responsibility for actions, whereas a person with information cannot help but take responsibility. FCT companies also share more information with their suppliers and customers than traditional competitors. In an FCT organization, information provides critical feedback, which unleashes learning and speed.

Information sharing means more than publishing figures. FCT competitors know that unless the context and meaning are clear, distributing information is wasted effort. FCT companies avoid information overload by defining the purpose behind the figures and only communicating the critical set of measures required, rather than everything they possibly can.

### *Make Decisions Locally in Real Time*

It is literally impossible to be fast if people have to seek approval at every step along the way. Speed increases dramatically when decisions are made locally, in real time. Doing this requires local decision-making capability supported by clear strategic direction, organizational alignment, locally available data, and a bias toward action.

Findings in an informal study conducted by Stanford University faculty member David Bradford showed that the best bosses knew only 40% of their subordinates' actual work. In today's turbulent environment, exception-based management stalls, because the exception has become the rule. Bumping each exception up to a senior manager shifts the decision process away from the locus of information and capability.

### *Employees Are Considered Appreciating Resources*

It is impossible to find a corporate values statement that does not acknowledge employees as the most important resource within the company. Paradoxically, it is rare to find an organization that invests in the preservation of its human assets as it does capital or technology assets. Increasingly, companies such as Motorola are requiring a fixed number of training hours per year for every employee. Motorola also bases pay in some operations on proficiency at multiple skills instead of seniority. Because FCT requires speeding up the rate of learning within an organization, investments that support learning can pay significant dividends. People are the only company asset that can redesign processes for increased speed.

In contrast to most Japanese firms, many U.S. firms continue to treat investment in employee capability development as a highly discretionary expense. Playing this belief out to its most dangerous consequence, firms that are suffering will cut back their development programs, which will cause them to suffer even more over time. If it is assumed that the half-life of useful technical knowledge continues to erode, then the organization that does not develop its people will become technically obsolete.

## Organization Architecture

FCT companies compete using a distinctively different organizational architecture from that of traditional competitors. In the Strategic Alignment Group study, the only attribute that showed up in *every* case studied was the use of innovative organization architectures.

Because the conversational use of the term *structure* in business limits itself to describing the organization chart, we use the term *organizational architecture* to refer to the broader set of structures and connections that organize the firm in a particular and unique way. A structure can be tangible or intangible.

In practice, organization architecture behaves like an iceberg (Exhibit 3.6). Although most visible, the tangible structures account for only a small part of the overall architecture. The intangible structures are where most of the daily work gets done. Because the intangible structures play such a major role, it is not easy visually to distinguish a traditional work environment from a high-performance FCT organization.

We are most familiar with tangible structures: organization charts, the personnel handbook, spending authorization limits, and the policy manual. Intangible structures include norms of behavior, beliefs held in common, style, and culture. The intangible structures capture the personality of each organization and remind us that organizations are *social* systems composed of human beings. Organizational effectiveness results from addressing human needs, not avoiding them.

Experience demonstrates that these architectural elements are at least equally powerful, if not stronger, determinants of employee behavior. For example, attempts to copy another organization's FCT capability often fall flat because only the tangible elements are copied. One can find many companies that have the same organization chart or product development process as Hewlett-Packard, Motorola, or Quantum without having their product development speed.

### *Dense, Mission-Focused Architecture Emphasizing Value Added*

FCT organizations build lean organizations around a sharply focused mission and strategy. Density implies that FCT organizations have a very clear focus, and their leaders keep them tightly in line with that focus. Potential investments that may be profitable on a stand-alone basis are assessed for their hidden overhead or distraction potential. Simplicity breeds speed.[8]

In a contrasting example, a high-tech component supplier began building its own test equipment because commercially available testers were not adequate to test its latest products. One of their customers inquired if the internally produced equipment was available for sale. Viewing this simply as an additional profit-making opportunity, the firm said yes. Its rationale was that it could recapture its own tester development costs through sales to customers. Over the years, the tester business generated modest profits.

As the business grew, the definition of the customer changed. As the external installed base of testers grew, external customers began to have more influence than the original internal ones. Tester development that used to be driven by internal needs was now driven by external needs.

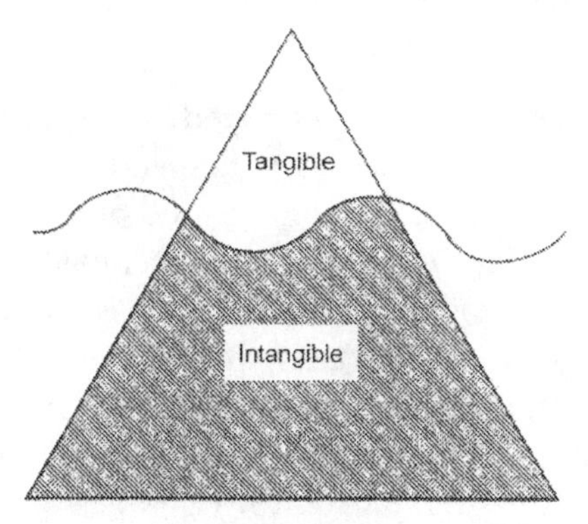


**EXHIBIT 3.6**

Moreover, as new testers were introduced, owners of previous generations demanded software updates and maintenance. What began as an opportunity to fund internal tester development rapidly became a distraction and a liability. More resources were devoted to managing customer dissatisfaction outside the organization than were devoted to supporting the core tester development process. Focus and density were lost.

*Flat with Blurred Boundaries*

FCT organizations keep themselves as flat as possible and blur their boundaries, both inside and out. A key difference is a change in the traditional span-of-control paradigm. Organizations grow taller when they fixate on a narrow span of control. If a company grows 30% per year and maintains a span of control of eight employees per manager, the physics dictate that after the eighth employee is hired, a new manager must be added. After eight managers have been named, a middle manager must be appointed. FCT leaders broaden spans of control to keep organizational units, such as divisions, to four levels or less from top to bottom.

FCT organizations align their structures to the work process, rather than the reverse. Management deliberately blurs boundaries between functional groups to ensure that people focus on the requirements of the work rather than on their home territory. FCT structures also provide hooks to facilitate inclusion of customers and suppliers in key decisions. For example, suppliers are frequently co-located within product development teams, or FCT companies co-locate their own employees at customers' locations for the same purpose.

### *Multifunctional and Team Based*

The Strategic Alignment Group study found that every leading FCT competitor used multifunctional work teams to speed products to market. The terminology used to describe the teams varied from firm to firm, but the underlying structure was the same. Labels included "concurrent development," "integrated product development," "simultaneous engineering," or "product teams." In each case, the structure created a dedicated, multifunctional team, usually co-located, working in real time toward a common goal. These are permanent work teams and not ad hoc task forces. Subsequent research looked for examples of firms that had reverted away from the multifunctional team, but none were found. Instead, many firms expanded the scope of multifunctional development teams to include product and business unit management.

The Japanese find multifunctional teams stimulate learning the development process. Rather than be concerned that one function might inappropriately meddle in another function's turf, the Japanese view meddling as useful. By forcing individuals with different perspectives to work on the same problem, they challenge and stimulate each other's thinking.[9]

### *Work Design Precedes New Work Technologies*

FCT organizations make it a practice to introduce new technologies such as robotics or computer-aided design tools into the work process *after* they redesign the basic work flow. Electronic tools such as CAD, CAM or CIM effectively accelerate a poor process as much as they do a good one. Making the same mistakes faster is not FCT.[10]

Process redesign is ongoing and incremental. Efforts are constantly under way to eliminate or consolidate steps that add marginal value and to reduce the time to detect or correct errors. The redesign process is a line management responsibility and involves those who will implement and work in the redesigned organization.

FCT process redesign pays special attention to establishing an effective interface between technical tools and social structures. Tools are chosen that reinforce team-based development, and teams are encouraged to expand their capabilities to use the latest tools.

### *Partnerships Are the Norm*

FCT competitors are not shy about establishing partnerships rather than traditional customer-supplier relationships. For example, the Ford Probe is a joint development effort with Mazda. The Probe's power train was developed by Mazda, whereas the body was designed by Ford. The Mazda Navajo is a reskinned Ford Explorer that is built in the United States and in fact competes with the Explorer.

### *Leadership*

FCT leaders use a model of motivation and control that parallels distributed data processing systems. Information systems have shifted from centrally managed, mainframes to distributed workstations that are networked directly to each other and use mainframe or minicomputers for selected operations. Similarly, FCT leaders distribute decision-making power locally and use networklike structures such as multifunctional teams to connect key resources. FCT leaders control the system by defining the strategic context, by setting high-level goals, and through the design of the network itself. FCT leaders define their job as enabling others by providing clear purpose, strategy, and structures.

#### *Define Mission and Goals, Fold Them into an Evocative Vision, and Communicate the Entire Package Endlessly*

The essence of the FCT leader's job is to set direction, evoke others' excitement and commitment to the direction set, and then get out of the way. Obviously, this is much easier to say than it is to do. Setting direction includes clearly defining the organization's purpose (mission) and folding the essence of the mission into an evocative challenge that captures employees' hearts as well as their minds (vision), including clear milestones (goals).

The mission statement defines the firm's core business, whereas the vision statement establishes a midterm performance target. For example, John F. Kennedy's "to the moon by the end of the decade" commitment established a target for the U.S. space program in the 1960s that energized NASA and the nation at large. FCT leaders often include an aggressive cycle time reduction target as part of their vision, such as reducing a new product development cycle time by 50% over three years. Each work unit develops measurable goals that nest within the corporate framework.[11]

FCT leaders persistently communicate and clarify direction. Internalized purpose and vision enable employees to self-select the tasks that add the greatest value to the end customer and support company goals. Control is the result of clear direction, enabled employees, and congruent organizational architecture.

*Initiate Strategy Development and Ensure its Execution*

A wise man once said that strategy is one-tenth inspiration and nine-tenths perspiration. If one examines a successful company's strategic plan from five years ago, the original strategy definition rarely describes the path the firm ultimately took. In the real world, business strategy is the result of incremental adaption and change.

The principal value of strategic planning is in the act of planning, not the plan itself. The planning process sets direction by building consensus among the leaders about the business and the environment it operates within. The FCT leader's responsibility is to make sure that strategy discussions are thorough and that *decisions are fully implemented.* In contrast, traditional firms focus their attention exclusively on the strategy discussion and assume implementation will take care of itself. Elegant strategy that remains solely on paper is worthless.

FCT leaders pay special attention to two strategic elements: the value proposition and ongoing capability development. The value proposition defines where the firm chooses to focus its value-added efforts. For example, Domino's and Little Caesar's are competitors in the pizza business, each having a fundamentally different value proposition. Domino's value proposition is home-delivered pizza, whereas Little Caesar's is pizza fresh from the oven. We'll discuss the role of the value proposition in greater depth when we discuss the strategic alignment process.

FCT leaders strategically map the capabilities required to execute their strategy and define how and when these will be acquired or developed. Technology, product, and supplier road maps are created and then aligned to the strategy and each other. This contrasts with firms who view capability development as a secondary, tactical issue. FCT leaders know that ongoing cycle time improvements are based on continually upgrading the firm's capabilities.

*Secure and Develop Resources: People, Financial, Technology*

FCT leaders provide rather than execute. They ensure that the organization secures or develops critical resources *before* they are needed. Resources are broadly defined, and leaders use many alternatives to acquire them. Options include technology exchanges, consultants, joint ventures, strategic alliances, and (of course) full-time employees. FCT leaders know that whenever the organization has to wait for resources, cycle time is hurt.

FCT leaders are not parochial about technology development. They are more likely than their competitors to use their suppliers to add value. Whereas a traditional firm may be concerned about who holds the rights to a particular technology, FCT leaders are concerned with long-term access. For example, Hewlett-Packard has dominated the PC laser printing market for five years, yet they do not make the printer's laser engine. Their value added is the integration, distribution, and service of the printer within the PC environment. Though one may question the long-term impact of outsourcing such a key component, H-P's results through the early 1990s speak for themselves.

*Design the Organization to Be in Alignment with Purpose and Strategy*

FCT leaders constantly test and realign their organization's architecture to be congruent with the company's mission and strategy. FCT leaders know that a good strategy will be compromised if the structure is out of alignment with the strategy (Exhibit 3.7).[12]

Misalignment can be the result of a rapidly changing environment. For example, Ford Motor Company, like GM and Chrysler, knew its product development cycle time was no longer competitive with the Japanese. Past efforts to increase development speed on products such as the Taurus had produced excellent vehicles but did not shorten development cycle time. Ford began several pilots using dedicated, co-located vehicle teams. After about a year, they found this structure was working, and further modifications were made to the teams and functional organizations. The tuning of that architecture continues to this day.

Strategic alignment is an ongoing leadership activity. In chapter 4, I will discuss the techniques used to do this.

*Ensure That the Organization Develops as a Learning System*

Business organizations are rotten places to learn. We constantly measure performance and reward those who succeed and punish or ignore those

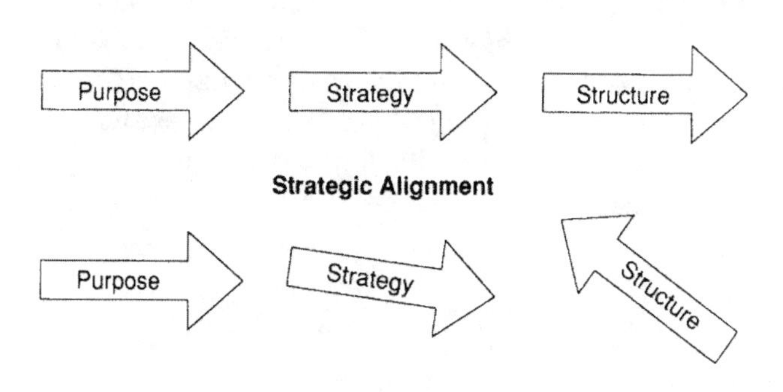


**EXHIBIT 3.7**

that fail. Mistakes are dangerous to make—and more dangerous to make in public. Because most people learn best from mistakes, and yet it is dangerous to make them, learning is compromised.[13]

FCT leaders accept that humans will make mistakes. The issue is to learn faster from those that do occur. Leaders make it safe for employees to *initiate* openly discussing errors. FCT leaders do not finish a tough discussion without asking what was learned and what actions are needed to make sure the learning is spread throughout the organization. This is particularly true when mistakes threaten human life. Curiously, our ability to control mistakes in commercial aviation surpasses that of most other industries. The difference is not because pilots are smarter than anyone else, but because we have learned more about what creates safety via intensive industry and FAA investigations of every crash.

### *Operating Practices and Business Strategy*

World-class FCT competitors use similar operating practices tailored to their specific industry requirements. The following examples include the most common and robust practices.

#### *Bold Cycle Time Reduction Goals*

FCT leaders use bold cycle time reduction goals to stimulate fundamental change and process redesign. A cycle time improvement goal of 25% can often be achieved just by working harder, focusing management attention, or providing additional resources. Where cycle time has been historically ignored, there is plenty of low-hanging fruit that can yield rapid improvement without major process redesign. Such single-shot improvements, while useful, do not create a sustainable competitive advantage.

FCT companies establish initial improvement targets in the range of 50% and up. By raising the standard to that level, it forces people to rethink the basic premises of their work process. Scaling a twenty-foot wall is a fundamentally different challenge than scaling a six-foot wall. The height of the twenty-foot wall immediately eliminates such obvious options as jumping over. Without a sufficiently strong goal, people will tend to "gunch" performance out of an inherently inefficient system.

#### *Overlapping Problem Solving*

FCT companies employ overlapping problem solving in many of their operations. In product development, overlapping problem solving has several names, including "concurrent development," "simultaneous engineering," "parallel processing," and "integrated product development."[14] The basic difference between traditional serial practices and overlapping problem solving is that the downstream group begins its work before the upstream group is finished. In certain situations, they begin work at the same time. Although the cycle time advantages are obvious, making the actual shift is quite difficult.

In serial problem solving, the handoff to the downstream function must wait until the article passes maturity criteria established by the upstream function. For example, development decides when the engineering is complete before an item is released to manufacturing. The majority of learning gained during development remains in the engineering organization; only the drawing moves. In overlapping problem solving, the handoff criteria changes. Instead of determining the handoff by the upstream group's definition of maturity, the downstream function defines handoff timing based on what it needs to begin its efforts.

Serial problem solving tests the maturity of the product sequentially, one function at a time. Overlapping problem solving focuses on the learning speed of the total system. Overlapping problem solving requires a supportive learning environment, because it exposes mistakes and requires a "one step backward, two steps forward" type of working arrangement in order to be effective. Co-locating the people involved is almost a requirement to make overlapping problem solving effective.

### *Process Development Pursued Jointly with Product Development*

FCT leaders pursue process development because it has tremendous leverage. For example, Texas Instruments employed "design for manufacturability" (DFM) in its engineering design process with significant success. Assembly time was reduced 85%, part count by 75%, assembly step by 78%, and metal fabrication by 71%. FCT leaders treat organization process development as a competitive weapon.

If the logic is clear, though, why is it so difficult to get companies to pursue process development? One reason organizations don't pay attention to process development is that significant improvements take time to design and implement; instant results are rare. In fact, while the process is being redesigned and implemented, productivity may decline. For example, when a group of engineers attends DFM training, their productivity falls, because they are not designing products.

Some managers overreact and expect that well-defined processes in and of themselves will produce dramatic results. The fact is that good processes are a necessary but insufficient requirement for results. Changing core behaviors, developing increased capabilities, and a can-do attitude are all required to make a good process translate into exceptional results. Process development should never become process paralysis.

The second reason companies do not pursue process development is the measurement system. Organizations have plenty of results measures and few process measures. Results measures tell us *what* we have achieved, but they provide little insight into *how*. Since we don't measure the process, people don't pay much attention to improving it. Knowing that Product A and Product B share the same defect will not help us know if the two defects share a common cause.

The third reason builds off the second: we measure those items that are easiest to measure. The dilemma created is similar to that of the drunk who only looks for his keys under the lamppost because that is where the light shines. Most organizations limit their process measures to the tangible, linear work processes such as those found in manufacturing. These processes are much easier to measure precisely than the nonlinear work processes found in development, marketing, or sales. Process measures for nonlinear work are not as precise, nor do they need to be. What is most important is to develop time-based measures that can aid improvement efforts. Relative measures that compare current cycle time to past times have more value and are easier to use than absolute measures.

### *Trade Cost for Time*

FCT competitors will spend money today to achieve a significant time advantage later in the marketplace. In a frequently quoted study conducted by the McKinsey Company, products that came to market on time but 50% over budget only lost 3.5% of their total profits, whereas products that were introduced on budget but six months late lost 27% to 33% of their total profits.[15] Experience demonstrates that the study stands up as long as one invests this money continuously throughout the project rather than trying to save a failing effort through a late influx of cash.

Trading cost for time requires multiple return-on-investment calculations based on potential completion dates. It may be ultimately more profitable to employ a more expensive component technology that gets to market faster. Doing so enables one to get critical customer feedback, which in turn provides guidance for enhancement as well as targeted cost reduction. Electronic products increasingly use more expensive field-programmable gate arrays because they are easier to modify than traditional arrays. This makes fixing and correcting problems a breeze as opposed to having to go to a foundry to manufacture a completely new chip. The implication is that cost is not a static item but one that should be assessed relative to time to market, competition, and customer requirements.

Trading cost for time also applies to the mundane aspects of development. Although a large corporate copy center may be more cost-effective for the total enterprise, its impact on a product design team may not be. We have seen countless projects suffer one-or-two-day delays due to slow turnaround time from a corporate copy center. The time-to-market delay is actually more costly than the purchase of a small copier for the local engineering team.

### *Time-Sensitive Performance Metrics*

Sadly, the measurement systems of most corporations are better equipped to serve the needs of Wall Street, auditors, and the SEC than they are those who run the business. Outside of some manufacturing and customer service operations, we have few metrics that expose the impact of time on business performance. People pay attention to what is being measured; if there are no time-based measures, people don't pay attention to cycle time.

FCT leaders develop time-based performance metrics for processes and results. The goal is to create real-time measures whenever possible. Imagine what it would be like driving a car if the speedometer indicated how fast you were going ninety days ago. This is obviously absurd, and yet we drive our businesses with the same lag-time handicap. FCT organizations use local, process-oriented measures to reduce the time to detect and correct errors. They focus these measures on the critical few business processes that are linked to their core competencies and business strategy, as opposed to trying to measure everything available.

### *Co-Location*

World-class FCT companies follow a simple rule: if you want people to work closely together, seat them together. This seemingly simple advice challenges the functional paradigm, in which people are usually seated with their functional peers. Because most value delivery processes require cross-functional efforts, the classic arrangement quickly becomes dysfunctional. Research demonstrates that when people are more than thirty meters from each other, communication effectiveness drops by orders of magnitude.

While this concept is clear and simple, its implementation is not. First of all, it is the rare individual who elects to co-locate. Typically co-location has to be driven, initially, by senior management. After one or two experiences with it, this problem disappears. Secondly, it is impossible to co-locate everyone who must work together all the time. Some specialized resources that serve a variety of groups cannot be in all places at once. Additionally, today's globally based corporation may have projects that involve people from several sites around the globe.

Co-location, therefore, requires thoughtful planning in order to achieve the correct balance. For example, co-location changes facility requirements. Dedicated co-located teams require a different physical layout, including movable walls, open space, and more conference rooms than a traditional functional organization.[16]

## The Limitations of FCT

There are two fundamental concerns that the reader should be aware of regarding FCT. The first is the intensity of effort required to compete in this fashion, and the second is its applicability to blue-sky research.

FCT companies operate with a level of intensity that is at once impressive and frightening. Although the strategy is based on working smarter rather than harder, there is no question that pressure builds in an FCT organization. The transition from a traditional competitor to an FCT company is stressful. In their enthusiasm, many slip into compressing time instead of redesigning core processes. Senior management must watch this at every step of the way. Whenever time compression is found, efforts must switch to redesigning the underlying process.

FCT does not speed up basic research or the invention process. FCT plays a central role in defining research priorities and allocating resources between blue-sky research and near-term developments. While we strongly believe that FCT has a vital role in technology transfer, we have seen little that fundamentally speeds up the invention of new technology.

## Summary

To an outsider, an FCT company may not look very different from any other firm. The capabilities that enable speed are essentially invisible. Much like the professional athlete, the successful FCT company moves rapidly but seemingly without effort. Every action and every process is based on one simple rule: be the first to provide consistently, reliably, and profitably, the greatest value to the target customers.

Fast cycle time is the ultimate close-to-the-customer strategy. No one in an FCT company can afford to lose sight of what the customer determines is added value or when they need it. The FCT competitor is always trying to reduce the time between the first customer itch and when the itch ceases to exist to zero. If they could, FCT leaders would change all the clocks inside the company walls to show the market clock rather than current time.

The traditional competitor has as many, if not more, technology resources than the FCT leader. One only has to look at the shift in growth within the personal computer industry to bear this out. The resources IBM had at its disposal did not prevent Compaq from becoming the fastest-growing company in its day. And the resources that Compaq acquired did not prohibit Dell Computing from doing to Compaq what it did to IBM. Technology plays a key role, but when the day is done, *FCT is more dependent on social innovation than it is on technological innovation.*

The FCT organization is an exciting one to work in. Leaders trust people's ability to learn and improve from their own actions. When leadership is required, the role is to focus attention, secure resources, and enable others to execute. To a significant degree, the leaders of an FCT organization serve as the public works department, responsible for making sure the roadways that lead to the mission are free of obstacles so that any "driver" does not have to take a pit stop or swerve to avoid a pothole as they speed forward.

The transformation to becoming an FCT company is also challenging and exciting. FCT requires behavior change at almost every level and dimension of the business. Executives have to crystallize new strategies that focus on value added and incorporate time-based measures. Project leaders have to shift beyond tightening schedules to fundamentally reconceptualizing the product development process as a learning laboratory.

# 4

# Systems and Organizational Learning

## *The Foundation for Fast Cycle Time*

The toughest FCT implementation challenge is to change the organization's fundamental operating behaviors. Until these behaviors change, FCT remains confined to one or two projects or, at worst, becomes management's "flavor of the month." In either case, until it is institutionalized, FCT does not produce a sustainable competitive advantage.

When organizations focus their energy on the easy-to-learn tactics and techniques of a new discipline and too little time integrating the concepts behind the techniques, change is not long-lasting. For example, "quality circles" became the rage of American business about ten years ago, and today their usage is virtually nil. Has Japan stopped using quality circles? Not at all. The issue is not that quality circles cannot work in the United States but that they cannot work unless they are a part of a more comprehensive culture change.

FCT faces a unique problem. The greater one's need is to reduce cycle time, the more one wants to get started quickly. The faster one wants to start, the more one is attracted to focusing on implementing tactics and techniques. This has two serious consequences. First, when we devote our time to learning tactics, we don't have enough time left to internalize the conceptual foundation that is required to support the tactics in the long term. Second, the more amenable a tactic is for instant use, the more likely it is that it's not very different from something we're already doing, or else we couldn't adopt it so fast. In our quest for rapid improvement, *we* create the flavor of the month. To gain its full benefits, FCT requires fundamental change in the organization's culture.

This chapter describes the conceptual underpinnings of FCT implementation, whereas the rest of the book applies the FCT implementation strategy and techniques. We will focus on two areas: systems thinking[1] and organizational learning.[2] Systems thinking provides an alternative to the functional paradigm that dominates organization structure, work processes, and problem solving. Systems thinking is the foundation of the "process orientation" that is embodied within FCT organization architecture, multifunctional teams, and process redesign. We will begin by detailing the traps within the functional paradigm that we refer to as "conventional thinking" by reviewing what happens during a simulation exercise. Next we will show how conventional thinking's focus on parts rather than wholes limits the functional organization's ability to be fast. We will then discuss the basic principles of the systems thinking alternative and apply them to the FCT organization alternative: team-based, network organizations.

We will then shift to examine how organizations learn. As we have stated, the ability to learn fast, rather than work fast, is the core of the FCT strategy. We will begin by discovering how dry the soil within organizations is for learning, due in large part to the impact of conventional thinking. We then will define the critical and often overlooked distinction between personal and organizational learning. Next we will show how our beliefs about learning curtail our ability to learn quickly within organizations and then argue that we need to "relearn" how we learn. We conclude by asserting that transforming an organization from a traditional competitor to an FCT "speed demon" depends mostly on how well one can unlearn current practices. We will provide specific suggestions for how to do so within your organization.

For those who are considering skipping this chapter, be forewarned. Merely implementing the strategy and tactics detailed in the remaining chapters without internalizing the fundamental concepts described herein will not yield lasting change.

## The Beanbag Exercise

Like people, organizational behavior follows the path of least resistance. Until that path is exposed and changed, behavior will continue as is. Change occurs when the current performance is no longer acceptable *and* the ultimate advantage of carving a new path clearly outweighs the old. If today's performance is close enough and the new alternative's benefits are a toss-up, most organizations will not change.

In traditional organizations, the path of least resistance for an employee is to please his or her immediate boss. The boss is typically in charge of a functional area, and if pleasing him or her conflicts with others' needs, including those of customers, so be it. If you doubt this, think of the last time you made a simple request of a bank or airline counterperson and were told that he or she had to check with the supervisor before granting your request. The path of least resistance is to check. Regardless of the answer received, the checking lengthens the service cycle time.

We observe this same dynamic in a simulation exercise we use to demonstrate FCT. Imagine a group of seven people seated around a circular table. A pile of fifteen small bean bags are placed in front of one individual. The task is to get the pile to the opposite side of the circle in the shortest amount of time while observing the following rules:

1. All bags must touch all people
2. Bags cannot be passed to a person directly on either side of you
3. Bags must be passed one at a time
4. All bags must get to the opposite side of the table.

Before the exercise begins, an instructor uses one group to demonstrate a star-shaped pattern of tossing the bags (Exhibit 4.1) as an example that is in accordance with the rules. All the other teams observe the demonstration. After the demonstration, the teams are given two min-

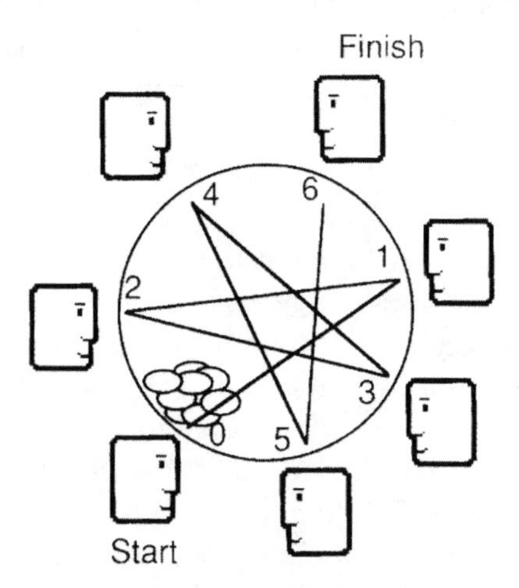


**EXHIBIT 4.1**

utes of planning time, and then the first round is conducted. During the first round, every team usually uses the star patterns. On average, the best times for the first round are twenty-five seconds. At the conclusion of the first round, the teams are given two more minutes of planning time, with the instruction to improve their cycle time *as much as possible.*

During the second round, most teams operate essentially as they did in round one, but with greater concentration on efficiency. Few change the basic star pattern. Most employ incremental alternatives such as standing up and placing their hands closer together. The best times for round two average about seventeen seconds, or a 32% cycle time reduction.

Before beginning the planning session for the third and final round, the instructor informs the groups that their top competitor has completed the identical task in under five seconds. The groups audibly gasp, followed by highly energized discussions. Without fail, every group uses a completely different process for the third round. The best times are often below five seconds. This represents an 80% cycle time reduction from the first round and a 70% reduction from the second.

The discussion that follows is very revealing. First, all groups immediately adopted the star pattern demonstrated by the instructor without entertaining alternatives, thus following the path of least resistance. Second, only incremental changes were made to the star pattern between rounds one and two—again following the same path. Third, it was not until the groups were given dramatic benchmark data of a competitor's capability that they questioned and fundamentally changed their process. Due to the new benchmark data, the path of least resistance shifted.

The most obvious lesson in the impact competitive benchmark data has on a system. The benchmark data created a miniature competitive crisis in the room. Knowing that a significantly shorter cycle time was possible, combined with the fact that a competitor had achieved it, changed the path of least resistance. Equally important, though more subtle, was that the star pattern demonstrated by the instructor became standard operating procedure with little debate. Even when asked to improve the process *as much as possible* between rounds one and two, the star pattern was not seriously questioned.

The same dynamics occur in our companies. For the most part, current procedures and organizational structures are the path of least resistance. Even when we see problems, we evaluate the energy required to "change the system" and often back down as a result. Improvement efforts are confined to making the present system function a little better; only when there is a crisis do we seriously consider an alternative.

Einstein is reported to have once said that the significant problems we face cannot be solved using the same level of thinking we used when we created them. Our experience is that the cycle time barriers within most organizations are created by how we structure our organizations and thinking. We refer to this mind-set as *conventional thinking*, which is the path of least resistance in Western education and business. Although FCT companies may not explicitly articulate the difference, they operate with a different mind-set that we will call *systems thinking*. In order to make the transition to systems thinking, one must first appreciate why and where conventional thinking does not deliver.

## Conventional Thinking

The hallmark of conventional thinking[3] is that it breaks wholes into parts and focuses its attention on the parts. It is a reductionist thought process. Once broken down, the parts are examined for fault. If fault is found, that part is either fixed or replaced. The assumption behind the entire process is that if all the parts are in good working order, success will occur. The part could be an individual in an organization work process or a component within a product. In either case, we are biased toward finding the "part" that does not work and fixing it. Conventional thinking fails to call our attention to the connections between parts in an object or process in an organization.

Although our interest in conventional thinking here is focused on cycle time, one should understand that it permeates every aspect of our lives. Consciously and unconsciously, our default mode for problem solving is to break problems into increasingly smaller parts, always hoping to find the part at fault. For example, our educational system teaches the complexity of business by breaking it into single-discipline study areas such as marketing, finance, computer science, electrical engineering, and so forth. We graduate with degrees that both certify our specialization and often become our self-definition. Then we join a company and are exhorted to meet customers' needs. Customers, however, don't break their needs into component parts. Possibly if business schools had a "meeting customer needs" degree, we would be better off!

An alternative mind-set is systems thinking, which considers the connections between the parts to be as important as the parts themselves. Systems thinking tells us that the parts must be connected *and* in balance to produce desired results. Thus, a problem is not a hardware or a software problem, but a product problem that is influenced by how the hardware and the software interact. Conventional thinking defines problems as "this or that," whereas systems thinking defines them as "this *and* that." Systems thinking is the root of understanding how process works. The FCT organization does not think of itself as a collection of engineering, marketing, and operations experts, but as in integrated set of processes that operates as a value delivery system for the benefit of end customers.

For example, an automobile will not start if the battery cable is disconnected. All the parts are in good working order, but the broken connection prohibits the system from working. Replacing the battery would be a waste of money. The same thing occurs when one element of an organization is disconnected from another. If a prototype part required by the design team is delivered to the receiving dock but engineering does not know it has arrived, work grinds to a halt.

The requirement for system balance is also essential. Consider what would happen if one installed a racing engine in a subcompact car. The engine may be the most powerful in the world, but the smaller car's transmission can only deliver a portion of its power to the wheels, or else it would self-destruct. The parts are connected but out of balance. When this occurs, the total system's performance is determined by the lowest-performance part.

The same is true when the performance goal is reduced cycle time. In the late 1970s, Toyota was able to *manufacture* a car in two days, but it took fifteen to twenty-six days for its sales organization to close the *sale and deliver* the car. The system was out of balance, because Toyota could build the car much faster than it could sell and deliver it. The ability to use the manufacturing improvement was lost, because a system only moves as fast as the slowest element in it. Part of this delay was due to inadequate information-processing systems in order entry and scheduling. Five years later, Toyota had cut the entire system's responsiveness to eight days (including manufacturing).[4]

Whereas conventional thinking breaks concepts and structures into pieces, systems thinking aggregates pieces into balanced wholes. Whereas conventional thinking minimizes the importance of interdependencies, systems thinking strives to understand interdependencies and to maximize their effectiveness. Again, systems thinking shifts us to a process orientation.

The conventional mind-set also treats people as simply a part in the organizational machine. Following this logic, people become disposable. When the organization does not perform, we look for the broken part. It might be Ed, in which case we either fix him or find someone else to do the job, such as Dorothy. If Dorothy fails, we look for someone else, and so on.

The machine mentality created by conventional thinking leads one to believe reducing cycle time in an organization is no different than speeding up an old computer by replacing a slow microprocessor with a faster one. One can change a computer chip without considering the machine's culture, but organizational change efforts flounder when the new "part" conflicts with the existing norms. Using the term *reengineering* to describe organizational process redesign efforts totally obscures the importance of culture change and the contribution of human spirit, creativity, and emotion in work. Treating the organization as a machine may be familiar, but it does not make sense.

Companies also try to fix the technology "parts" of their organizations to speed them up. This is why many organizations' first attempts to reduce cycle time often begin (and end!) with purchasing machines such as tools for computer-aided design (CAD). Paradoxically, CAD tools are only as productive as the underlying process and people's willingness to use them.

Conventional thinking takes our attention away from process and focuses it too narrowly on the parts. Are good parts required for speed? Certainly. Are good parts sufficient for speed? No. Just like the teams in the beanbag exercise, when we use conventional thinking blindly, we take *how* for granted and focus our attention on *what*. Conventional thinking also focuses our attention only on the parts we can see. For example, measurement systems focus on easy-to-measure tangibles such as cost but do little to account for such intangibles as the revenue that is lost by being late to market.

The most tangible impact of conventional thinking on FCT is the sluggishness of the functional organization structure. Its limitations become increasingly apparent as the global rate of change and competition continue to increase. The functional organization must change if one is to become an FCT competitor.

## The Functional Structure and Its Limits

The organization diagram in Exhibit 4.2 is familiar to all. Based on conventional thinking, the structure breaks the organization into its component parts: sales, marketing, engineering, operations, and so on. Each part then specializes on doing its job correctly. The behavioral characteristics of the functional structure include the following:

*Work is divided into specialties.* The organization is broken into groups based on technical or administrative expertise. These groups sit together

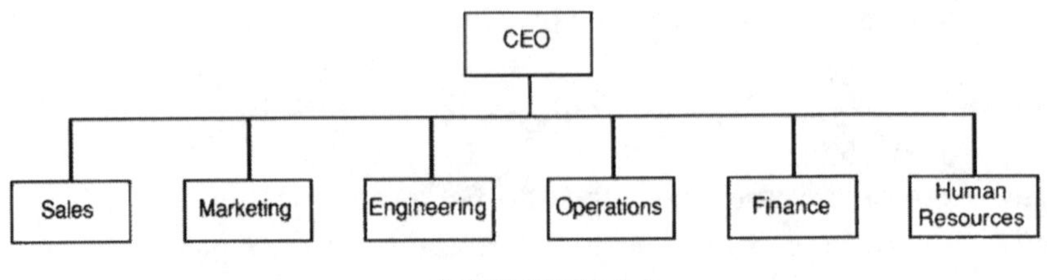


**EXHIBIT 4.2**

and often have subgroups within each function that are also defined by expertise.

*Control comes down from the top; problems go up.* The boss of each function runs that unit, and the chief executive office directs the function bosses. Every work unit leader is individually accountable for his or her unit. If someone has a problem, the path of least resistance is to bump it up to the boss.

*Conflict between units is resolved above and outside the units.* The bosses of the units and the CEO are the only ones who have formal authority to resolve conflicts between units.

*Product development is serial.* Sales gives input to marketing that is then shaped into product requirements. Engineering translates the product requirements into a specification, develops the product, and forwards it to manufacturing.

*Integration is the boss' responsibility.* Because only the bosses of the units have the authority to make decisions for their units, integration between units is dependent on them.

*Performance is defined by standards set within each function.* Each unit boss establishes the performance criteria for his or her unit. Measurements and monitoring systems are functionally based.

*Accountability is to the function and its leader.* Members of each unit are keenly aware that their job is to please their boss. Organization-wide initiatives are endorsed to the degree the unit boss endorses them.

*Physical layout is by function.* People sit with people having a similar background and work experience. Separation from this group puts one out of the information loop and possibly off the career track.

*Communication between functions is through bosses.* Communication with other units is primarily through the boss, who in turn uses subordinates to prepare his or her position and presentation.

*Customer contact is limited to those with formal functional responsibility.* For the most part, those outside of sales and marketing are crossing turf lines when they deal directly with the customer. Certain groups such as customer service and quality may have some direct contact, but each is very careful about what they feel they may talk to the customer about.

The combined impact of these elements can be disastrous. Because each function has its own goal, it is possible to have every function excel and still not meet the customers' needs. Furthermore, conflicting interpretations regarding customer needs are bound to occur. Each person uses his or her own functional lens, and the result is akin to the twelve blind people who each hold a different part of an elephant: one thinks it's a hose because of its trunk, while another thinks it's a tree by the shape of a leg. The limited contact makes it very difficult for any one group to understand a customer's total solution requirements. Work processes, such as new product development, are characterized by "over the wall" handoffs as each function washes its hands of the problem as it moves to the next function in line.

Specialization, functional accountability, and control mechanisms create a suction that pulls decisions upward. This is especially true if there is any risk involved. Since conflicts are resolved by "bumping up" problems to the next level, leaders often find themselves in the position of being asked to resolve problems for which they have little information, knowledge, or technical skill. As the number of levels in the firm increases, the leader's distance from the information and skills required to make the decision becomes a liability. This is particularly true for those problems that do not remain neatly within one function. Not only are they bumped up, but finding a knowledgeable person willing to own the problem can be extremely difficult.

This is exacerbated in bad times, because top management typically wants more involvement when the perceived risk of making a wrong decision is higher. This increases the suction and pulls even more decisions upward. One pays a large cycle time price for each issue elevated. Individuals waste time deliberating whether they should make a call or bump it upstairs. If one chooses to bump, then there is time spent communicating the issue, plus meeting any request of the boss for further information. Each boss involved might have to repeat this deliberation. A similar sequence is followed once a senior person makes the decision, because each level must be communicated with as one moves back down the ladder.

*By far the most serious problem with the functional structure is that it serves its members better than its customers.* Functionally biased processes and procedures force one to swim against the current to serve the customer. People become more invested in their functional world's success than they are in the customer's satisfaction.

Do people within functional organizations find them effective? Those who like clear boundaries and sharp role definitions do. A more important question is, can this organization work in an increasingly fuzzy, fast-paced business environment? Our belief is that it has to be modified. Too many who work within these structures complain about the functional silos or chimneys. The pervasive concern with turf protection becomes most obvious when changes are suggested—for the issue becomes did "we" win or lose, as opposed to whether the customer won or lost. Cycle time and effectiveness both suffer.

Like any other format, the functional organization in practice does not work exactly as described above. Task forces attempt to create bridges between functions. Reward systems include a component for overall organization performance such as profit sharing. Those companies who use quarterly and annual objectives establish some for companywide performance. But the fact of the matter is these are patches and only go so far. In the eyes of employees, the carrot, the stick, and their careers are in the hands of their functional manager, and thus functional needs come first.

Is the functional organization going to be replaced? As we know it today, yes. Will the requirement for technical or administrative specialization also disappear? Clearly not. The need for such expertise will continue to grow as products and business at large become increasingly complex. What will change is the dominance of the functional structure. It will continue to give way to architectures where the customers' needs prevail.

The functional organization is just the organizational heirloom of the reductionist mind-set inherent in conventional thinking. Conventional thinking is so ingrained, it is highly possible that if all the functional organizations in the world were destroyed on Monday, they would be back in operation by Friday, because that is how we were taught to think!

## Principles of the Systems Alternatives

Whereas conventional thinking principles provide the base for the functional organization, systems thinking provides the foundation for the FCT organization. Before we describe the FCT organization itself, the reader should understand a little more about systems thinking.

If there is a single systems principle that is absolutely central to FCT, it is that structures, tangible or intangible, drive the behavior of systems. The policy manual is a tangible structure, and unstated norms of behavior are intangible structures. "We don't do it that way around here" may not be written down, but it has the same (if not greater) impact on people's behavior as the policy manual.

The impact of structure is easiest to see using tangible structures. For example, there is little difference in humans' basic biochemical composition versus that of any other mammal. All mammals are composed of carbon compounds, each organized in a unique manner. Thus, we are composed of the same materials as a giraffe, yet how these are structured makes our appearance, capabilities, and behavior quite different.

As noted in Chapter 2, the conversational use of the term *structure* in organizations limits itself to the organization chart; we use the term *organizational architecture* to refer to the broader set of structures and connections that organize it in a particular and unique way. Because the architecture shapes the behavior of the organization. FCT organizations constantly assess and modify their architecture as business conditions and strategy change.

The design of an FCT architecture focuses on maximizing the effectiveness of value delivery to the end customer. Let's briefly examine five additional operating principles that apply to FCT organizations.[5]

### *Structures Can Accelerate or Inhibit Movement Toward Goals*

Graduate students in systems dynamics at the Massachusetts Institute of Technology once labeled this principle the "Callahan Tunnel effect."[6] To drive to Boston proper from Logan Airport on a Friday evening, one must pass through the two-lane Callahan Tunnel. Traffic narrows from eight lanes to two in the space of approximately one hundred yards. If there is any volume at all, traffic quickly grinds to a halt. The physical structure of the roadway inhibits the flow of traffic from reaching Boston proper.

In exactly the same way, tangible and intangible structures can stop a project as quickly as the Callahan Tunnel does traffic. Consider the impact on cycle time when spending authorization limits are set too low. What if an engineer's boss is out of town when he needs to authorize a $175 component purchase, which exceeds his $100 authorized limit? The spending limit is part of the organization's tangible structure. If the component is critical to moving the project forward, development must wait. Let's assume the acting manager decides to wait a couple of days until the traveling manager returns, because earlier in his career he faced a similar situation, approved the purchase, and was chewed out for doing so. The acting manager's choice to wait is intangible but no less impactful. FCT companies size approval limits for speed as well as control.

On the other hand, structures can accelerate progress to goals. Nordstrom has become one of the best-known retailers for its impeccable and speedy customer service. The entire employee handbook for Nordstrom's is one page in length. It clearly states that the primary corporate goal is to serve the needs of Nordstrom's customers. Only one rule exists: use your best judgment in all situations. The content and one-page format create a compelling structure.

### *Every Structure in a System Has Its Own Goal and Payoff*

In a traditional functional organization, each function sets goals relative to its internal needs and priorities. Manufacturing will typically be very cost sensitive, whereas engineering will be attuned to reducing technical risk. Yet 70% to 90% of the product cost is locked in during the design phase. Changing a design after it reaches the shop floor costs ten times what it would in engineering, and one hundred times as much midway through the production run.[7]

In contrast, the FCT organization establishes goals for each process. These goals integrate rather than separate functional activities. For example, achieving a cycle time goal for new product development at the very least requires the involvement of marketing, engineering, and manufacturing experts. Multifunctional teams are the most common structure used to manage processes that extend beyond a single expertise.

FCT leaders and managers spend their time ensuring that the goals of each team and the centers are aligned to the firm's mission and strategy. One of the principle advantages of the FCT structure is its high degree of flexibility. When strategy changes, it is much easier to realign a process or team-based structure than a division or functional one.

### *Unspoken Rules Take Priority over Spoken Rules*

Every person in a company maintains an invisible gauge inside his or her head that tracks management's current interest. We like to call this gauge the *management apparent-interest index*. The needle on this gauge (Exhibit 4.3) only changes based on what management *does* rather than what it says.

For example, at Mighty Tech's quarterly management off-site, Mighty Tech's leaders introduced FCT as *the* strategic initiative to focus on for the next five years. Cycle time improvement goals were set and reviewed.

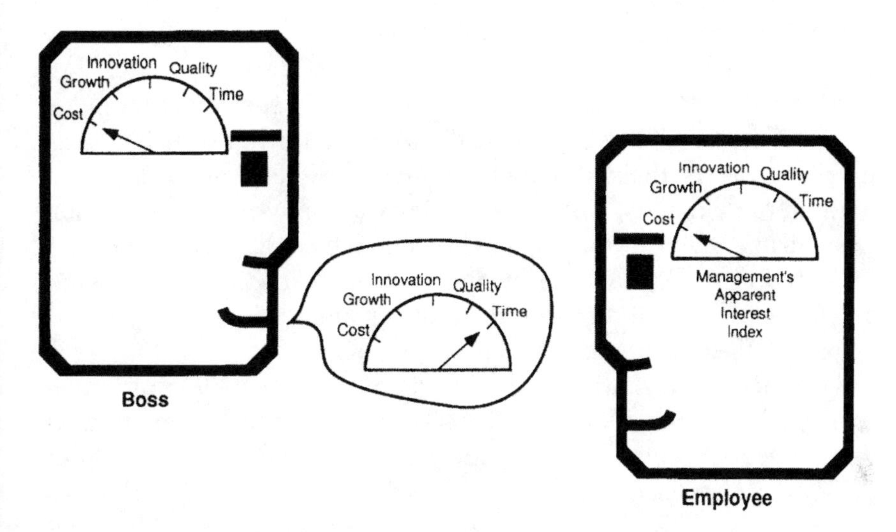


**EXHIBIT 4.3**

A lot of hoopla and time were involved in laying out the FCT program. Previous to this, Mighty Tech was renowned for its ability to squeeze every nickel of cost out of any product design through its monthly cost reviews.

Immediately after the off-site, senior management held its monthly cost review. Over the next few months, the monthly cost reviews continued as before, with relatively few questions from senior management about FCT implications. Where do you think the needle on individuals' indexes pointed—cost, or FCT? People will always modify their behavior to be in line with management's apparent interest, regardless of what management says it wants.

During change, people are highly sensitized to look for the first signs of confirming or conflicting evidence. Companies that explicitly identify high-visibility processes that are not in alignment with the FCT strategy and terminate or transform them increase speed rapidly. It is quite useful for senior management to examine how it spends time publicly and privately, for this is the primary determinant of the index. When management changes its behavior and devotes time to FCT, others take notice and follow.

### *Different People in the Same Structure Produce Qualitatively the Same Result*

If one put the best and the worst salespersons in the world in a Yugo car dealership, it is reasonable to assume that both would have an equally troublesome time. If one placed both of them in a Lexus dealership, however, on a relative scale they would both be better off.

Flagstaff Devices makes custom equipment for the computer industry. Over the past five years, Flagstaff has terminated three manufacturing managers for their inability to improve cycle time and yields. Each one entered with great fanfare, only to leave abruptly in great frustration. One might argue that Flagstaff has not found the right person, but this is unlikely. Flagstaff is run by an engineer who is also the founder and chief executive officer. He focuses most of his time and the majority of Flagstaff's financial resources on product design.

Historically, Flagstaff's manufacturing process capabilities are added to only after a crisis. During the creation of each annual operating plan, each of the respective manufacturing managers tried fruitlessly to increase the manufacturing budget. Due to the bias of Flagstaff's CEO, each was unsuccessful. Development resources were always added in anticipation of needs, but never manufacturing resources. The intangible structure created by Flagstaff's CEO doomed any manufacturing manager to failure.

The reason FCT organizations pay close attention to structure is that it is where the root cause of the majority of organizational and personal performance issues rest. This is not to say individual capabilities are unimportant, but that is not where the leverage is. There may well be a manufacturing manager somewhere in the world who could convince Flagstaff's CEO to budget more funds for manufacturing; however, it is a long shot. Building an organization around principles that require herculean efforts to do base business is not fast or effective.

### *Cause and Effect Are Not Closely Related in Time or Space*

Every year for three years, Wonder Workstations doubled its sales and the size of its sales organization.[8] At the beginning of the fourth year, sales fell below the historical growth rate. At a staff meeting, Wonder's CEO asked her sales executive to explain the drop in sales force productivity. The sales executive declared that his people were pushing as hard as ever, but the company needed to increase its marketing investment due to a significant increase in the number of competitors. A marketing program was initiated, and sales growth returned to historic rates for three months and then slackened again.

When Wonder's CEO raised the issue a second time, the manufacturing manager surprised everyone by saying she knew what caused the problem. The real problem wasn't sales productivity but manufacturing capacity. She reminded everyone how reluctant they were to invest the capital required to expand the manufacturing floor nine months ago. Now, manufacturing was operating at close to 200% of the facility's rated capacity. Boxes, systems, and cables nearly filled the building from floor to ceiling. At the end of the month, one could hardly move a box without moving another box to make room for it.

As a consequence, shipments were increasingly configured inaccurately or shipped with the wrong cables, software, and manuals, often to the wrong location. The manufacturing manager said the young company's credibility as a reliable supplier was being actively questioned by many customers. A quick check with regional sales directors confirmed this perception. Even current customers who were excited about the product were holding back additional orders because of their concerns.

Wonder Workstations incorrectly defined the problem as a sales issue because that was where the problem surfaced. Processes within systems work in different rhythms. Accordingly, there is frequently a time delay between the birth of a problem and when it is visible. The problem often shows up somewhere other than where it started, as was the case at Wonder Workstations. FCT organizations use flat, multifunctional team-based structures to increase the flow of knowledge and therefore the probability that problems will be spotted sooner.

## The FCT Organization

The FCT organization is conceived and operated as a system whose goal is to deliver value to the firm's customers rapidly, accurately, and reliably. The work required by and between each *value delivery process* determines the configuration of the organization and its technical resources. The three questions one asks when designing the FCT organization are as follows:

1. What are the core value delivery processes?
2. What are the other required processes?
3. How should the above processes be structured and integrated to deliver the highest value in the shortest amount of time?

*Core value delivery processes.* Value delivery processes are those processes that directly produce value for end customers.[9] For example, the product development process transforms customer requirements into a reproducible design. The order-to-fulfillment process takes the order, manufactures, and delivers the product to the customer.

*Other required processes.* Most organization processes do not directly add value to the customer. Some experts estimate that only 0.05% to 5% of all work is value added. The non-value-added processes are required to support the value delivery processes, but they do not directly deliver value themselves. A simple example is the performance appraisal process. The organization may use performance appraisal as a basis for compensation and development, but the customer has little interest in it. FCT competitors constantly try to shrink, combine, or eliminate any process that does not directly deliver value.

*Process integration and structure.* The FCT organization focuses on designing the interface between structures and processes with a bias toward speed. For example, multifunctional teams are a commonly used structure to speed the new product development process. Formal reporting relationships and informal champions combine to create interfaces between the teams and other organization elements.

The FCT organization attempts to mirror the work flow that would be seen if one simply observed people working without regard to title and functional home. As illustrated in Exhibit 4.4, when one overlays the functional organization on the actual work processes, the artificial segmentation of the functional structure is plainly visible. The FCT organization uses the natural work processes as the primary basis for organization.[10]

Startups function in this manner. When fifteen people work day and night using rented furniture in less than ideal surroundings, there is little room for titles. If the venture capitalists request a financial report, the person who knows how to use spreadsheet software becomes the Chief Financial Officer for that moment.

Startup decision-making processes are more informal than those of a more mature organization. As organizations grow, they begin to formalize how work is done. An early manifestation of this trend is specialization, which ultimately transforms the startup into a functional organization. As this occurs, people report that the fun quotient deteriorates and speed is lost.

## Value-Added Versus Non-Value-Added Processes

Value is always determined by the end customer, and never by "internal customers." The "internal customer" terminology helps people understand the interdependencies of business processes, but it is a serious mistake to equate employees' needs with those of end customers. End customers generate revenue, while internal customers generate costs.

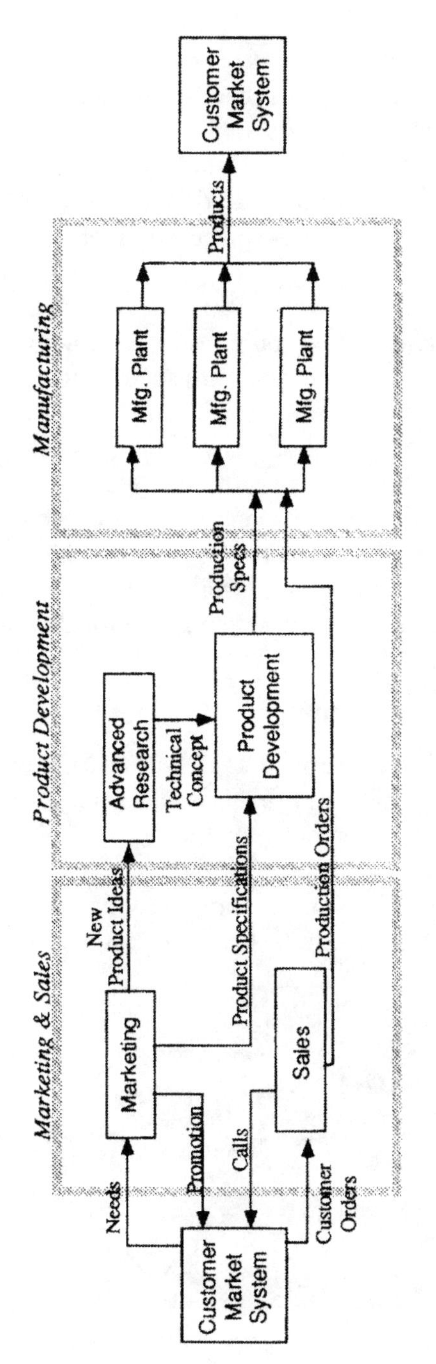
Marketing & Sales
Product Development
Manufacturing
Customer Market System
Needs
Promotion
Calls
Customer Orders
Marketing
Sales
New Product Ideas
Product Specifications
Production Orders
Advanced Research
Technical Concept
Product Development
Production Specs
Mfg. Plant
Mfg. Plant
Mfg. Plant
Products
Customer Market System

**EXHIBIT 4.4**

Several firms (including Motorola) are doing away with the term *internal customer*.

One can easily add value for an internal customer without doing anything for the end customer. For example, the creation of a new product to process engineering change orders may appeal to program managers, but it does not add value for the end customer. To test this logic, think of the last consumer product you purchased. Was your buying decision strongly influenced by how they manage their engineering change process?

The experts who cite the low level of value-added work base their comments on work flow studies.[11] They only count that time when a person or machine is transforming the product into something of greater value that directly meets customer requirements. The reason the percentage of value-added work is so low is that many of the processes required to produce a product either compensate for our lack of process and product understanding or are required to support the organizational infrastructure. As one develops better control over the technical variables at play, one can eliminate or compress non-value-added processes. We will discuss this in greater detail in the section on process analysis in Chapter 6.

## The FCT Organizational Model

The functional organization is easily drawn, but the FCT organization is not. Exhibit 4.5 captures the main features, although it cannot fully illustrate the dynamic interaction between them.

What we used to think of as functions are now centers of technical and administrative expertise. The bars are purposely drawn horizontally to emphasize the shift in power. Multifunctional teams are networked to

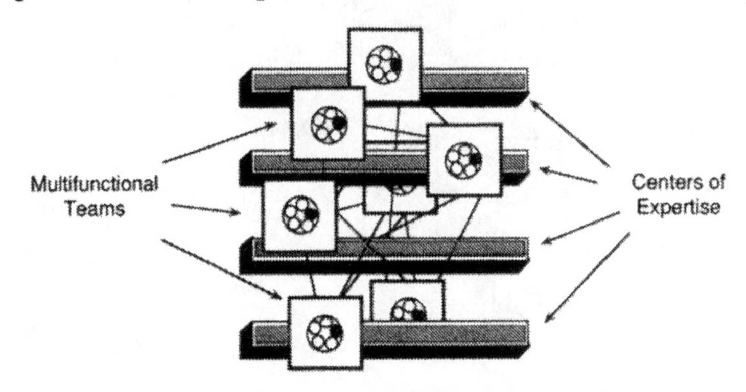


**EXHIBIT 4.5**

each other and to the centers of expertise Were it possible, this diagram would be shown as a pulsating, three-dimensional figure, with teams shifting back and forth to reflect the changing priorities of end customers. Furthermore, network connections would appear and disappear as required by the business strategy and work flow.

This model does not eliminate dedicated groups of similarly skilled people, but their needs and perspectives are focused to support the value delivery processes. They are augmented by a set of multifunctional teams, which are designed around complete processes and are responsible for execution of these processes. For the purposes of this book, our focus will be on the new product development process and the teams associated with it.

The multifunctional teams possess the critical mass of technical and administrative skills required to complete the process for which they are responsible. The multifunctional structure places the people who need to work together in real-time direct contact with the bulk of the resources they require. The teams are the primary value delivery structure.

The centers of expertise provide technical resources to the teams, either in the form of team members or directly. To guarantee an ongoing supply of technical talent, the FCT organization maintains a strong technical ladder. This provides a career path within the center of expertise for selected technologists who will be primarily based in the centers rather than on the multifunctional teams. If multifunctional team participation is the only career path, there is a danger of losing critical technical competencies.

To work effectively, there has to be a redistribution of power in the organization. Whereas the functions dominate decision making in a traditional organization, the multifunctional teams have 51% of the clout in an FCT organization. The slim majority reflects the fact that technical expertise *and* integrated processes are required to add value. In practice, the majority of issues are resolved without impasse, and this never becomes an issue. What the 51% implies is that when an impasse is reached, the balance will tip toward the teams, for they are the primary mechanism that delivers value to end customers. In Chapter 5, we will discuss in detail how one designs and implements this structure.

## A Closing Thought About Organizational Systems

Creating effective structures to channel work rapidly through the organization is central to transforming your organization into an FCT competitor. Any change—no matter how big—that does not change the organization's architecture, including its core work processes, will not endure. At the same time, any change—no matter how indirect or small it seems—that affects the organization architecture is going to alter the firm's long-term behavior. Stan Davis echoes and expands this point:

> Marginal reductions (10–20%) generally can be accomplished by improving efficiencies: reductions in multiples (50–100+%) generally require reconceptualizing the production, distribution, and/or delivery processes themselves. The transformative quality lies in the elimination of any waiting at all—zero-based time. . . . Speaking practically, whatever your business, think about how you create products and services in real time that you can deliver instantly.[12]

We have focused most of our attention on aligning the work structure to the value delivery process but have not spoken much about speeding up the work flow itself. The FCT competitor has a second concern: increasing the rate of organization learning. Product development gains velocity in proportion to increases in the rate of learning. Let's turn our attention to organizational learning and explore how one accelerates it.

## Organizational Learning: The Heart of FCT

A common difficulty faced during FCT implementation is that people equate working faster with FCT. Senior management usually states the strategic rationale for faster product development, but does not say much about how it will be achieved. This feeds the speed-up perception. Since most people have experienced a rush project at one time or another, the perception cannot be dismissed as myth. John Sculley, chairman of Apple Computer, understands this point: "It isn't getting engineers to work harder; they work extremely hard as it is. It's getting decisions to be made faster, and getting the integration between manufacturing and what's shipped in the marketplace and what is happening with the product decisions."[13]

FCT competitors view learning as a continuous improvement process that feeds on itself primarily through multiple small victories. The vast majority of successful new products are not breakthrough discoveries but existing knowledge blended in a slightly different way. A turn of the lens enabled Sony Corporation to take mature audiotape technology and create the Walkman. Chrysler's built-in child seat introduced, in the early 1990s, requires no new technology. All too frequently, development specialists artificially limit their definition of learning to dramatic breakthroughs such as Polaroid film or cold fusion.[14]

Although many development organizations talk about learning, only the FCT organization pursues increasing the speed of learning as a strategic objective. In contrast, traditional organizations treat learning as a want instead of a must. They fail to make the connection between the rate of learning and their firm's long-term competitiveness. The responsibility for learning is singularly relegated to the training department. If the business comes under economic pressure, the commitment to learning is visibly tested, because training is one of the first items managers cut from their budgets. FCT organizations view speeding up learning as a strategic imperative. For example, Motorola has one thousand educational specialists and devotes 1.5% of its revenue to employee development.

Yet learning is not something organizations do well. In a fascinating book, MIT professor Donald Schön explores how professionals learn their craft.[15] He examines four professions: clinical psychologists, urban planners, architects, and business people. With the *exception* of business people, each profession has a deliberate apprenticeship process that grooms future professionals. In addition to the absence of a process to groom professionals, Schön finds that the majority of tangible and intangible structures within business undermine learning. In the broadest terms, business organizations reward those who already know and punish those who do not. If you have any doubts about this, think of the number of times you use or hear the expression "please don't shoot the messenger."

Those who have experience working with Japanese companies see a different orientation. Learning is considered an integral part of the job, and they understand the difference between personal and organizational learning. The Japanese spend a much longer time developing a *collective* understanding of a problem before they act. Their "slowness" in making decisions is outweighed by their speed of implementation, which results in faster elimination of the original problem. When they finally take action, implementation and problem resolution happen quickly whereas Western firms often require several sets of decisions and actions to solve the same problem. This underscores the fundamental distinction between making rapid decisions and solving problems quickly.

### *The Difference Between Organizational and Personal Learning*

Our concept of learning is strongly influenced by our experience in school. For the most part, the focus of school learning is on the individual. Tests, for example, are taken individually. Furthermore, the methodology of school education is to have the students solve problems given to them by their teachers.[16] As a result, we grow unconsciously dependent on others to define problems for us. In business, appraising a situation and defining the right problem are often 90% of the battle.

Our concept of organizational learning is even less developed. Most treat organizational learning as the sum of individual learning. Organizational learning is much more than that; it is *the continuous testing and transformation of experience into shared knowledge that the organization accesses and uses to achieve its core purpose.*[17]

The firm's operating experience is the raw material for organizational learning. The critical factor is devoting time to testing and judging operating experience so that the most valuable nuggets are extracted and transformed into knowledge that others can use. How fast this occurs paces the rate of organizational learning and cycle time. Simply compiling large amounts of data is not learning. We have yet to encounter an organization that lacked sufficient data, but rarely find one that has enough usable data or knowledge.

Once the transformation of experience and data into knowledge is complete, it must become available for others to use. When available, people can access and use knowledge *if* they know it exists and can find it. Often one design team learns something about customer requirements or product or process technology that would be useful to all teams, but it never gets outside the original team. Ideally, there should be no delay between the time that knowledge is created and when it becomes known and accessible to others. This will not happen unless the creation and distribution of knowledge are actively led and managed as resources.

The most basic format for capturing knowledge is the written word. Increasingly, new technologies are providing additional opportunities to ensure that what is written gets used. For example, data bases can provide easy storage and retrieval, but these are still not easy to use. A further step is the development of expert systems. Design tools for electronic circuit design incorporate real-time design rule checking to guide the development of new circuits.

Intel has used this technology to reduce its development cycle time while increasing the complexity of its chip designs. Beginning in the late 1980s, Intel spent $250 million testing and incorporating new design knowledge into its CAD tools. The spending represents approximately 20% of the firm's total R & D budget. Since 1985, it has cut chip development time by more than half, to an average of forty-four weeks. The lead time for the 486 model chip was shorter than for the 386, even though the newer chip is a lot more complicated.[18]

For knowledge to be useful, it must be in alignment with the organization's mission and strategy. Intel's expert system development would have little value for a specialty steel company. Once again, the importance of clearly articulating where and how the firm adds value for its end customers is critical. If people do not understand the value proposition of the organization, they will not be able to focus their learning efforts.

By contrasting individual learning with organizational learning (Exhibit 4.6), one can quickly see the dilemmas inherent in creating a healthy corporate learning environment. First, each of us has our own unique learning style. Some learn best by doing, others prefer to read, and still others like to watch. Second, individual learning is invisible. It is impossible to tell when someone is learning simply by watching him or her. Last, the motivation for learning can vary greatly between people in the same situation. Most attend management training classes to learn, but some go because they are substituting for someone else or because it would look bad if they didn't go. Each attends, but with different agendas in mind.

The primary difference between personal and organizational learning is the social requirement of organizational learning. For example, FCT competitors conduct postmortems on development programs in order to capture the learning before the team disbands. The postmortem creates a public forum where people's thoughts regarding what worked and what didn't are exposed and possibly contested and/or criticized.

A distinguishing feature of the postmortem is that it provides a forum that makes publicly discussing mistakes legitimate. We all recognize mistakes are a fact of life and a basis for learning, but the actual experience of making a mistake or discussing it publicly is not necessarily pleasant. As effective as the postmortem is, it occurs after the project is finished. A real-time mechanism that created the same discussion when the problem first occurred would be far more effective.

*The primary obstacle to real-time learning is the perceived risk.* Discussing mistakes when they happen is difficult. People are disappointed and sometimes angry; the degree to which one deems the environment

| ***Personal Learning*** | ***Organizational Learning*** |
|---|---|
| Personal | Social |
| Invisible | Public |
| Self-defined Purpose | Collective Purpose |

**EXHIBIT 4.6**

safe either inhibits or spurs the discussion. As Schön's study corroborates, most businesses are replete with "don't shoot the messenger" metaphors that speak to the hazards of public acknowledgment of mistakes.

### *Relearning How to Learn*

FCT organizations distinguish themselves by continuously improving their learning processes just as they do their value delivery process. This is not easy, because our beliefs about *how* we learn are as invisible to us as water is to a fish. These invisible beliefs inhibit our learning speed just as effectively as the Callahan Tunnel constricts the flow of traffic. Until they are visible, we cannot change them. Until changed, individual and organizational learning suffers. FCT organizations need to create new rules for learning that support speed and become part of their corporate culture.

Test and see if the following beliefs are part of the invisible learning processes that influences you and your organization.[19]

1. There are right answers and wrong answers
2. It's wrong to be wrong
3. For me to be right, you have to be wrong
4. Someone knows the right answer; just wait and they'll tell you
5. Learning is not work

The first inhibiting belief creates a binary choice between right and wrong that leaves little room for "it depends." Originally taught to us by our parents, school examinations cement this belief into our unconscious. In addition, bringing home low test grades quickly teaches us the second inhibiting belief. These seemingly simple notions have considerable implications for FCT. Because of these beliefs, many avoid speaking out until they are absolutely sure of their answer. Time is wasted while people privately assure themselves and others that their answers are correct. It also encourages people to position their ideas carefully and leave plenty of room for backpedaling in case they are wrong. Obviously, these two beliefs do not create an environment for measured risk taking.

When one views being wrong as untenable, the third belief emerges: for me to be right, you have to be wrong. Since being wrong is not acceptable, we will avoid it at all costs. This can take a seemingly fruitful discussion and quickly degrade it into a personal attack. When combined with the power hierarchy found in organizations, "for me to be right, you have to be wrong" obscures the truth when one is concerned about the boss's reaction. Nothing wastes time more than trying to ferret out the truth or operating while knowing that one has only half the story.

It is easy to see how these intangible beliefs about learning can have a greater impact on product development cycle time than specific technical issues. When people spend more time covering their rear anatomy rather than dealing with the issues head-on, valuable time is wasted. It is not nearly as visible as missing a program milestone, but it has the same (if not bigger) impact. The black-and-white split between right and wrong is particularly inappropriate in new product development, because there are usually several right and wrong answers for any issue. The consequences people associate with being wrong inhibit experimentation, risk taking, and the very nature of scientific inquiry. For example, the use of feasibility studies expands beyond ensuring technological feasibility to justifying or protecting one's standing. Commissioning a feasibility study can become an indirect way of saying no.

The fourth belief that permeates organizations is "Someone knows the right answer; just wait and they'll tell you." Comments such as "if they would only tell us what they want, we'd be glad to do it" reflect the essence of this belief. Cycle time increases invisibly as people wait to be told what to do next. One of the major challenges facing organizations today is convincing people that empowerment is a two-way street. All too often, our first efforts at enabling others through a redistribution of power are thwarted by their own internal beliefs, which wait for the right answer to be given to them.

The last belief has the most serious implications: most people and organizations do not define learning as work. Work is defined as making decisions and taking action, whereas learning is a passive activity that occurs in the corporate training facility or on your own. If this were not true, why would so many describe those who are away attending a seminar as being on a "boondoggle"? When learning is not work, then devoting time to it, by definition, is waste.

To overcome the momentum of all these beliefs, leaders in FCT organizations must become leaders of learning. Without a dedicated effort, the current beliefs and their implications will continue unabated. FCT leaders lead learning by challenging the dependency the beliefs create in themselves and others. Our experience suggests that FCT leaders can lead learning more effectively if they reframe this challenge as *leading unlearning*.

### *Unlearning*

Our experience is that most seasoned product development managers have worked on at least one fast cycle product development project, although it probably wasn't called that at the time. This usually happens when there is a crisis and, for whatever reason, the normal rules of behavior are suspended. The project receives all the support and visibility it needs, because for the moment it is the most important thing going. There is a palatable change in the human energy field as well; people are excited and things get done quickly.

The problem is that these situations are the exception, not the norm. Once completed, we return to our historical behaviors. In order for the exception to become the norm, we have to give up some of our normal ways. In other words, *learning requires letting go as well as adding on.*[20] Remember the traditional pyramid display of oranges at the end of a grocery aisle? Learning is the process of placing a new orange on top of the pyramid and simultaneously removing one from the bottom. The challenge is in removing the bottom orange. Experience suggests that all organizations want to improve their cycle time; they just don't want to have to do anything differently!

Unlearning is a difficult process for people to go through and a tough one to lead. The following are suggestions and methods that have proven useful in cycle time reductions across a variety of industries and technologies.

### *Allocate Time for Unlearning*

FCT asks product development specialists to develop new products incorporating the latest technologies by using a new development process that itself is untested. If people do *not* resist such a challenge, we should be worried! Before people are going to step up to such a challenge, they must have time to engage with their leaders about how and why this will work.

Taking time to engage others fully in discussions about FCT, process analysis, and business strategy resets everyone's management apparent-interest index to redefine learning as work. The early stages of FCT require some pushing by leadership, otherwise it would not be a change. When people see management spending its time pushing itself as well as others, it sends a clear signal that learning is indeed work.

The time spent should be a two-way dialogue that is an honest airing and exchange of ideas and suggestions rather than a one-way indoctrination session. This could be in the form of a brown-bag lunch meeting, training, or an FCT process analysis project. Whatever form it takes, if those who have to change are not allowed the time to test the suggestions against their experience, the change will not be sustained.

### *Design Forums for Learning and Unlearning*

Just as college faculty create curriculums and courses for learning, one needs to design similar structures and processes for unlearning. We think of these as learning forums—places where people can publicly test their experience and transform it into knowledge that others can access and use.[21] Generically, the forum should increase awareness and facilitate open inquiry into the issue at hand. Shortly we will examine alternative learning forums that FCT organizations use; for now, let's use FCT process mapping to illustrate what a learning forum is. We will discuss process mapping techniques in much greater detail in Chapter 7.

Mapping teams include those who are directly involved in the process being mapped, since they have the best information about it. Their first task is collectively to create a map defining how the process works today. Some disagreements always emerge, but these are usually minor. The disagreements help loosen people up because they are usually just different perspectives of the same issue. Next, the group analyzes the map, looking for potential cycle time improvements. This is the first step onto new ground. Last, they build a map outlining the new process that incorporates their choices of what to hold on to and what to let go.

By detailing the current process first, it honors people's experience. As a result, they are willing to explore alternatives and eventually let go of selected current practices. The letting-go component can be accelerated by involving an outside facilitator. A facilitator is sufficiently distant from the work process to ask naive questions that challenge the status quo, as well as to serve as a disinterested third party to guide the discussions.

### *Tell the Truth Publicly; Reward the Truth When Told*

The most difficult aspect of leading unlearning is telling the truth publicly and encouraging others to do likewise. With rare exception, organizational lies are well intentioned. Each of us has attended too many meetings where executives, managers, and employees consciously and unconsciously talk their way around issues. It is as though there is special code of conduct that is invoked when discussing a sensitive problem. The lies conceal the real issue and smooth rather than highlight differences that exist; the motivation is to protect people's feelings and egos. If you want to know the truth in such a meeting, wait until there is a break, then listen to the conversation in the bathroom. Ninety percent of the time there is more truth told there in five minutes than in the entire meeting. Leaders bring the bathroom conversation into the conference room.

Not only is truth avoided, but so is any discussion of its undiscussability—a serious double bind. If you doubt this, next time you're in a meeting where people are politely but obviously talking around the real issues, try telling the group just that. Regardless of your job title, nine times out of ten the group will become extremely defensive and deny or excuse its behavior.[22]

The organization pays a significant price for not telling the truth. Our concern is outside the realm of business ethics: the operational inefficiency and negative impact on learning and decision cycle time are blatant. First, the lack of truth telling wastes more time than technical issues. Simply add up the expensive meeting time spent ferreting out the truth from conversations containing half-truths, hidden agendas, and the like. Second, any learning based on half-truths is either useless or terribly dangerous. It is useless because the data it's based on are corrupt, and it is dangerous because someone may not know that and take action based on it. Third, count the time and energy wasted encoding and decoding these half-truths.

For example, assume an issue is not resolved during the meeting because it becomes obvious that the parties involved are working hard to further their individual interests but don't say so. Because of travel and vacation schedules, another meeting cannot be scheduled for a month. A one-month delay has just occurred. None of this is measured, but it extends throughout the development process. Simply telling the truth would enable everyone to focus their attention on the right issues quickly.

The most powerful FCT leaders we witness are those who succinctly identify critical issues and make it safe to discuss them. They do this publicly and privately, with groups and individuals. These leaders are particularly tenacious with data, yet compassionate with people. They do not let their concern for people cover the facts, nor do they let the facts erase another person's dignity.

These leaders will not hesitate to name the real issue under discussion. We refer to this as "pulling the dead horse out from under the table." This picturesque phrase is useful to executives because they can adopt it and use it in meetings as a code to get the real issue out in the open. FCT leaders will not sit long through a conversation that is dancing around an emotional topic without pulling the horse out from under the table so all can see it.

### *Increase Reflection During Daily Business*

When our bias for action and experimentation is overutilized, learning and unlearning are trampled. New insights come from poking an issue from a different angle and thinking about it a little differently. When we are constantly pushed to act, we deal only with what is on the surface. Just like a rock causes the ripples on the surface of a stream, constant action deals just with the ripples and never the rock. One should never leave a meeting without taking the time to ask, "What did we learn from this, and what changes, if any, should we make in our process or structure to keep it from happening again?"

Reflection slows us down enough to see when we are making leaps in abstraction. An engineer might say to a colleague, "Don't use that vendor, they're always late." Without digging any further, that vendor may be chopped off the list of potential suppliers when in fact the engineer's experience might be eight years old. The reader saw in the beanbag game how quickly one can transform small pieces of data into formidable belief systems.

For reflection to support unlearning, it must balance inquiry with advocacy. Inquiry is the process of understanding the thinking and assumptions behind others' positions and advocacy requires exposing one's own thoughts. In complex matters, this takes time and effort. It is critical to keep a balance between the two. When that balance is lost, one slips into "for me to be right, you have to be wrong."

Reflection can keep us straight on management's apparent-interest index. When we are too consumed with action, we lose sight of how our actions are being read by others. When what we say and what we do are out of sync *and* we are unaware of it, the organization discounts any leadership initiative.

### *Expose Current Behavior with Measures*

The power of measurement is that people pay attention to what is being measured. Well-designed measurement systems guide behavior. If one wants an organization to focus on cycle time, establish cycle time measures for key value delivery processes throughout the system. If the data shows that cycle times are either rising or not falling as expected, people will dig naturally behind the issue and start the learning/unlearning process. Chapter 8 presents FCT measures in detail.

A powerful example of using measurements to stimulate unlearning is benchmarking. This was demonstrated in the beanbag exercise. When one is confronted with a competitor's capability to achieve performance that is considered internally impossible, unlearning soars as all sorts of options open up.

### *Use Crisis as Opportunity*

Crisis is the most powerful driver of unlearning there is. When the situation can no longer be handled by conventional means, minds open up to new options. When Roger Penske took over Detroit Diesel, the company had become internally focused and was losing money badly. He started by requiring all managers and distributors to call or visit four customers a day. He also invited employees from forty independent distributorships to visit Detroit Diesel's Canton, Ohio, warehouse. These customers suggested 250 changes that helped cut spare part delivery time from five days to three. Emergency orders now take less than twenty-four hours. Today, Detroit Diesel makes money—$21 million in operating profits on $971 million in sales in 1990. Market share for heavy-duty truck engines grew from 3% in 1987 to nearly 6% in 1989.[23]

## ***Learning Forum Examples***

One of the amazing contradictions about people is our capacity to change despite our dislike of change. With rare exception, when an organization consistently devotes time and energy to a problem, improvement results. The dilemma is defining which issues to spend time on or, as is more frequently the case, which issues to accept as is. For learning to become part of work, there must be structured forums where time can be effectively spent learning. The following are examples from successful FCT competitors.

### *Project Postmortems*

Project postmortems should be conducted just before the team dissolves and moves on to the next project. It ought to review the critical incidents in the product and process development efforts with an eye toward identifying required changes that should be made to speed up the overall product development process. Questions that identify key learnings should be asked, such as "If we could have done only one thing differently, what would it have been?"

### *Technology Reviews*

Technology reviews are similar to peer or jury reviews at technical conferences. The focus is on the technology itself. The review should be designed to facilitate dialogue between participants rather than one-way communication from the podium.

*Debates*

We are all familiar with the debating format from our school days. This technique was used frequently by Rod Canion, former CEO of Compaq Computer, to facilitate the surfacing of conflict. When dealing with problems that have high emotion and as many solutions as causes, select two teams and stage a debate. Follow the format of opening statement, rebuttal, and closing statement. Don't be shy about getting into the theater of a debate by using a podium and asking each team to argue as vigorously as it possibly can for its position.

The point of the process is to make it OK for people to express their beliefs fully. The fun and theater of the format help people release their responsibility for managing others' egos and feelings and dig into the issues. One can spice up the debate by asking those who would naturally advocate one position to be responsible for advocating the opposite one.

*Benchmarking*

As noted, benchmarking can create a superb learning forum. It is far better to have those who must produce the new result take responsibility for conducting the benchmarking analysis rather than a corporate staff group. Be sure to benchmark the process required to make the product and part count as well as product performance. Always assume that if the competitor has an advantage, they are doing something differently.

*Strategic Thinking*

Strategy sessions that focus on defining changes required in key operating assumptions such as industry structure and competitiveness are superb forums. Again, the common thread is increasing awareness and an active dialogue that surfaces the assumptions lying beneath our daily thinking. Focus on defining the right questions rather than getting the right answer.

*Process Mapping*

As discussed, the process of mapping the current process and then redefining a new process creates a natural learning forum. This work is best done using half-day increments at a minimum. Chapter 6 will describe how to do this in detail.

*Steering Committees*

Experience shows that a steering committee can play a major role in facilitating the transition to become an FCT competitor. The charter of an FCT steering committee should be to make sure learning about FCT success spreads throughout the company. Its members should visit other companies and bring back new ideas.

## Summary

Implementing a fast cycle time culture requires adopting a new work paradigm. Conventional thinking inhibits one from understanding process dynamics and opportunities, whereas systems thinking illuminates them. Once illuminated, the key process one must speed up is the learning process. Organizational learning is bigger than the sum of individual learning and requires ongoing executive attention. To lead learning, executives within FCT organizations must relearn how to learn for themselves and then lead others to do likewise. This is deeper than techniques and becomes the strategic focus for internal capability development.

# PART TWO

*FCT Implementation*

# 5

# Strategic Alignment

## *Moving Up and to the Left*

The road to becoming a new product development dynamo starts long before any single development begins. Experience clearly demonstrates that the further one moves upstream in thinking, planning, *and* action, the faster the ultimate speed of the firm is. We call this up-front work *strategic alignment* because the focus is to ensure that the firm's purpose, strategy, and structures are aligned to each other in order to minimize any distraction or disruption once development begins. Any misalignment will reduce speed and waste energy in the race against the market clock and the competition.

This chapter will briefly highlight why strategic alignment is critical, who is responsible for ensuring that it occurs, and how to do it. We will use the *strategic alignment planning model* as an implementation template. This model provides a step-by-step approach for achieving strategic alignment, but it obviously is not the only approach. We offer it as a starting point that we fully expect each reader will tweak and tune to meet his or her specific needs. We will close the chapter by introducing the Core Products case study. For the rest of this book, we will visit with Core Products, Inc., and see how it implemented the FCT concepts. People and products are disguised, but otherwise Core Products provides a real example that will help the reader translate the purity of concept into the pragmatic choices that one must make along the implementation path. Let's begin with a brief overview of the role of strategic alignment.

## Why Strategic Alignment Is Essential for Fast Cycle Time

Cycle time delays follow a consistent pattern. Specifically, the root cause of any delay is always upstream of where the delay itself surfaces. Additionally, the best leverage for resolving the delay is from a vantage point higher than where the delay originally surfaces. We've seen this phenomenon so often that we call it Meyer's Law: the "Up and to the Left" rule, because the root cause of any cycle time problem is up and to the left (see Exhibit 5.1).

For example, one of the most common delays in new product development is reaching agreement on product specifications. Yet, what often appears as a delay in setting product "specs" is actually caused by other factors, such as the absence of upstream planning. Let's examine what happens to a design team's specification-setting effort when the company lacks an overall product plan.

A product plan defines the company's target markets and the products they will develop for each market. The product plan establishes high-level product definitions within which design teams detail their product's specifications. Because the overall product plan integrates individual products into a unified product slate, it should be created from a higher vantage point than that of a single development team. We use the term *vantage point* because it doesn't necessarily have to be a higher level organizationally; the task may be done by a corporate product planning or strategic marketing group. The group's scope of responsibilities enables it to look across products and markets to create a coherent plan. A design team lacks the perspective, data, and frequently the analysis experience required to make these choices.

Within each design team, specification discussions have to resolve trade-offs among time to market, performance, and cost. To do this in-

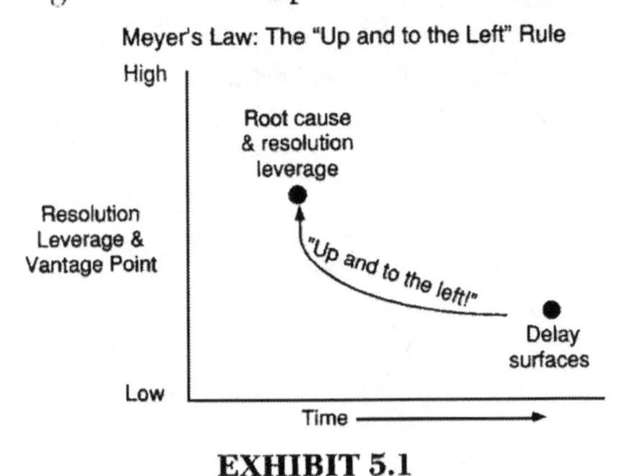


**EXHIBIT 5.1**

telligently, each design team establishes decision criteria. If criteria are established without regard to other products in development, the final specifications could easily overlap or conflict with other products under development. Thus, to develop a specification that is good for the program and the company, the team has to understand where their product fits with other program concepts and priorities. This is normally provided by the high-level definitions within the company's product plan.

When an overall product plan is missing, each design team is forced to create its own high-level product definition. And because it knows that its product ultimately has to complement other development efforts, it also has to re-create high-level definitions for the other development efforts. The team thus stops setting its own specs and switches to understanding the market targets of the other development efforts. Because it may lack data or perspective, the discussions of other programs are often based purely on opinion.

Knowing it is on shaky ground, the team sees unhelpful behaviors emerge. It can become gun-shy and avoid any issue where there is conflict. It may seek agreement for agreement's sake and therefore end up with weak specs that cannot stand up to substantive challenge; this invites further delay when the inevitable challenges occur. And because there are no previously agreed-to high-level specs, discussions about feature trade-offs are often unconscious attempts to reverse engineer the missing high-level product definition. In sum, business and product strategy are poorly addressed by essentially the wrong group, and the resulting specs are often weak. And, of course, the whole process is an enormous time sink. We have seen specification setting linger like this for six months or longer.

In this and many situations, the design team's delay is simply symptomatic of the lack of upstream planing. It would be a mistake to try to fix the design team because of the delay in setting the specs. The effective solution would be to have a product plan established long before any development effort begins. The root cause of the difficulty in setting the specs is thus "up and to the left." One way to think about this concept is that whenever a development effort has to stop or change direction, senior management should look up (in terms of vantage point) and to the left (in terms of the time line) and ask, "What process or structure should we have put in place that would have prevented this?"

A similar situation often happens when a company examines its product development process for the first time. A common finding is that each development effort tries to do too much invention during the development effort. In response, the companies adopt a strategy wherein they develop "bookshelf technology modules" upstream of the design effort that the design teams figuratively pull off the bookshelf and use in their developments as is or with slight modification. To make this strategy work, one again has to move up and to the left. First, the bookshelf technologies have to be selected. The strategy has the greatest payoff when the bookshelf technologies are leveraged across many products at once. To do this, one has to define future products, timing, and technical resource requirements and assess the technological difficulty required for each module. Each step takes one further up and to the left.

Organizations that do not heed the Up and to the Left rule find themselves living in constant reactive motion. There is no center of gravity to the business. They are driving as fast as possible to define a product when all of a sudden they swerve to address product quality issues, only to brake a moment later to address a competitor's new product announcement. Once in the reaction mode, it is very difficult to stop, because the behavior itself is so addicting.

Why is it that senior managers don't devote the required time upstream? Three reasons stand out. First, many senior executives mistakenly believe that FCT is primarily the responsibility of middle management. FCT is considered a tactical rather than a strategic issue. It is true that middle management leads specific new product development efforts, but their ultimate speed is clearly constrained by the degree of strategic alignment.

We like to explain it this way. If one wanted to speed up public transportation in New York City, one could exhort the bus, taxi, and subway drivers all to drive faster, or one could ban all private cars from the city. Obviously, the second choice is where the leverage is, because it changes the fundamental structure of the city's traffic problem: too many vehicles. Development teams are like vehicles in a city. They can only go as fast as other traffic or road conditions permit. They cannot change the basic structure themselves; only senior management can.

Second, the work required to create strategic alignment is less satisfying than that for resolving operational issues. Most executives got to their position by taking direct action and solving problems. In contrast, creating strategic alignment is more dependent on defining the right question to prevent problems than it is on finding the right answer to solve problems. This cuts against the grain of many executives' education and experience.

We all like the feeling of accomplishment. A CEO we know once asked his vice presidents why they got so much enjoyment out of fighting fires or, in his words, "killing alligators." Each day, they proudly reported to their colleagues and families about the various alligator-sized crises that had occurred and how they slew them. Our friend then asked his vice presidents where alligators came from. The vice presidents laughed and told him they came from baby alligators. When the CEO asked why they didn't kill the babies, they laughed again and said because the babies don't bite. There is much less innate satisfaction, visibility, and reward for preventing problems that there is in solving problems. Perhaps performance appraisal and interview criteria used when selecting high-level managers should focus on how good they are at preventing problems rather than solving them.

Third, in contrast to the operational problems, strategic issues are essentially wicked in that they have multiple causes and multiple solutions, and there is no immediate way to test if the decision is correct. The time span between setting a strategic direction and learning if it is right often exceeds the executive's job tenure. In the United States, senior executives and young high-potential managers often change jobs so frequently that they rarely live with the consequences of their actions.

For these reasons, we find that executives grossly underestimate the importance of strategic alignment and overplay the value of downstream product development tactics, such as computer-aided design technologies. While not as easily measurable, either in cost or contribution, strategic alignment creates a context that focuses the organization's energy and resources. *The responsibility for strategic alignment rests with senior management.*

A final word before we introduce and demonstrate how to apply the strategic alignment planning model. Although today's management literature is replete with exhortations to empower people, the issue is more appropriately the elimination of disabling actions.[1] People are born fully powered. One only has to spend an hour with a three-year-old to understand that he or she doesn't need to be empowered! Organizations that lack strategic alignment effectively disable others from acting because there is no contextual basis for people to know if their actions help or hinder the achievement of organization goals. How can one ask people to focus on value-added tasks if one has not defined what is valued added and what isn't? Any organization leader who seeks to "empower" people should first create a clear strategic context that enables others to use the power with which they were born.

## The Strategic Alignment Planning Model

The strategic alignment planning model (Exhibit 5.2) provides a template for defining the key elements in the space that we refer to as "up and to

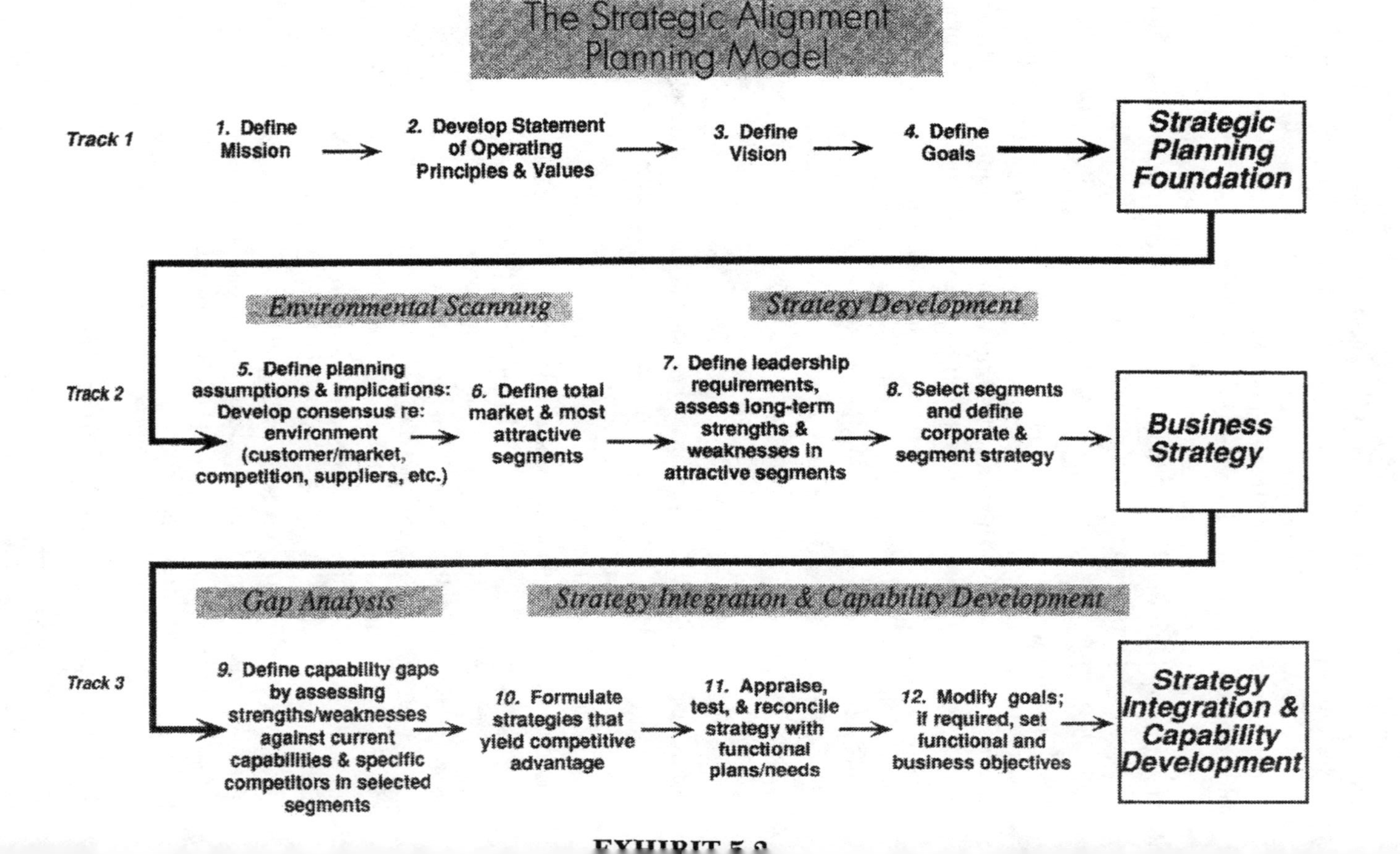
The Strategic Alignment Planning Model
Track 1
1. Define Mission
2. Develop Statement of Operating Principles & Values
3. Define Vision
4. Define Goals
Strategic Planning Foundation
Environmental Scanning
Strategy Development
Track 2
5. Define planning assumptions & implications: Develop consensus re: environment (customer/market, competition, suppliers, etc.)
6. Define total market & most attractive segments
7. Define leadership requirements, assess long-term strengths & weaknesses in attractive segments
8. Select segments and define corporate & segment strategy
Business Strategy
Gap Analysis
Strategy Integration & Capability Development
Track 3
9. Define capability gaps by assessing strengths/weaknesses against current capabilities & specific competitors in selected segments
10. Formulate strategies that yield competitive advantage
11. Appraise, test, & reconcile strategy with functional plans/needs
12. Modify goals; if required, set functional and business objectives
Strategy Integration & Capability Development

the left." As it is a template, the reader should fine-tune and emphasize those elements that are most relevant to his or her particular business requirements. The model itself does not attempt to predefine every potential upstream exigency. Rather, it poses the right questions that steer the user to define the most important issues for his or her business. In contrast to other planning models, the strategic alignment model was designed for FCT and therefore emphasizes internal capability development and strategy implementation. We will describe the basic elements of the model and how to use it.[2]

The model has three horizontal, sequential tracks. The first is the development of the planning foundation. The planning foundation defines the mission, operating principles, visions, and goals for the organization. Combined, these four elements establish the boundaries of the business, define baseline behavior expectations, and set targets and direction. Just as an inadequate building foundation can cripple the growth of a physical structure, a poorly defined planning foundation inhibits the growth of the business. Our experience is that FCT companies keep their planning foundation simple, clear, and openly supportive of FCT philosophies.

The second track defines the firm's business strategy. This track is probably the most familiar to the reader, as it incorporates many business planning basics. Because of familiarity or urgency, many rush through the planning foundation in order to get to the business strategy "meat" quickly. Our experience suggests that this is unwise. When firms do this, many conversations that are seemingly about markets and products are actually unresolved discussions of mission, vision, goals, or operating principles. The most important element of track two is the environmental scan. This is the one point in the process where attention is focused *outside* the organization. The scanning process generates a set of planning assumptions about the business environment that, if incorrect, can render the entire process and result worthless.

The final track focuses on strategy implementation and execution. The new strategy is tested against the firm's capabilities and its original goals. Using gap analysis and gap filling, organizational capability improvements are defined and designed as required. Strategic alignment is only a good intention until it changes core structures, such as resource allocation decisions. The most important aspect of the last track is that it merges strategy with the organization's annual operating plans and individual functional plans. As a consequence, the strategy becomes part of the daily operating behaviors of people, departments, and functional groups.

## Implementing the Strategic Alignment Planning Model

By far, the most important consideration to keep in mind when using the planning model is that the value added is in the planning discussions, not the written plan. The plan itself is an artifact that represents the collective agreement of those involved in the process, but it cannot and should not attempt to capture every nuance or detail. This written product should fit easily within a half-inch binder. Keep in mind that the purpose of the activity is to create operational alignment between purpose, strategy, and structures. Operating alignment occurs when people act out the agreements they discuss during the planning process.[3]

Accordingly, a typical planning team should include the unit's work leader or CEO and his or her direct reports. As a working guideline, keep the size of the working team to twelve or less; when the group becomes too large, it is hard to have effective discussions. Groups larger than twelve can use the process with modifications such as subgrouping and strong self-discipline to keep the interaction effective.

A facilitator is often used to guide the overall process. The role of the facilitator is to ensure that the group addresses the important issues head-on and thoroughly. It is extremely useful if the group understands the dynamics of the business, although it must manage its participation in order to cause the correct questions to be asked without becoming the focus of attention itself.

The planning process requires a defined time horizon. Before one begins the process, establish a planning time horizon that is at least three years long and in most cases less than seven years. Time frames shorter than three years do not force enough forward thinking. Select the end point based on the requirements of your business and the rate of change in your industry. The higher the rate of change, the less useful a long time horizon is.

The time it takes to complete the process varies from firm to firm, primarily depending on how many elements it already has in place and the rate of change within the business. Experience shows that the first couple of times through the cycle take longer because the thought processes and many of the activities are new, and because the planning foundation must be constructed for the first time. In subsequent cycles, the planning foundation remains relatively constant, with the exception of updating the goals and sometimes the vision.

One should schedule all meeting dates at the beginning of the cycle and adhere to them with nearly fanatical devotion. The dilemma we always find is that companies have time to fix problems but never to prevent them. Rest assured, there will always be an urgent issue that challenges taking time to create long-term strategic alignment. The consequences of not creating strategic alignment are easily identifiable, but the pain is not felt for some time, whereas today's problems hurt right now. If the organization's leaders do not hold tight to the planning process, it will always give way to working on today's problems.

Ideally, one would complete the strategic alignment planning model prior to development of annual budgets and operating plans. One could then easily integrate strategy choices into resource allocation decisions. Most importantly, however, *one should not jeopardize the quality of thinking to fit within this time constraint.* Better to do the work right than to go through the motions just to meet a deadline.

In fact, one could argue that it is preferable to view strategic alignment as an ongoing strategic thought process rather than an annual undertaking such as budgeting. When the strategic alignment process evolves into a seasonal routine, it marches to the company clock rather than the market clock. For example, if the strategic alignment process is conducted between August and December each year, what happens if a new technology or business opportunity surfaces in February? Waiting until August to start addressing the opportunity is the antithesis of FCT. If the alignment process is tied too tightly to the company clock, potential opportunities may be masked or missed entirely.

With appropriate prework, each track of the planning process can be completed in two to four days. The meetings should be at least one day long, and preferably two. It takes half of a day for executives to let go of daily operational thinking and shift to the strategic mode. Good strategic thinking focuses on testing basic assumptions rather than formulating more answers. Our experience is that if there is a gap of more than two months between planning sessions, it takes at least a couple of days to get back in the rhythm.

## Creating the Planning Foundation

The planning foundation defines the boundaries the corporation operates within (mission), how it chooses to conduct itself (values and operating principles) and its high-level goals (vision and goals). To jump start people's thinking, we recommend providing team members with several examples of missions, values, operating principles, and visions from other organizations. One quickly sees there is no universal format or definition. The examples serve as a mirror to help gather one's thoughts.

***Mission Statement***

The mission statement should be a dry statement of what the organization does and for whom it is done. Done well, mission statements appear so obvious that one expects them to be easier to write than they are. In practice, each word is contested as executives compare the meaning they personally attach to each term. It is useful to focus the group's thinking by having someone draft a straw-man mission statement. An example of a good mission statement comes from Quantum Corporation, a manufacturer of disk drives:

> Quantum is an integrated designer, manufacturer, and seller of mass storage products for computer and noncomputer applications worldwide.

The mission commits Quantum to design, make, and sell, but leaves open the opportunity to pursue additional mass storage opportunities beyond their current disk-drive products. Quantum's mission provides a firm foundation for defining what is value added and what is not.

There is always the dilemma of spending too much group time wordsmithing sentences versus generating understanding. The group should avoid settling on language merely to resolve conflict if it blurs the statement's meaning. If the process bogs down, leave the wordsmithing and outline the key elements or concepts that the group is trying to express. Then have one person synthesize this into a draft over lunch and resume discussion.

The mission statement is an important FCT tool. As Jan Carlzon, president of SAS Airlines, describes, it helps his employees focus on value-added work and eliminate non-value-added work:

> We said we want to be the preferred airline for the frequent business traveler, and we are not allowed to invest one penny or spend one resource in any activity not related to the business market. We went through the entire company asking ourselves, "Is this service, is this production, is this person related to the business traveler's needs or not?" If the answer is yes, we have to ask ourselves if we have enough or too much of that resource, and should we increase or decrease it. If the answer is no, we have to get rid of it immediately. Because it's more important to be 1% better in the right detail than to be 100% better in the wrong detail.[4]

***Values and Operating Principles***

The values define the baseline behavioral expectations within the company, and the operating principles place the values in the context of daily decision making. Values are typically expressed in one to three words, such as "honesty" and "customer focused." Operating principles are phrases that define how the value is acted out in daily operations. An international chemical company has an operating principle for honesty that states, "All business dealings shall be conducted openly and well within the spirit as well as letter of the law in the communities we operate in." Just as the mission statement defines the boundary of the business, the operating principles define the boundaries of expected business behavior and identify those most desired (as well as those prohibited) by the organization. Below are Ford Motor Company's values and operating principles.

### *Values*

*People.* Our people are the source of our strength. They provide our corporate intelligence and determine our reputation and vitality. Involvement and teamwork are our core human values.

*Products.* Our products are the end result of our efforts, and they should be the best in serving customers worldwide. As our products are viewed, so are we viewed.

*Profits.* Profits are the ultimate measure of how efficiently we provide customers with the best products for their needs. Profits are required to survive and grow.

### *Operating Principles*

*Quality comes first.* To achieve customer satisfaction, the quality of our products and services must be our number one priority.

*Customers are the focus of everything we do.* Our work must be done with our customers in mind, providing better products and services than our competition.

*Continuous improvement is essential to our success.* We must strive for excellence in everything we do: in our products, in their safety and value—and in our services, our human relations, our competitiveness, and our profitability.

*Employee involvement is our way of life.* We are a team. We must treat each other with trust and respect.

*Dealers and suppliers are our partners.* The Company must maintain mutually beneficial relationships with dealers, suppliers, and our other business associates.

*Integrity is never compromised.* The conduct of our Company worldwide must be pursued in a manner that is socially responsible and commands respect for its integrity and for its positive contributions to society. Our doors are open to men and women alike without discrimination and without regard to ethnic origin or personal beliefs.

FCT organizations often have operating principles that set expectations regarding speedy decision making, empowerment, teamwork, and quality. For example, a computer company states, "We believe in focusing our internal resources on those few things critical to achieving fast time to market with our products." Another states, "Individuals *and* teamwork are essential for our success." As was the case for the mission, there is a delicate balance in using group time for building common understanding and wordsmithing. It is often useful to break up into small groups and have each group refine one or two operating principles in service of the total group.

Obviously, drafting the operating principles is just the first step. They must be disseminated throughout the organization and continually reviewed and championed. Although they are not something one talks about daily, FCT organizations make sure they are reviewed with all new employees and reinforce them with all employees on a regular basis.

Action-oriented executives often underestimate the importance of operating principles relative to other elements in the strategic alignment process. Over time and with work, they lead to speed in the same way that citizens' understanding of traffic customers and laws enables us to drive quickly and safely without tremendous effort anywhere throughout the country. Imagine the impact on one's average driving speed if there was no agreement between states about what side of the road one should drive on.

The use of operating principles should be assessed periodically. The assessment should test how well they are being followed, as well as their continued relevance. Rapidly growing organizations should test them more frequently, since growth dilutes a culture's cohesiveness and its values.

### *Vision*

Whereas the mission statement is a dry description of the firm's business, the vision statement paints a picture of the future that evokes the emotional commitment and energy of employees at every level. A good vision unleashes passion in those that are exposed to it. The vision presents a challenge that is not so crazy as to be unreal and yet still stretches people's imagination. It is said that when Vincent Van Gogh was asked how he created such beautiful art he responded, "First I dream my painting, and then I paint my dream." A good vision is created by dreaming of the future and then painting it in such a way that others are compelled to join in.

Some vision statements do this by using a quantitative dimension, such as "Becoming a ten billion dollar company by 1995," or "Reducing new product development cycle time by 50% in three years." Often expressed as slogans, vision statements can focus on qualitative achievement, such as Chrysler's Lee Iacocca did with his "Not the biggest, just the best." The vision creates an evocative challenge that speaks to all employees. It should be a milestone along the endless journey defined in the mission and fit within the planning horizon. As with the mission statement, the vision statement is senior management's definition of what they want the organization to achieve. There is no standard format, although clarity suggests that the statement be shorter rather than longer.

The most important factor about the vision is, does it challenge and excite people? A good litmus test is to assess the excitement the vision generates among those who drafted it. If it does not excite these people, it is doubtful that it will inspire others.

### Goals

Within the planning foundation, the mission sets the broadest boundaries, and the goals establish the narrowest. Setting goals plants a stake in the ground that serves as a vector for the business strategy discussions that follow. Without quantitative goals established, it is impossible to define strategy, since "any road will get you there if you don't know where you're going." Goals further define value added and provide a baseline of progress measures.

By far, the most common goals include revenue, profitability, growth, quality, returns for investors, and employee satisfaction. Some prefer having one superordinate goal with supporting goals, while others are comfortable with a set of four or five equal goals. Goals should be measurable and limited to five or less in order to maintain focus. A good test for the total goal set is to ask, "If we achieved only these goals, would we have taken a major step toward our mission?"

The goals should be easy to understand at all levels in the organization and fit within the planning horizon. When a longer planning horizon is used, milestones should be established as well. For example, if a five-year planning horizon is used, there should be five-year goals and one-year milestones.

### *Implementing the Planning Foundation*

At this point, it is critical to halt the planning process and share the output with a broader audience of managers. Never lose sight of the fact that all the work involved in the planning foundation does not generate strategic alignment unless people are exposed to the results and use the planning foundation to guide their daily actions. FCT competitors use a combination of department and companywide meetings to review and stimulate reaction to the planning foundation. Central to this process is designing the communication to be two-way and application oriented rather than a one-way briefing. Department meetings are the best forum to discuss how the planning foundation affects daily work.

## Creating the Business Strategy

The firm's business strategy defines the answers to two questions: where do we play and how do we win? Operationally, this becomes the basis for allocating company resources. In conjunction with the planning foundation and based on factors such as customer needs, internal capabilities, and competitor actions, the firm must further refine where and how it will add value. The choice and how well it is executed ultimately differentiates one competitor from another. Execution is critical; as noted earlier, business strategy is 10% inspiration and 90% perspiration. FCT competitors recognize this and steer clear of complex strategies that are extremely difficult to implement.

The discussion of strategy development here will be limited to defining the steps required to generate the basic elements essential for creating strategic alignment. We will also identify where FCT competitors focus their attention.

### *Environment Scan*

The first step is to define the future environment within which the firm must function. The easiest way to do this is to break the environment into a set of variables or "domains" and assess the changes anticipated in each. The most common domains include customers, competitors, suppliers, technological developments, and international and macro socioeconomic trends. Next, characterize each domain today and define the changes that are expected to occur by the last year of the planning horizon. Pay particular attention to the cycle time requirements and trends within each domain. Expect to find differences within the planning group regarding its view of today's issues as well as anticipated changes.

The data for the environmental scan come from internal and external sources. Tapping the organization for input can improve the quality of the discussion, and it seeds the organization for eventual implementation. FCT executives often gather input for the environmental scan within their own organizations prior to the planning meeting. The focus of the data gathering is to generate broad understanding without driving toward consensus too early. Typically, there will be much more agreement than disagreement. Where there is disagreement within an organization, the executive should note it but not strive to resolve it; resolution should occur within the planning group.

In larger organizations, one has to balance the amount of involvement and the time required to collect it. On the one hand, involvement helps generate buy-in, which later converts to greater alignment. On the other hand, the added value of each additional increment of input diminishes, and the time required to collect and sort it increases. Experience shows that when executives conscientiously involve their direct reports, the process works well, but extending involvement beyond that is highly variable in its usefulness. Obviously, it is impossible to predefine the appropriate balance for every organization.

The internal perspective should be balanced with external views. The primary purpose of outside research is to ensure that the internal view is not contaminated. Firms often commission outside studies to look at all or selected domains. Outside research can also be useful to delve deeper into a particular issue that the working team would not have time or the resources to undertake itself, such as competitive benchmarking. It is useful to minimize the amount of contact the outside study team has with internal players when conducting their study. Although this can make the researcher's job somewhat more difficult, our experience is that the difficulty is more than compensated for by the lack of contamination and the increase in original thinking. External researchers should be asked to identify the implications of their findings.

The environmental scan discussion is one of the most enjoyable parts of the strategic alignment process. The discussion always illuminates some aspect of the business that has been unattended, as well as confirming the importance of past and current action. The primary objective is to build a consensual set of assumptions about the future environment and its implications for the business.

Once the expected changes have been agreed to, one has to define the implications of these changes. For example, one trend may be that the supply base is undergoing consolidation that apparently will continue. An implication is that each competitor may have a more difficult time gaining suppliers' attention if the suppliers' customer base does not shrink. These implications become the planning assumptions upon which the rest of the strategy is based. *Developing assumptions carefully is critical; if they are flawed, the strategy will be.*

### *Defining and Segmenting the Market*

After the environment scan is completed, the firm needs to define the markets in which it will compete. The first step is to identify the total available market that fits within the mission statement. For example, if one's mission were to be the world's largest supplier of advanced avionics, one would start by including all purchasers of advanced avionics without regard to volume, geography, or ultimate use. Anyone who purchased avoinics would be a member of this first group. Defining the total available market ensures that one does not overlook potential customers based on past experience. It is usually easier to expand current capabilities into new markets than to develop or acquire new capabilities.

The next step is to segment the total market into smaller pieces and select the most attractive ones for the company to attack. How one segments the market is as critical as the choice of segments to attack; segmentation ultimately increases or decreases the visibility of changing customer needs. The segmentation process groups customers based on like needs. Grouping can be by price, geography, technology, end use, customer values, or any other common denominator. For example, when segmenting by price, customers within each segment are willing to pay only up to a certain price for a product, regardless of performance.

Segmentation by geography may be appropriate if the needs of European customers are significantly different than those of North Americans. A firm that segments its markets by price might not be aware of fundamental differences between customer requirements in different geographic areas. For example, Japanese luxury cars such as the Lexus have made significant inroads into German luxury car sales in the United States due to their lower price. In Germany, the same cars at approximately the same relative prices have not fared well, as a result of the German customers' demands for increased high-speed handling and safety requirements. For the purposes of this example, segmenting the U.S. luxury market by price makes sense, but it does not illuminate the unique high-speed handling and safety requirement that a geographical segmentation would have revealed.

Perhaps the value of segmentation is best described by examining what happens when a firm does not do it. These firms attempt to be all things to all people. Rarely are they well differentiated in the marketplace as having a particular expertise. Internally, people are whipsawed as the definition of who the customers are and how the firm is trying to serve them changes. In short, there is no focus—and without focus, it is impossible to be fast. FCT competitors distinguish themselves by having a crystal-clear focus on who they serve and who they pass by. Knowing who we say no to saves time to serve those to whom we say yes. No one basis of segmentation is perfect, nor does it last forever. A firm must retest its basis for segmentation during each planning cycle to ensure that it remains useful.

### *Defining Leadership Requirements*

After the most attractive segments are defined, the firm tests its ability to win by identifying the leadership requirements for each segment and comparing them to the firm's historical strengths and weaknesses. Examples of leadership requirements include time to market, cost, distribution requirements, product performance, availability, and service. One looks at historical strengths and weaknesses in order to measure the degree of change that would be required to succeed. It is much easier to extend an organization's existing capability than it is to invent a new one.

FCT competitors typically focus their attention on segments where their capability for speed gives them a distinct advantage. In 1989, Conner Peripherals became the fastest-growing company in the United States by providing the smallest available frame size in disk drives before any of its competitors. Although Conner's drives did not distinguish themselves in performance or quality, their customers found their early availability a compelling buying proposition.

It is highly unlikely that any firm would attempt to address all segments within its total available market. By dividing the total available market into segments, one can target the segments that create the best match between the organization's capabilities and its goals. Growth opportunities will differ between segments, as will the organization's ability to serve each segment. FCT competitors typically select only those segments where they can excel relative to customers and competitors. If the firm's goals cannot be achieved within those segments, than additional segments are added one at a time. *The FCT competitor is very careful to not spread resources too thin.*

### *Defining Corporate and Segment Strategy*

This is where the business strategy is created. It incorporates everything up to this point, from the mission statement through the definition of segment leadership requirements. The strategy details where the corporation will add value and outlines strategies specific to the selected segments.

Logically, one should try to craft the corporate strategy prior to defining the segment strategies. In practice, there is a mutual dependency between the two that must be honored. Establishing the corporate strategy first provides initial direction, but it should also be influenced by the segment strategy. Strategy development is a nonlinear process that recycles different options from both a corporate and segment perspective. A new segment strategy may drive the redefinition of a corporate strategy, and vice versa.

Road maps for products, technology, and suppliers are important tools that FCT firms use to clarify, integrate, and communicate strategy (Exhibit 4.3). Product road maps illustrate all the product development efforts' initiation, introduction, and expected-end-of-life points. Technology road maps illustrate the technology development focus for the firm. By using the same time scale on the x-axis, one can overlay the maps to ensure that the technology development pace supports the product development needs. Similarly, the supplier road map captures the supplier strategy and should match the timing of the two other road maps. Product road maps are updated every six months; supplier and technology road maps have more stability and are updated annually. If the product road map is changed, the technology or supplier road maps may need to be modified if they were not modified earlier.

Exhibit 5.3 illustrates the road map concept via a product road map. The y-axis depicts the different market segments, and the x-axis defines timing. Note how the visual depiction quickly illuminates several issues. In the low-cost segment, there is a significant gap between Noble's end of life and the production of the follow-on product, Duke. The Puma and Duke product families have five products going into production at approximately the same time, raising a question about the company's ability to handle that many new product introductions at once. The value of road maps increases when you overlay the technology development and supplier road maps on top of the product road map; mismatches in tim-

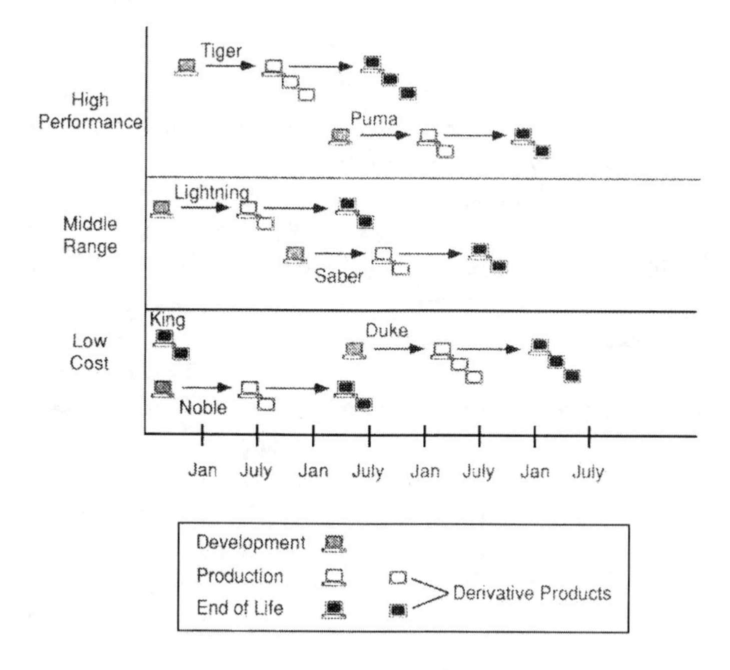


**EXHIBIT 5.3**

ing frequently show up. Road maps help one make "up and to the left" more tangible and visible.

The added value of strategy is that it further sharpens the firm's value delivery focus and enables targeted resources allocation. *The goal is to keep the strategy as simple as possible.* The strategy minimally should define the set of products and services, underlying economic model, technology requirements, and key features that define how the firm will outperform the competition.

A recent experience with one FCT competitor causes us to insert a caution for those who incorporate reducing product development cycle time as a central element in their strategy. This competitor defined and successfully executed the FCT strategy by reducing new product development time by over 30%. At the time the strategy was developed, everyone believed it was the right thing to do, but understandably no one knew how successful they might be with it. Accordingly, they played it conservatively and did not examine what might occur if they were successful.

The good news is that they were able to reduce their new product development time dramatically. As they had hoped, demand for their new products skyrocketed, with margins that easily beat any historical trend. The bad news was that they did not have nearly enough manufacturing and technical capacity in place to meet the demand for products and customer service that they now generated. In retrospect, they created and executed a fine strategy but did not really act as though they believed they could do it. The result was that they were unable to maximize their success as much as they should have, and because of the customer problems created, they slowed their ability to get started on their next generation of products. The moral of the story is that if that if you adopt an FCT strategy, make sure that you think of the systems implications of its success and act accordingly.

Further discussion on strategy development is beyond the boundaries of this book. Our intent is to illustrate the critical connection between clear strategy and the ability to achieve FCT. One often hears about the countless hours lost due to the lack of a clear strategy. The hours are countless because they are mostly upstream, where the work is invisible and not measured. A missed project milestone is obvious at the time that it is missed, but the time lost due to a unclear product road map is rarely counted or discovered until long after one can do much about it.

### *Implementing the Business Strategy*

A clear business strategy is absolutely essential to become an FCT competitor, but it too is useless until it is understood and embraced by those who must execute it. At the end of track two of the planning model, the business strategy should be shared with a broader circle of senior managers. This is best done in a large meeting rather than through the individual department meetings. A large meeting ensures that all elements of the strategy receive equal attention across all groups. It is useful to provide a breakout section in the meeting where work units and development teams can meet separately to identify implications the strategy has for their work. One approach that is particularly useful is to challenge the breakout groups to identify potential capability gaps that managers see as they contemplate executing the strategy. Capturing this information provides input for the gap analysis when the planning team begins the third track.

With each planning cycle, senior management creates the next page of their strategic road map, which leads to the organization's mission and defines its chosen route. This enables others to go full speed on their current tasks without fear of driving off the edge of the map. When there is no map, each individual and group must slow down and plan as they go. These folks have little choice but to pull into the slow lane and let their FTC competitors blow by them.

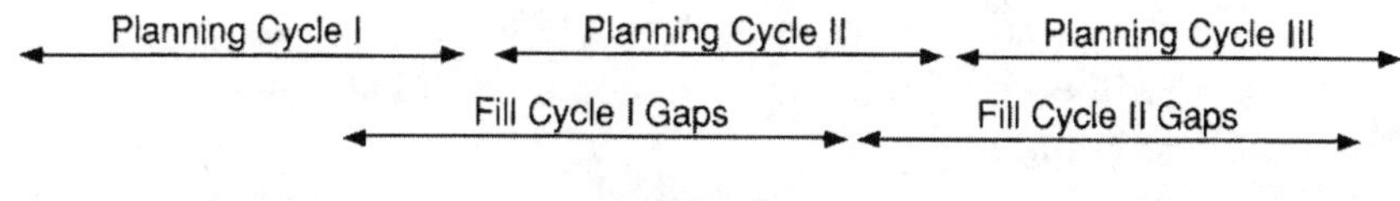


**EXHIBIT 5.4**

## Strategy Integration and Capability Development

The purpose of strategy is to set a vector to which the organization's resources are then aligned. Once aligned, the organization initiates actions that enable the firm to win in the marketplace. Regrettably, too many planning processes end after the strategy has been defined but before the realignment process begins. Results only come when the organization's resources, processes, and structures are realigned to support the strategy. Without this last step, there is very little value to the entire process.

Typically, this phase of the strategic alignment process last longer than any other but is less intense. The gap-filling process in particular occurs over the course of approximately a year. During the current cycle of the planning cycle, the previous cycle's gap-filling plans are developed and implemented; this overlap is illustrated in Exhibit 5.4. Integration of strategy with functional plans also takes more time than the other elements of the planning process. Transitions have to be planned and executed that facilitate changes in direction without sacrificing near-term performance.

### *Defining Capability Gaps*

The first step is to define the gaps between the strategy's requirements and the organization's current capabilities. The gap definition identifies what is missing that would inhibit implementing the chosen strategy. For example, requirements for success in a parts-and-service business firm included the need for a superior logistical capability. The firm chose to expand its parts-and-service business, but found a gap between its inventory systems and those that were required to win. The initial gap definition was, "We don't know where our parts are twenty-four hours a day."

The gap definition process comprises ten steps:

1. Each executive compares the business strategy with his or her unit's current capabilities and defines gaps; collect and compile data
2. As a group, delegate gaps lacking organization-wide consequences to functions, unless special situations require total organization attention to close the gap

3. Combine repetitive versions of the same gap
4. Gaps identified by three or more people should advance to the second stage immediately
5. Gaps identified by only one person should be dropped unless more people can be convinced the gap is critical
6. Each member votes for two from the remaining list of gaps
7. Advance those receiving substantial support to the second stage
8. Discuss second list and repeat above steps as required until gaps are less than or equal to eight
9. Hone final gap definitions
10. Assign gap champions to lead filling each gap

It is not uncommon for the working group to identify more than forty gaps in the first pass. We find that limiting each individual to eight items or less helps keep the total size of the first list manageable. Prioritizing the list and reducing it to a manageable number takes most of the time. The goal for the gap-prioritizing process is to have a substantive conversation about the gaps rather than to follow the above process mechanically. The final list should be limited to the eight gaps that have the most leverage for achieving the organization's goals and require senior management's involvement to close. If there are gaps that are specific to a single market segment, it is best to have the business unit responsible for that segment address the segment gap. Only when a segment gap is dependent on an underdeveloped corporate-wide capability (such as manufacturing) is it appropriate to have that remain within senior management's responsibility.

Once the final list is agreed to, the gap definitions should be reviewed and honed. Then assign one person to act as "gap champion" for each gap. The gap champion works in service of the working group to define the set of actions that will fill the gap. Our best experiences in support of FCT have been where a champion was selected to lead the filling of each gap. The gap champion serves the working group, since most gaps require cross-functional efforts to resolve. Gaps find a natural path to their champion based on the champion's ongoing work assignment.

### *Gap Filling*

The first task for the gap champion is to form a team to work on the gap and rigorously sharpen the definition of the gap. The team is composed of those people whose expertise or job is central to resolving the gap. The group also defines how they will know the gap is filled. In other words, how would the organization have to behave for people to say there wasn't a gap anymore?

FCT companies often have gaps related to increasing business process speed. For example, one organization defined the lack of an agreed-to financial model for managing the business as a major impediment to making quick resource allocation decisions. The basis for knowing the gap was filled was when the new financial model was actively used and resource allocation decisions took half the time. This prompted the gap champion to look beyond just building the financial model to make a tool that was easy to use.

Defining the gap focuses the gap-filling activities and makes it easier to prepare a plan to close it. The plan should include key tasks, measurable milestones, and timing. The gap champion should present the plan to the planning group and define what actions, if any, he or she needs from them. The planning group should actively monitor the gap based on the timing in the gap-filling plan.

*We have found that success in the gap-filling process depends greatly on the focus and visibility the original planning group maintains on the gap during the course of the year.* Keep status reporting succinct and use most of the time for discussion and decisions. If the gap disappears from the planning group's view once a gap champion is selected, the chances of it drifting into a third or fourth priority increase tremendously. Don't forget that each gap represents a capability development *required* to execute the business strategy. It is very easy for the gap to become subordinated to everyday tasks that are always urgent, although rarely as important.

### Functional Integration

The next step is to deploy and integrate the business strategy and gap-closing plans with the organization's budgeting and resource plans. Although FCT organizations use multifunctional teams as the core value delivery structure, most resource allocation processes such as budgeting are still functionally based. Over time, this will shift as the organization becomes more used to operating in the FCT mode, but until then one must ensure that functional plans are in alignment with the gap-filling and business strategies.

Aligning strategy with functional plans presupposes that functional plans exist. For our purposes, functional plans are defined as plans that define the specific contribution and expertise required within each function to achieve the firm's goals during the plan's lifetime. Functional plans typically include current and future capability requirements, resourcing strategy, current and future operating structure, and a migration path using the same time horizon as the strategic alignment process.

The task at this time to guarantee that focus of functional activity is aligned to the business strategy. For all the reasons cited earlier in the discussion of conventional thinking and functional organizations, it is very common to find functional barriers creeping back like weeds in a garden. By testing functional plan alignment to the strategy within the planning group, senior management creates the visibility to check this behavior.

This last point cannot be overstated. Too frequently and with the best intentions, organizations pursue strategy development with a serious discipline, only to stop dead when it comes to integrating the strategy with functional plans. Since the budget process is the primary resource allocation process in the organization, if the strategy is not clearly reflected in each function's budget allocation choices, then there is a low probability it will serve the organization as intended.

### *Approval and Completion*

The last step in the planning process is to incorporate final changes, confirm the plan's integrity, and gain corporate or board of director approval as appropriate. Changes are integrated throughout the planning process. At this point, the primary concern is to address any issues uncovered during functional integration that require modification.

The plan should receive one last test. The critical question is whether the plan, properly executed, will achieve the goals outlined in the planning foundation. Because the major issues have been addressed along the way, the answer is normally yes. In rare cases, however, the answer may be no, in which case one can either modify the plan or adjust the goals. Experience suggests that if the answer is no this late in the process, one has to question seriously how the strategic alignment process has been conducted. The length of time it takes to detect such an error is symptomatic of a larger problem.

One should also use this opportunity to test the plan's vitality and usefulness. If the agreements behind the plan appear (even in the slightest way) to be accommodations for the purpose of mechanically completing the process, stop. *Strategic alignment only results when people act in accordance with their agreements.* Never forget that the plan itself is merely an artifact of conversation and by itself is only a communication and tracking tool. Confusing the paper product with the goal of creating an operating consensus and strategic alignment is a serious mistake.

### *Implementing the Final Plan*

At this point, the plan should be summarized and communicated to senior managers, with a focus on the identified gaps. The gap championships are the best ones to explain each gap and how they are working to fill it. The task of integrating functional plans with the strategy typically involves senior managers within each functional group and therefore needs little additional communication.

Last, a single-page summary of the strategic alignment planning results should be prepared and distributed broadly. The single-sheet approach forces one to be clear, simple, and focused. Success and perfect communication are defined as getting the same answer from any employee asked, "Where is the firm going, and how are we going to get there?"

## Real Life: Core Products, Inc.

Just as strategy is never played out exactly as it is outlined, neither is the strategic alignment planning process ever executed in lockstep with the model. To help the reader better appreciate the dynamics of the planning process within the context of an operating business, I will introduce Core Products, Incorporated. Core Products represents an actual case example that has been disguised to preserve confidentiality. We'll rejoin Core Products later to see how they link the strategic alignment process with their FCT efforts.

Core Products (CP) is a ten-year-old supplier of advanced technology components to the computer manufacturers who integrate them into their systems. Today, CP's revenues easily exceed one billion dollars, and it is a Fortune 500 company. CP products have a historical reputation for high performance and quality, but not swift time to market. Their products are selected by computer manufacturers after a rigorous qualification.

Like many companies, CP recognized the need for creating strategic alignment, although it did not use that terminology. CP's CEO, Brad Worster, was the driver of the effort, and he employed an external consultation to guide the firm through the process. Worster's management team was operationally skillful but had been burned several times in the last months by the lack of forward thinking. Based on this, they were willing to use the strategic alignment model to develop strategy based on a three-year planning horizon. We'll visit CP as it completes each of the three tracks of the planning model.

After making good progress on its mission, CP got caught in a rut when it came to translating its values into operating principles. Its management team had trouble agreeing, and several members minimized the disagreements as semantic issues when in fact they were more than that. The truth was that two members were quite impatient and wanted to get to the "meat," which they referred to as "gap analysis." They had little patience for the planning foundation and made this known both directly and indirectly.

This is a common occurrence among action-oriented managers. Rather than continue to knock heads over the value of the operating principles, the outside resource suggested that the senior managers stop trying to write them as a group and commission a subgroup to do that. They summarized points of contention and turned the task over to a subgroup. The subgroup brought in its recommendations at the next meeting. Almost all were adopted, but there were a few more concerns. The subgroup went away again, and by the third meeting the operating principles were finished.

A straw-man vision statement was brought in by Worster. The most important aspect of the vision debate was a long conversation over wording that described CP as "among the leaders," since some felt the target should be "the leader." The discussion was quite valuable, for it exposed the differences behind each executive's assumptions regarding ultimate goals and growth rates. Once exposed, people found there was more agreement than disagreement. The final vision statement defined a specific revenue target within three years. The vision discussion forced a clear agreement on growth rates that was ultimately expressed by the three-year revenue target.

The next meeting was supposed to complete the planning foundation, but there still was significant resistance from some of the impatient group members. Worster and the outside resource met and concluded that the goal of strategic alignment would soon be compromised if the impatient members continued to resist. The primary basis of their concern was that the group was talking about what to do in three years, and they weren't sure the group knew what to do in the next six months. The outside resource suggested that they devote the next session to defining the issues faced in the next six months and a road map for addressing them. Then they would return to the strategic alignment process.

It turned out that despite all the comments about "meat," the real issue was that marketing and engineering had not agreed to a product road map and it was time to start new projects. More importantly, marketing and engineering were going through the motions of having discussions, but they were not really talking to each other. The good news is that once the issue was discussed, resolution was easily reached. The obvious bad news is that they had not been talking to each other.

Our experience is that this type of disruption is not uncommon. The strategic alignment process coexists with many other business pressures and needs. One firmly has to preserve the planning time required to move up and to the left, or FCT will never occur. At the same time, one has to keep the overall process of strategic alignment paramount, rather than the mechanical completion of the individual steps. We would argue that the strategic alignment process here served to surface the problem; if CP had not taken this diversion, at least two critical members of the planning team would have physically or mentally "checked out" of the rest of the process. Also note that the actual work done during this diversion was useful for developing the business strategy in track two of the planning model.

The management team returned to the planning process at its next meeting and had an excellent discussion that resulted in a set of goals. Interaction at this meeting was the best of any. The group elected to set a revenue goal but also established goals for product development, operations, quality, and people.

CP shared the results of the planning foundation at the midyear managers' meeting. Much of the presentation was devoted to explaining the planning progress. Managers were anxious to learn about the work, because everyone knew the executives had been meeting. Others were pleased because they had been personally burned by the lack of long-range thinking when problems surfaced in recent months. As one might expected, the mission statement and operating principles did not evoke a great deal of response during the presentation. These were printed on coffee mugs and distributed to each of the attendees. The vision and goal statement raised a couple of questions, which were easily answered.

In the weeks that followed, planning-group members were surprised by the unsolicited positive feedback from their people. Further conversations were held during staff meetings, and more questions were asked and answered. The effort generated dialogue that in turn provided greater clarity regarding CP's future.

The planning group moved into track two feeling a lot better about its ability to work together and about the value of the work. One member noted that although the efforts on the operating principles were not fun, he was glad they had stayed with it, because the work helped bond the working group. This is a common occurrence and an indication that real alignment is beginning to form.

The environmental scan discussion went extremely well, as did the definition of the total market. During the environmental scan, CP spent much of its time trying to understand what was driving some of the dramatic changes in its business. Older, larger competitors were struggling, while a younger one was growing very rapidly. CP was growing, too, but not at the rate of the younger company. The senior managers used the discussion of the factors behind the younger company's growth to test their own assumptions about the business.

Their learning was profound. The younger company did not have the same level of performance or quality in its products as CP, but it was consistently early to market with them. Computer manufacturers told CP leaders that its products were often better, but they could not afford to wait for them.

The conversation that followed was both difficult and eye-opening. It was difficult for the managers to accept that CP's traditional strengths of higher quality and performance were no longer as compelling as an adequate product that was available earlier. Time to market had always been an issue in the industry, but this evidence clearly showed it was more important than they had thought. The bright side was that if they could increase their speed and retain their traditional performance and quality advantages, they could be very successful. They decided that fast cycle time was critical to their corporate strategy moving forward.

The next session focused on defining the total available market, selecting segments, and defining leadership characteristics. By using a market model developed in advance by a senior marketing manager, the team was able to quantify and identify the most attractive segments quickly. Based on market growth rates, it became clear that CP could not reach its revenue goals if it did not expand into an additional market segment. The choice of an additional segment was obvious so that it did not require much discussion.

As the senior managers began to identify leadership requirements and compare them to CP's historical strengths and weaknesses, the requirement to become an FCT competitor was reinforced. There were different performance requirements in each segment, but all segments needed products faster than ever before. Based on the work done during the earlier diversion, the managers were able to create product and business strategy for each segment quite quickly and thus concluded track two. Although they discussed sharing the results of track two at a managers' meeting, they elected to wait until the conclusion of track three. Instead, each briefed his or her own department managers on the outcome of track two.

At this point, the company's annual operating plan and budgets were being prepared. Worster, the CEO, wanted to make sure the learning and decisions made were incorporated into the resource allocation process without rushing the completion of the planning process. In conjunction with the team and the outside resource, Worster prepared a summary of the strategy to date and a forward look at some of its implications. The forward look captured discussions about implementation and capability requirements implied by the strategy. Though not a full-fledged gap analysis, Worster was trying to maximize the guidance on the operating plan's preparation. Worster referred to his summary as "hitting the print button" on the planning process, much as one would hit a print button on a word processor.

Track three went very smoothly. By now, there was a great deal of alignment within the planning group. There was more openness and challenge between members, as well as better understanding of the key assumptions that drove the business. The first pass at gap identification yielded over fifty gaps. The prioritization process went well, and by the time they were down to eight gaps, everyone was very pleased.

At least three of the gaps were related in some fashion to developing an FCT capability. One manager questioned the internal structure's ability to sustain growth and speed. A second cited a gap in the firm's access to strategic technology required to compete in the future. A third noted that all had agreed that FCT was central to the strategy, but there was no overall FCT plan of attack. The members chose to sharpen the gap definitions in the planning group before selecting gap champions.

Once the gap champions were selected, Worster and the outside resource established a process for ensuring that progress on the gaps was updated regularly. Within four months, two gaps were virtually completed, and one had been dropped. The dropped gap focused on landing a specific customer who in turn had elected to become a competitor in CP's markets. Another gap lagged behind the others; the champion for that gap was not providing the necessary leadership. This became a serious problem down the road, and the gap championship was eventually replaced.

The team next turned to integrating the strategy into the resource allocation and budgeting process. Worster immediately saw that each member of his team had not thought much about the long-range development of his or her respective functional capabilities. Since there was no functional plans into which to integrate the strategy, Worster did two things. First, he asked each leader to show the planning group where next year's operating plan supported the strategy and where it did not. Then he asked each leader to prepare and present a complete functional plan during the next six months.

The absence of functional plans is quite common. As much as entire companies do a poor job of looking up and to the left, units within companies do even worse. Once again, the key is to balance the pragmatic essence of the strategic alignment and over time increase the capability of leaders to think further up and to the left. Worster's near-team approach worked quite well. Adjustments were made to priorities, resource allocation, and spending choices.

The last session for this cycle was not required. The level of agreement and testing of the strategy that had grown throughout the process was substantial. Instead, a presentation was prepared for the board of directors, who were extremely pleased. Following board approval, one hour was spent at Worster's staff meeting evaluating the entire strategic alignment process and making recommendations for how to improve it next time. Thus, the planning aspects of the first cycle were formally closed, although gap monitoring would continue throughout the year.

It is quite difficult to capture the totality of CP's experience. The preparation by the team and Worster before each session is not very visible, nor is the immediate impact that many of the discussions had on their daily business. Although they used a three-year time horizon, they made many discoveries that were implemented immediately. The strategic alignment process created a learning forum that CP leaders used to focus strategy and resources in both the near and long term.

Moving up and to the left is the only sustainable method of reducing time to market. Most firms have already picked the low-hanging fruit available within development or manufacturing process cycle times. The firms that will win in the 1990s are those that grapple with the less obvious upstream issues and assumptions that constrain speed throughout the rest of the system. If one focuses on creating clear purpose, focused strategy, and aligned structures, speed will continue to accelerate over time.

# 6

# Structuring for Speed

## *Designing and Implementing Multifunctional Teams*

Organizing for innovation means flattening the organization hierarchy, giving more responsibility to the lower levels, and scuttling discipline-oriented departments in favor of ad hoc mission-team groups.

—MIT Productivity Study, *Made in America*

If there is a single visible element that distinguishes FCT competitors from others, it is their extensive use of multifunctional teams. Multifunctional teams establish the structure that brings the necessary people, regardless of technical expertise or functional base, into real-time contact to accelerate the speed of learning. The multifunctional teams provide a common forum for overlapping problem solving.

Multifunctional teams have long been used as temporary task forces, most recently as part of quality improvement programs. Next they migrated into product development, and some now use them to manage complete businesses as a replacement for stand-alone divisions. The trend is toward full-time teams that have increasingly broader responsibility.

Multifunctional teams in product development have many labels that mean the same thing: concurrent engineering, concurrent development, integrated product development, or simultaneous engineering. We use the term *multifunctional* rather than *cross-functional* to stay clear of the perception that the functional organization remains intact, and the teams are just a veneer pasted over it. We also avoid using the term *engineering* because it implies that the traditional engineering function dominates. The term *business team* or *strategic business unit* (SBU) is used when the team manages a complete business.

In this chapter, we will detail how to design and implement multifunctional teams. We begin by summarizing why multifunctional teams are essential and discuss the two central redesign issues: the scope of the change, and power redistribution. Then we will contrast multifunctional teams with other organizational architectures. Third, we will detail the multifunctional team itself: who is on it, and how is it managed. Next we will define the fifteen critical elements of organization architecture that must be in place before the team itself is launched. Fifth, we will discuss the requirements for the design of the team, including realignment of organization reward and recognition systems. Next we will detail how to develop the multifunctional team into a fully functional work unit, including the typical problems one faces during implementation and how to address them. Last, we shall return to Core Products, Inc., and see how an actual redesign and implementation was conducted.

## Why Multifunctional Teams Are Required for FCT

During the discussion of systems thinking in Chapter 2, we showed how structure drives behavior. Functionally oriented structures cause people to optimize their function's performance at the expense of the overall system and, most importantly, the customer. The multifunctional team creates a new structure that sets in motion the distinct set of behaviors required to achieve FCT. Specifically, the multifunctional team has three characteristics that make it indispensable:

1. Establishes a forum for iterative learning (which is essential for rapid new product development) including overlapping problem solving
2. Creates a customer-focused value delivery culture instead of internally oriented, functional silos
3. Provides greater flexibility for managing change than other organization structures

The first point is central for FCT. New product development seldom occurs in a linear or static fashion. The process is an iterative one that requires idea generation and testing from multiple perspectives over time. The multifunctional team enables this to happen without delay by providing a structure that holds people together and forces real-time interaction between different functional perspectives. This contrasts with the functional organization where individual disciplines work serially, in relative isolation from one another.

A fear expressed about multifunctional teams is that while they may be effective, they are not necessarily efficient. Specifically, there may be *too much* participation in solving issues. Team members report sometimes receiving too much "help" from team members who, in their mind, lack the technical qualifications to help. This complaint is common and symptomatic of someone operating in a multifunctional team while using the old functional mind-set.

Rather than maximize the skill difference and overlap created by the multifunctional team, those operating with the traditional mind-set continue to break the team's task into component parts and distribute them separately to team members. The fear of meddling is also driven by a model that views new product development as *information processing* rather than *knowledge creation*. While excess information could be superfluous from an information processing efficiency standpoint, qualitatively it enriches the context and reliability for knowledge creation.[1] The information overlap stimulates creative thinking, because different perspectives on the same data lead to the creation of new meanings and ideas.

To support learning, multifunctional teams are co-located in a working space designed for that purpose. Teams often establish a regular meeting room that they turn into a "war room." They cover the walls with schedules, charts, team goals, and other information. The war-room concept facilitates surfacing issues and keeping them visible to all until resolved.

The second reason for multifunctional teams is that they provide a permanent work structure whose goal is to provide customer solutions—in contrast to the functional organization, whose goal too frequently is to serve the function. Without multifunctional teams, the customer does not have a unified voice within the organization; customer needs are divided and arbitrated between functions. Even with the best intentions, no single function has a 360-degree view of the customer's needs. The multifunctional team creates a customer center of gravity in the daily work flow.

Last, the multifunctional structure is more flexible than other organization designs, including the stand-alone division. The stand-alone division is led by a general manager and contains all the resources required to run the business, but operates as a functional organization. When technology or markets change quickly, a division may find that its charter is no longer effective and is possibly in conflict with another division. For example, as the power of personal computers has grown, the workstation and personal computing divisions of broad suppliers such as Hewlett-

Packard often find both divisions vying for the same customers. Multifunctional teams are much easier to change and therefore broaden an organization's strategic and resource allocation options. We will revisit this concept later in tracing the implementation of multifunctional teams by Core Products, Inc.

## Critical Redesign Issues: Scope and Power Redistribution

Two issues influence multifunctional team implementation more than any other. The first is the breadth of the redesign effort, and the second is the redistribution of power. Let's examine design breadth first.

One cannot merely overlay multifunctional teams on a functional organization. *Successful implementation of multifunctional teams requires a fundamental redesign of the entire organization.* The task of implementing teams is like a new addition to an existing house. If one doesn't break through the walls of the existing structure and install a door, as well as integrate the design, furnishings, plumbing, lighting, and so forth, the space will be underutilized (Exhibit 6.1). Just as one has to make these changes to change the flow within the house, one must do the same to change the flow of work within an organization.

A fundamental implementation problem is the failure to devote the same attention to the redesign of the existing organization that one pays to the initial design of the multifunctional team. The existing organization must complement the team, and vice versa. In a team-based organization, the traditional organization changes how it operates for those off the team as well as the team itself.

The second challenge one faces when implementing multifunctional teams is changing the balance of power in the organization.[2] Organizations operate by the golden rule: those who have the gold (or power) make the rules. To achieve the benefits described earlier, some of the power that used to belong to the functional organization must transfer to the

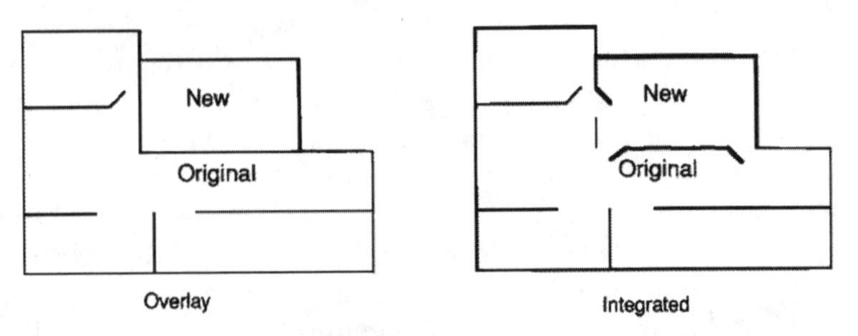


**EXHIBIT 6.1**

teams. People will participate initially in the teams because they make sense and are truly fun to work in. But if the power shift does not occur, the team's actions will soon conflict with the existing functional organization. If the power issue is not addressed, the functional organization wins by default. Once burned, team members rapidly become disillusioned, they withdraw and the entire structure is viewed as a sham.

The power will only shift when those who currently hold it choose to redistribute it. No one can give away management's power on its behalf. Therefore, the process of designing the teams and redesigning the existing organization must start with unit-level management's personal involvement. The political nature of the power shift and its implications must be discussed openly by executives, and later by middle managers and the teams. Once the shift has been designed, senior management must ensure that middle management and teams accept the accountability as well as the power.

## Alternative Organization Architectures

Hayes, Wheelwright and Clark provide a useful model that contrasts four alternative organizational models for product development.[3] Each one has a different philosophy regarding power (Exhibit 6.2). The most familiar is the functional organization where the working engineers live and breathe within their respective function, as has been discussed many times earlier. The "lightweight" model evolved as it became clear that a greater degree of cross-functional coordination was required. In the lightweight model, the functional manager retains control; the project leader does not have operating control of the working engineers but influences them through a liaison. Project managers in this structure have the responsibility but little authority. In contrast to the lightweight structure, the "heavyweight" model gives control of the working engineers to the project leader. Many of these resources are full-time on the team, plus they have the ability to access additional resources from their function.

Multifunctional teams are based on the heavyweight model. They can be used for product development projects or complete businesses. Because FCT organizations use teams as their primary value delivery mechanism, the latter must be able to act quickly. As a rule of thumb, the teams have 51% of the vote in conflicts, versus 49% for the functional organization. In practice, most of the issues are resolved by mutual agreement—yet, when push comes to shove, the team is empowered to make the decision. This must be discussed publicly, agreed to at the most senior levels and acted out by functional as well as team leaders. If the state-

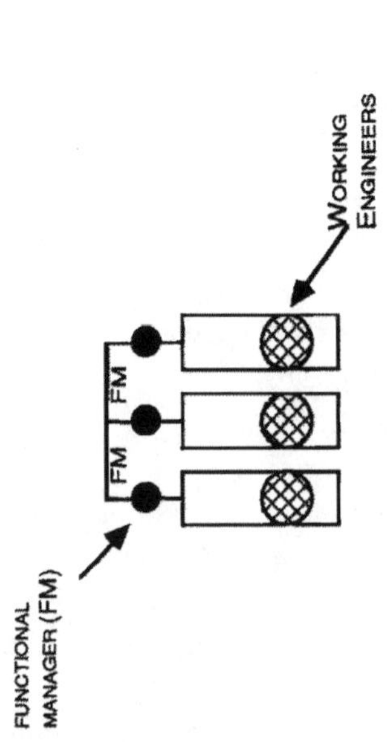


LIGHTWEIGHT PROJECT MANAGER

FM FM FM FM FM

L L L L

LIAISON PERSON

PROJECT MANAGER (PM)

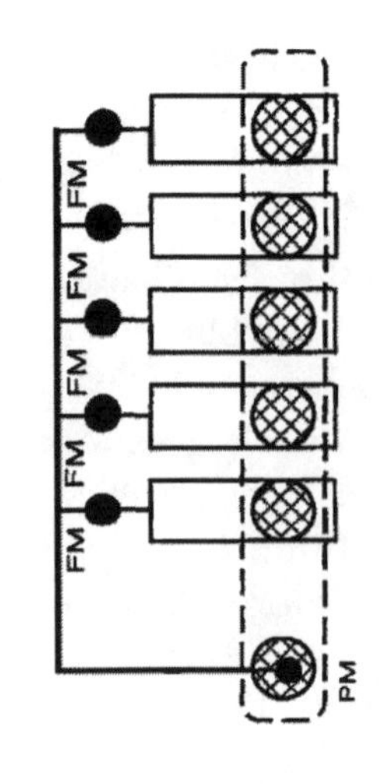


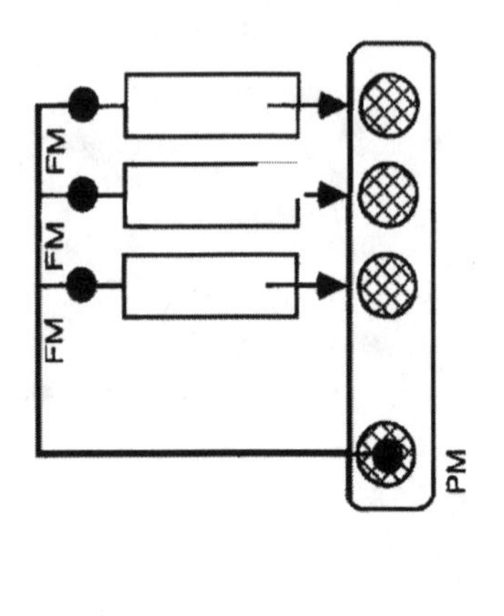


**EXHIBIT 6.2**

ment is simply mouthed without actions, the team management structure will quickly regress to a lightweight structure.

Heavyweight project managers or team leaders are senior managers. In some organizations, they are at the same level as or even outrank functional leaders. The team leaders spend approximately 20% of their time working as part of an extended management team, as outlined by the L-shaped box in Exhibit 6.3. Their involvement with senior management ensures that the team's strategic needs and capability requirements are clearly visible and integrated into strategy and operations. If they spend more than 20% of their time with the traditional management group, their ability to perform the team leader role is compromised.

The last alternative, "tiger teams," typically operate outside the confines of the current organization. In other words, a tiger team takes resources from the organization and minimizes any ties back to the formal organization. Like a skunk works, it is often physically located completely away from the main organization. Skunk works received a great deal of attention in the 1980s; management gurus touted their rapid speed and lack of bureaucracy. The fact of the matter is there are many downsides to tiger teams that greatly limit their long-term effectiveness.

One reason for using a tiger team is when the situation is dire. If there is no way possible to work through the existing organization and the need is critical, then a tiger team becomes the only resort. Tiger teams might also be useful when a firm is entering a new area of business that requires fundamentally different behaviors. In this situation, the tiger team enables a fresh start that facilitates the development and sustaining of new behaviors.

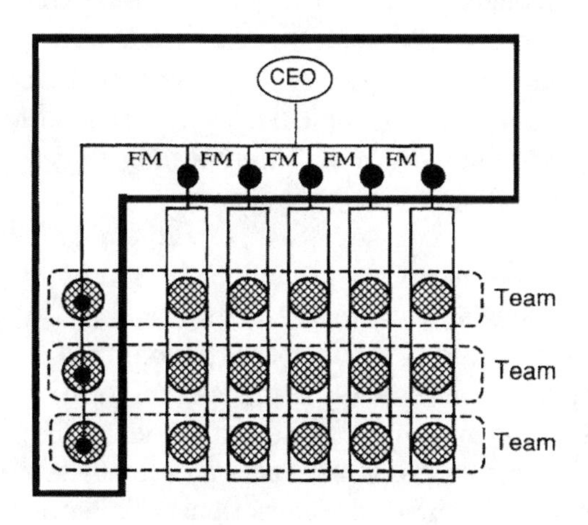


**EXHIBIT 6.3**

Under most other conditions, using a tiger team or skunk works is an admission that the core organization is so flawed that one cannot work through it. If that is the case, then it is far more appropriate to fix the core organization than to run from it. When you create a tiger team, it carries little history and knowledge beyond each individual's experience. More importantly, any success the tiger team has is very difficult to reintegrate within the existing organization.

We would be remiss if we did not contrast briefly the multifunctional team with the classical matrix organization. In a matrix organization, people have two bosses: functional and project. Multifunctional teams are *not* the same as a matrix organization. The primary difference is that the team leader has the authority to make decisions *and* the redefinition of the functional organization supports him or her in doing so. Employees working in multifunctional teams work for the team leader.

## Detailing the Multifunctional Team

Let's begin by reminding ourselves of the context within which these teams operate. Exhibit 6.4 reiterates the FCT organization architecture. The teams are the primary value delivery mechanism, and the centers of expertise provide technical support and team members. We purposely use the term *center of expertise* to differentiate their operating behavior from traditional functions. As we progress, we will discuss how a function operates as a center of enterprise.

With the context refreshed, let's define the elements of a generic multifunctional team. Exhibit 6.5 details the multifunctional team. All the circles within the black square are members of the team; the core group leads the team, and the solid dot is the team leader. The term *core group* is deliberately chosen because those outside the circle but inside the square are also team members. One does not want a hierarchy within the team. Those within the circle have different roles than those outside the circle, but they are all members of the team.

The core group includes the key areas of expertise required to run the business or deliver the product. Core group members in product development minimally include engineering, manufacturing, and marketing. Each business must define what additional disciplines are required in the core group.

The core group members serve as the conduit for their respective area of expertise. This means they must be able to deliver their functional organization's resources and support. These are usually senior middle managers with project and management experience. The core group members' contribution directly hinges on how well they deliver their function's ca-

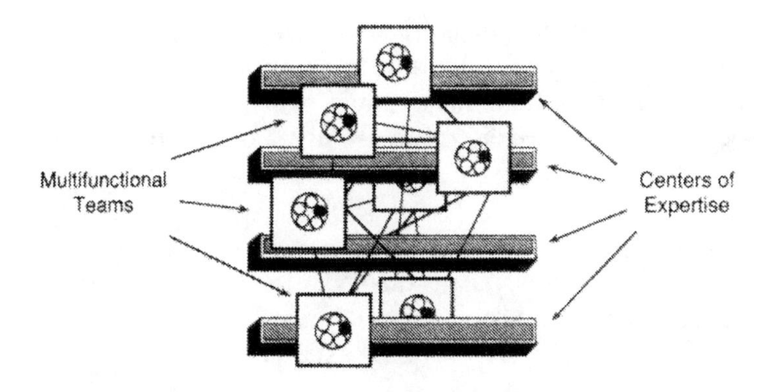


**EXHIBIT 6.4**

pabilities to the team. Commitments made but not fulfilled quickly destroy the effectiveness of a core group member and of the team at large. The core group member does not need to have the personal capability to do every task but must be able to access solutions for the team. This is done by bringing either information or additional resources to the team.

Preferably, the members outside the circle but within the boundaries of the square are full-time team members. They include engineering, product marketing, manufacturing, or other experts working on the team's mission. They take daily work direction for core group members and, like the core group itself, are typically co-located with their colleagues and work tools.

A common question is whether team members must be full-time. The answer is that it is not essential but highly desirable. This eliminates the

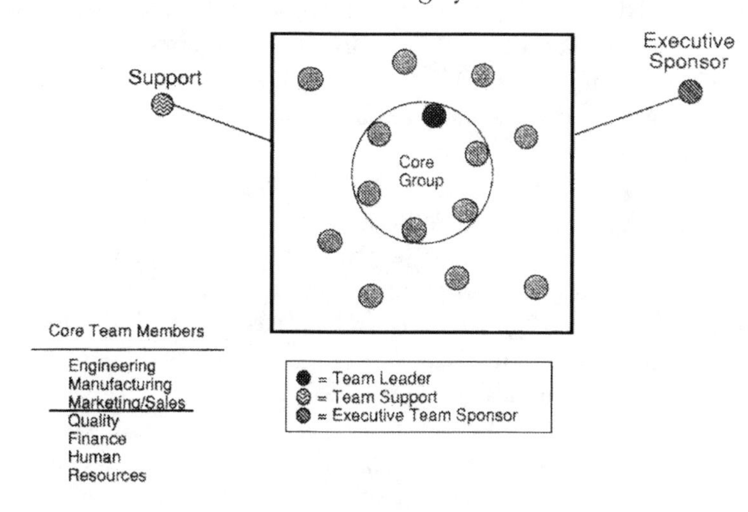


**EXHIBIT 6.5**

"tin-cup" feeling that the team and part-time members experience as they juggle conflicting priorities. The same answer does not apply to expertise that is not required full-time. For example, many organizations have technical specialists or finance or human resource people who participate on more than one team because the demand for their services is not an ongoing requirement.

Behind this question there is a fundamentally more important issue. The full-time/part-time debate is driven by the number of projects versus the total resources available. Most organizations take on more development efforts than they can adequately staff, meaning that each project contains the critical mass of resources required to execute the task within the agreed-to schedule. Many organizations don't do a good job of saying no to marginal projects. They lack either a simple mechanism, enough discipline, or both to match total project resource requirements against total resource capacity. Rather than eliminating marginal projects early, they start more than their experience shows they can finish. The organization slips into a survival-of-the-fittest modality, where projects are weaned over time due to lack of support. We will discuss how to avoid this problem in Chapter 7.

The circle labeled "support" to the left of the box in Exhibit 6.5 indicates resources who are not team members. These scarce resources are required by multiple projects and used rarely. For example, an aerospace company has a senior technologist who is an internationally respected expert in the fluid dynamics of trailing air flows from airplane wings. This individual is one of three in the entire world who thoroughly understands wing design requirements. His knowledge is required on each of the airframe projects under development, and it would be foolish to assign him to only one program. The same can be said for functions (such as legal) that are required during a patent filing but are not necessary on a full-time basis.

The executive sponsor is a critical role, particularly during the initial transition to multifunctional teams. The traditional role of the sponsor is to mentor and guide the team. In this capacity, the sponsor operates like a driving instructor, who teaches the student to drive without grabbing the wheel himself unless the situation is life threatening. In this capacity, the sponsor helps build capabilities and processes within the team to achieve its goal rather than applying his or her individual talents to the team's issues. The mentor also provides information and guidance on current business issues and corporate direction. For example, this could include helping the team request additional resources such as capital. A good sponsor will help the team decide when to make the request and how to prepare for it, including sensitivity to other resource requests that management is considering.

There is a second sponsor role that is more critical and yet rarely discussed. The sponsor role provides a vehicle that teaches senior executives how to work with teams and to transform their own function into a center of expertise. As much as the team members need to learn how to work on a team, senior executives need to learn how to lead a team-based organization.

This is significantly different from leading a functionally based organization. In a functional organization, those who rise to leadership are "doers" who are not shy about giving direction or making decisions. As the organization changes toward multifunctional teams, the same doers are now asked to facilitate and coach multifunctional teams that will, in part, deliver the value previously based within the functions. Take-charge executives lack a clear model of what *facilitate* and *coach* mean in practice.

It is very difficult to comprehend fully how these teams actually work until you've been on one. Making functional leaders sponsors enables them to see firsthand how the teams work and what they must change within their function to support them. Those who do not serve as sponsors miss this experience and rely on anecdotal reports picked up in hallway conversations. Without direct experience, they inappropriately process the spotty data with little context, using their old functional lenses. They may become even more concerned and try to "help" in ways that are not necessarily helpful from the team's point of view.

For example, to influence a traditional functional organization, you go to the leader. If you can get his or her attention, then you expect action. In a team, you go to the team leader, but he or she may want to talk with the core group and possibly others, depending on the issue. The decision process varies from issue to issue, and although it is usually clear to members, to outsiders it causes uneasiness because they view it as indecisive. Viewing the team and leader as indecisive implicitly equates making a decision with solving a problem. Multifunctional teams at certain times take longer to make a decision, but they will usually implement a complex solution much faster.

One needs a different influence style with teams. When executives are not sponsors, they do not learn how to work with teams or to appreciate their capabilities. Thus, making executives sponsors provides an excellent forum for unlearning functional preconceptions and biases.

## Fifteen Critical Architectural Elements for Successful Implementation of a Team-Based Organization

As noted earlier, a common impediment to successful implementation is the lack of senior management involvement in defining the overall team-based organization architecture. Teams are set up with little or no attention on how they should work, and minimal changes are made to the existing organization. If the redesign task is delegated, senior management limits its role to approving the recommended changes. The approval process typically is oriented toward the most tangible and formal elements of the new structure, whereas it is the attention given to the less tangible and informal elements of power that is more important. Furthermore, the active involvement of senior management eliminates any questions within the company regarding their support of the new structure.

The process of designing the new architecture starts with the following fifteen elements in the order listed.[4] Once implementation begins, additional issues will surface and should be addressed as quickly as possible. Tuning the architecture is a continuous process that lasts the life of the teams.

### *1. Clear Purpose for Multifunctional Team Structure*

Management has to define concisely why it is implementing multifunctional teams and what are the benefits it expects to achieve. It should also define the scope of the teams' responsibility. Specifically, are these teams limited to new product development, or will they be used as business teams to manage operations? Typical goals include the need for FCT, improved cross-functional interaction, better learning, and enabling the right people to make the right decision in real time.

### *2. Defining Program Management Expectations*

Senior management should reach a collective agreement about its definition of a well-run development program or business. The natural tendency of a functional organization is that it speaks with one voice within a function but uses multiple voices and expectations across functions. When team members get different signals from their functional leaders regarding expectations and priorities, work grinds to a halt. For example, one functional leader may want project reviews to be internally oriented, while another wants them to be communication vehicles to the outside world. The team loses time as it sorts through the conflicting messages. Coming to a common agreement helps establish common expectations and facilitates the charter discussion that follows.

### *3. Team and Functional Organization Charter Definition*

The charter for the multifunctional team must be created from scratch, and the charter of the functional organizations must be modified to support it. *The best way to do this is first to identify what are and are not the*

**Team Charter**

| Is | Is Not |
|---|---|
| | |

**Function Charter**

| Is | Is Not |
|---|---|
| | |

**EXHIBIT 6.6**

*respective responsibilities of the multifunctional team and the functional organization* (Exhibit 6.6). The is/is-not approach sharpens boundary definitions as well as identifies gray areas where roles overlap. It is important to make sure all the items in the gray areas are identified but resist the temptation to resolve every one immediately (as shown in Model B of Exhibit 6.7). Apply common sense to keep the size of the gray area under control and then resolve the remaining issues as you gain experience with the new structure. Model B is intellectually attractive because it is neat and defines clear ownership, but like the functional organization itself, it reflects how we would like the world to be rather than the way it is.

The charters detail the major deliverables and responsibilities of each group and should be tied to the business' overall goals. In product development, teams are typically responsible for the delivery of a new product, often through the bulk of the mass production ramp. When multifunctional teams are used to run entire business segments, teams have broader responsibilities that can include profit and loss. Some organizations find it useful to limit a business team's responsibility to the gross margin line because overhead and capital spending are not controlled by the team.

Functional organization charter changes must reflect the shift of responsibility to the multifunctional team. In addition, the functional charter changes should reflect additional functional responsibilities taken on to support the teams. For example, a functional leader may now be responsible for ensuring that all teams have common CAD tools to execute their tasks.

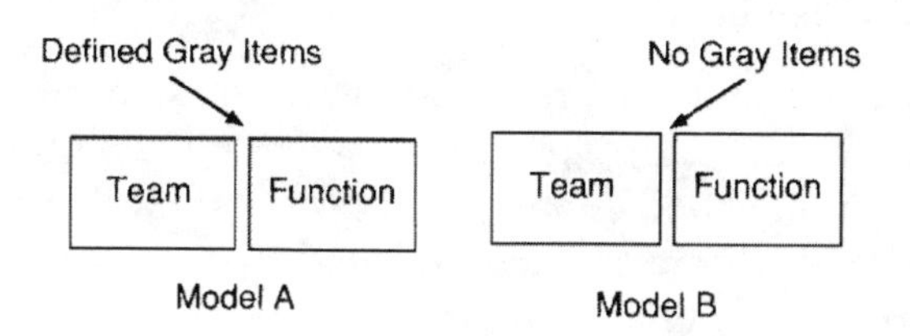


**EXHIBIT 6.7**

### 4. Core Group Membership and Leader Responsibilities

The primary responsibilities of core group members and leaders should be detailed. The list includes all or some of the following:

1. Responsible for achieving team goal
2. Delivers functional capabilities and results to team
3. Directs team tasks and subgroups
4. Manages team process with others
5. Trains and develops team members in content and process
6. Proactively identifies, prevents, and resolves conflicts with the functional organization
7. Escalates problems within the team and the functions until results are achieved
8. Defines and stewards budgets

The team's leader has additional responsibilities. He or she is the person management ultimately holds responsible for ensuring the team's goal is met. The team leader is responsible for making sure the team moves through conflicts effectively. He or she works closely with the team sponsor and represents the team within the organization.

### 5. Core Group Member and Leader Capability Requirements

Senior management has to define the baseline capability requirements for team leaders and core group membership. Rather than listing competencies on paper, it is much easier to identify one or two obvious leaders or core group members and use them as benchmarks to define the selection criteria.

We recommend keeping core group membership to within two organizational levels. Even though team members may agree to take their stripes off their sleeves when they work within the team, there are figurative tan marks that others see. Differences greater than two levels increase the chance that a counterproductive hierarchy may form. This is particularly true for the first generation of teams.

### 6. Number of Teams

The number of teams required is a function of their purpose and need within the company. Care should be taken to use multifunctional teams only where the functional integration plays a critical role in delivering value to the end customer. There is a tendency for organizations to create too many teams rather than too few.

In practice, the number of teams is a compromise between the number of teams desired and the individuals within each function who meet the capability requirements defined earlier. The process of matching resources to requirements is easily done using a matrix, as shown in Exhibit 6.8. As you fill the cells, it is normal to find that you have too few people with the required capabilities for the number of teams you would like to have. This is a revealing and often disturbing message. The good news is that the process of implementing teams surfaces capability gaps that often go undiscovered in a functional organization.

The typical experience is to find that the organization has plenty of people, but the mix is wrong. There are too few people who have solid technical competence combined with the broad perspective required to work well on a multifunctional team. There are also too few people who are sufficiently rich in technological capability to serve within the centers of expertise as resources to the teams. For this reason, *a team-based organization must have a viable technical ladder in order to attract technical specialists without driving them into teams.* Last, there are too many who have basic functional competence but are not outstanding technically and are not disposed to working cross-functionally.

One may need to hire a few people to run a team-based organization during the initial transition. Hiring is the short-term solution to fill the holes required to staff the number of desired teams. As the teams gain momentum, one often discovers a middle management surplus, because much of that role is now taken care of by the teams themselves. Development programs are required to retrain those who are interested.

When you assess the number of teams required against the resources available, avoid implementing more teams that you can adequately resource. We once unintentionally colluded with a client to stretch its resource capabilities to staff three teams when it only had enough resources for two and a quarter. The results were disastrous. The third team was filled by doubling up on some team members from the other two and by using others who barely met the lower limits of the defined capability requirements. This business team became known as "the business team

| **Members** | **Team 1** | **Team 2** | **Team 3** |
|---|---|---|---|
| *Marketing* | Mike B. | Mark J. | Sarah E. |
| *Operations* | Susan H. | John S. | Tim F. |
| *Engineering* | Ken L. | Pat M. | |
| *Quality* | Ken P. | Kathy R. | John P. |
| *Purchasing* | Jim B. | | |

**EXHIBIT 6.8**

from hell." It took over three years for the organization to fix this team. Our experience is that the behavior patterns of teams are set very early in their lifetime; once set, they are very difficult to change, even when you change all the original players and the sponsor.

### 7. *Team Goals*

Management should craft a goal for each team it establishes. This goal should be a simple, one-paragraph statement that defines the team's prime deliverables, the time frame within which the latter are required and budget requirements as appropriate. For example, a Fuji/Xerox team's goal was to bring in a copier at the same performance level as the existing model at one-third the cost by a given date.

The reason management drafts a goal is to set the team's expectations and to focus their efforts. Teams have a tendency to take on more tasks than they can handle. By providing a simple, clear goal, management helps focus the team. The goal as defined by management must be taken, chewed, and digested by the team to make it its own. If ownership of the goal does not switch to the team, the commitment required to achieve it will be lacking. Should the team choose to modify the goal, it must come back to management and discuss the modifications.

### 8. *Team Reporting Mechanism*

The trick to defining to where the team reports is to consider all the options available and choose the one that gives the team the best potential for success. Teams typically report either to the full executive staff or to individual senior executives responsible for a particular part of the business. Although common, it is not a requirement that the senior executive have a direct link to the piece of the business within which the team works. Organizations that go this route effectively cross-train their executives.

When the teams run businesses within marketing segments, it is quite common to have them report to the full senior executive team. In these situations the teams are the primary value delivery arm for products and services and, therefore, require direction and support from the most senior multifunctional team. Teams that focus exclusively on developing a new product will report either to the senior management team or to a single executive.

If the team reports to a single executive, that executive should not be the team sponsor. Doing so compromises his or her ability to act as a coach; the team will not know when the sponsor is coaching and when he or she is acting from an authority position. As described by a team leader who was caught in such a reporting relationship, he felt he was in a boxing match, and all of a sudden the referree slugged him!

### 9. *Co-Location*

Without question, one of the most powerful productivity accelerators for a team-based organization is co-location. Co-location means that the people who need to work together on an ongoing basis are located together. The most obvious benefit is that this both enables and drives real-time communication. Additionally, the high visibility of co-location sends a symbolic message to the entire organization regarding the team's importance.

The three levels of co-location, in descending order of impact, are sight, walking, and campus. Sight co-location means that I can see you from my office; thus, if I have a question or simply want to bounce an idea off you, all I do to make contact is raise my head. The practical limit of sight is approximately one hundred feet. Research proves that communication effectiveness, which can be difficult face-to-face, drops off dramatically when people are more than one hundred feet apart. Walking co-location means that I cannot see you, but I can walk to your office within a few minutes. Although significantly less effective than sight, access is not prohibitive, and in the case of larger teams, such co-location is unavoidable. Campus co-location is an abuse of the concept. Being in another building on the same campus is better than being across the ocean, but often one might as well be.

*The senior management group must lead the transition to co-location.* Our experience is that most people resist co-location if they have never done it before. One's office is the most personalized space one has in an organization; therefore, there is high sensitivity to any action which challenges the status quo. Asking people to move away from their functional peers evokes multiple concerns centered on being "out of the loop," be it regarding information, fellowship, or careers. In Chapter 7, we will discuss details one must consider when implementing co-location. At this point, it is critical to note that senior management develop a clear policy to implement it.

### 10. *Reward System Alignment*

The overwhelming majority of organization reward systems focus exclusively on individual performance. When one implements multifunctional teams, the reward system must be altered to reward individual *and* team results. The requirement to realign the reward system is driven by the fact that people's behaviors are strongly influenced by how they are measured. It is foolish to ask one behavior while you reward another.

To be sure, reward systems are a lagging indicator of organization change. In large companies, multifunctional teams and FCT are well under way before major changes are made in the reward system. In smaller companies, the reward system changes can happen much more quickly. In either situation, the actual change in compensation may not vary dramatically after the implementation of multifunctional teams. Changing the reward system, however, represent a very clear and powerful symbol of management's commitments and expectations.

### *11. Managing Gray Areas*

Defining the process for how gray areas will be managed frees all parties to operate cooperatively without artificially rigid charters. If there is one thing we know for sure, it is that the world will not behave exactly as we have planned. Rather than try to predict the unpredictable, management sets expectations for how the unexpected will be handled by establishing a clear process for identifying and managing gray areas. Senior management should make sure the resolution process uses the team's knowledge and capability whenever possible. It is poor practice to resolve every gray area by elevating the decision out of the team.

The gray areas identified during the initial charter discussion should be revisited and a process established that at the very least (1) defines known gray areas, (2) identifies responsibility for initiating the resolution process, and (3) defines ownership and authorities within the resolution process. For example, even though the charter of each development team may state that it is responsible for its product's definition, a change at a major corporate account may require a corresponding change in one or more products under development. In this case, the senior corporate accounts sales manager might be responsible for initiating the resolution process. The process should involve the affected teams as well as representatives from selected functional organizations such as marketing. The decision authority could rest with the senior marketing executive.

### *12. Training and Development*

Teams do not spring forth fully grown and capable. In fact, teams initially operate as miniature functional organizations and have to go through a series of development processes to begin behaving as a team (Exhibit 6.9). Team development for a multifunctional team is signifi-

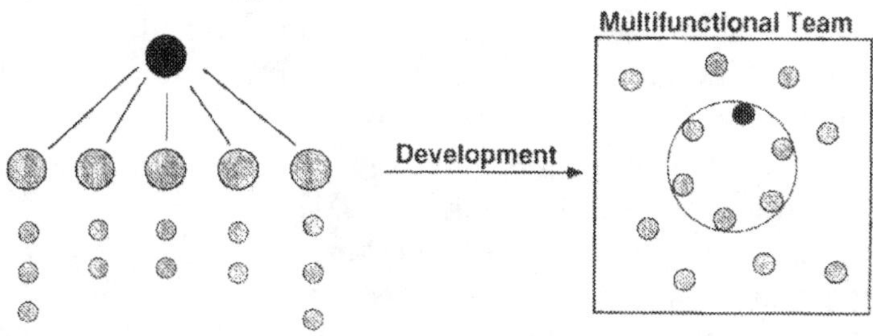


**EXHIBIT 6.9**

cantly different from traditional team building. Whereas a single-function team varies primarily because of the personalities and capabilities of the individuals, a multifunctional team brings together people who have fundamentally different worldviews based on their functional education and work experience.

At this time, senior management has to outline the training requirements and ensure resourcing and execution in a timely manner. The key deliverable of team development is to increase the capability of each team to manage itself and become a learning organization. The learning-organization component is critical, for it is here that the multifunctional team achieves its FCT potential. We will detail the training and development process later in this chapter.

### *13. Performance Measures*

The unit's management needs to define and inform the teams regarding how it will measure the teams' performance. The team should review and negotiate any concerns it has. The measures should access team results and team capability development.

Management should define what it expects the new teams to accomplish in their first 90 and 180 days. For example, one corporation asked its newly formed teams to develop first-quarter development and schedule objectives, as well as establish a training and development plan for the team. Particularly in the early phases, it is important to have clear performance objectives agreed to by the team and senior management. This guarantees alignment between team behavior and management's expectations.

### *14. Rollout*

An effective rollout of the new architecture can ensure a rapid startup and preempt later problems. The rollout effort establishes the team's presence in the organization. Not only do team members need to know what is expected of them, but so do functional organization members. The extent of the rollout depends upon the breadth of change and the responsibility the multifunctional teams have.

Senior management should define the key constituencies they want to reach and the key messages for each one. Within this framework, the detailed planning can be delegated to others. Typically, one cascades the rollout, beginning with team leaders, team sponsors, and functional leaders. The content of the rollout reviews the elements of the new organizational architecture. Care should be taken to allow ample time for the concerns of those not on the teams, as well as those who will be.

It is useful to prepare a single question-and-answer handout, plus a list of what is different and what is the same. This guarantees a clear and consistent message across teams and functions. The rollout to team members should be staged in such a way that team leaders and sponsors have an opportunity to meet and influence the rollout to their team members. Frequently a senior executive joins the team for a brief period to review the team architecture. This demonstrates management support but also provides an opportunity for queries regarding the program.

### *15. Implementation Management*

Although the initial architectural elements may be defined, one can be sure that new issues will arise as the teams begin to get their feet wet. We strongly recommend that senior management place on its staff agenda "team management implementation" as a standing item for a minimum of three months following launch. Doing so ensures that emerging problems are seen early and resolved as rapidly as possible by senior management. Although not included in this list of fifteen elements, the issue of replacing team members will also come up at some point. This issue does not need to be addressed until it occurs, but when it does, it should not be decided by the teams. The unit-level management cannot delegate responsibility for the overall team-based architecture. It should ask the teams to bring forth proposals as appropriate, but the ultimate success or failure of the team management program is its own. The quicker it identifies and removes roadblocks or spreads successes, the more effective the multifunctional teams will be.

This completes the initial definition of the team-based architecture. By defining these fifteen elements crisply, a sufficient context is created for the teams to succeed. We find it usually takes two days to resolve these fifteen issues. Without exception, executives push to do this in one day;

where there is preexisting dialogue about team management and strong initial consensus concerning team roles and responsibilities, this may be possible. Experience shows, however, that most management teams do not share a common understanding of what is required to create a multifunctional team architecture.

## Designing the Multifunctional Team

After the executives define the overall architecture for the team management program, the teams are created. Metaphorically, we have now built the addition to the house, broken through walls, and created an integrated structure. Now we have to make sure the room itself is usable. To design effective teams, the following factors should be considered and agreed to by the unit's executive management.

### *1. Critical Mass of Leadership and Energy*

Teams need to have a critical mass of leadership in the core group. Whereas a functional organization can get by with a single leader, a team cannot. The core group should have sufficient leadership depth so that the team still functions if the leader is away. If there are eight members in the core group, approximately three of them should be capable of leading the team for brief periods.

Energy is also critical to a multifunctional team. Teams are a social environment and require people who are comfortable in group settings; a core group composed of eight introverts will rarely be effective. Senior management should examine the potential core group members and assess if there is enough energy in that group. People who may be viewed as a bit outspoken or brusque in the functional organization often work quite well on teams. Their outspokenness helps keep the team moving, and the teams easily control the downside of this behavior.

### *2. Clear Goals and Charter Owned by the Team*

The team has to take the charter and goals given to it by management and work with them until they become the team's rather than management's. With aggressive goals, this requires conversations between the team and management to reach a meeting of the minds. If this step is skipped, you can be sure that at the slightest hiccup, the team's commitment will quickly erode.

Teams have a tendency to add elements to goals and the charter rather than take them away. Management should be careful to extend goals and charters only where the need is obvious. The broader the charter becomes, the less focus there is, and therefore the less speed the team can attain.

### *3. Team and Members Held Accountable for Performance*

In the early stages, senior management often adopts a hands-off approach to the teams. It overcompensates in the coaching role and hesitates to identify issues or problems the team is not addressing. The focus should be to keep accountability always visible and within the team while encouraging, pushing, and supporting the team to resolve issues itself. When senior management must step in to resolve a problem, it is as much a failure of senior management as it is of the team. Senior management's role is to ensure that teams have the resources and structure to be successful, and it is only in rare situations that it must take control of the team.

Regarding individual performance, teams are normally better at exposing poor performance than a traditional organization. Still team members may collude and defend each other from criticism under the assumption that this equals good teamwork. In fact, this is the antithesis of good teamwork. Teamwork requires honest and rapid identification of problems in order to speed resolution; shielding team members from direct feedback is inappropriate. Sponsors, team leaders, and senior management must all work to make sure performance issues are dealt with promptly.

It is important to note that during the early implementation phases, those who resist the team concept will constantly point to mistakes the teams make. The fact is, people will make mistakes in teams just as they did outside them. The appropriate response from senior management should be, "Would it be any different in a functional organization?" In 90% of the cases the answer is no, with one exception: in functional organizations, the problems might never become visible, because a functional organization offers more nooks and crannies to hide in than a team-based structure. Team-based organizations do not create more problems, but they make the problems you already have much more visible.

### *4. Small Size with Critical Functional Representation*

The teams should be no larger than required to accomplish its goal without lacking any critical resource. In some industries, the team can be as small as five to ten people, whereas in industries such as automobiles, it is very difficult to keep the team size below two hundred people. One can easily argue that two hundred people are a horde rather than a team, but in fact, through co-location and focused effort, it is quite possible to have a large group operate effectively. In such cases, co-location is absolutely essential.

People should not be added to the teams simply for the purpose of inclusion. Every individual added to a team creates a potential interface problem at a geometric rate. Large-scale teams, such as in aerospace or auto firms, typically require unique governing and coordination mechanisms that add overhead.

### *5. Continually Updated with Relevant Information*

When an organization converts to multifunctional teams, it must rewire the information system to provide the teams with the information necessary to do their jobs. Some information that used to go to the functions should be rerouted.

New information needs will emerge, because the multifunctional teams require information that enables them to manage cross-functional value delivery processes. This was only required by the functional organization for its top management. A common need is team- or project-specific financial information. Core group members from finance or information services will typically be looked to in order to provide this for the team. It is critically important that the leaders of these functions make the redesign of the information system a top priority.

### *6. Expectations Clear Within and Between Teams*

Team members wear three hats: a team hat, a functional hat, and a corporate hat. The team and functional hats are most familiar. The functional hat is worn within the team when advocating the team's requirements.

The corporate hat is worn on those occasions when the team must put aside its needs to serve a greater organization need. For example, a team may be asked to give up a critical resource to another project. Because teams become extremely focused on their goals, they will naturally fight this. By clearly defining the three roles at the beginning, these situations are less disruptive. Senior management always retains the responsibility for managing cross-team issues.

### *7. Trained in Teamwork and Process Management*

Because we will cover this subject in greater depth shortly, let us just note that each team must receive training over the course of its life to ensure that it operates effectively.

### *8. Team Members Are Willing to Step Out of Roles*

You will know your teams are working the day an engineer begins sounding like a marketer, or vice versa. Effective teams operate like a small startup in that people take whatever role is required, with little regard to function or rank. Leadership roles will also rotate when the team is working at peak effectiveness. The designated leader will step back and let leadership emerge from the parties either most knowledgeable or responsible for the issue under discussion. There is not an absence of leadership, but rather an increase and balance of leadership from all team members.

## Aligning Organizational Reward and Recognition Systems

Organizational reward and recognition systems are among the most powerful structures within organizations. A change in either system is a clear indication that management is serious and committed to FCT and multifunctional team structure. The recognition system has the most direct impact on daily behavior, yet the formal reward system is the focus of most employee's testing of management's commitment. Organizations that implement multifunctional teams must change their reward systems so that team *and* individual achievements are the basis for rewards. We will first address the formal reward system (specifically, compensation and advancement) and then turn to the recognition system.

Ideally, one wants to realign compensation and advancement to support the FCT strategy as quickly as possible. The older and larger the organization is, the more difficult reward systems are to change. At times it seems as though the formal reward system is kept under lock and key within a concrete reinforced bunker, hundreds of feet underground. Rather than being used to drive new behaviors, most of these systems change *after* the organization is practicing the new behaviors.

Most employee attention is focused on the compensation system. Some experts argue that even if changes are made, the average amount of variable compensation is small to begin with, and thus changing how it is distributed should have little impact on behavior. Others suggest that the recognition system is the true motivator and that the need to change the compensation system is grossly overstated. We believe otherwise for two reasons. First, because compensation systems are so resistant to change, changing them sends a very powerful symbolic message that management is serious about multifunctional teams and FCT. Frankly, we are hard-pressed to think of a single action management can take that demonstrates its intentions more clearly. Making the change also puts an end to the time and energy that is wasted in conversations of why, how, and when this should happen. Without question, rarely is someone's motivation dramatically changed by the change's financial impact, but it does remove a serious dissatisfier.

Secondly, one must remember that compensation is only half of the formal reward system; the promotion system is the other half. Redefining promotional criteria *does* have a significant financial impact over the course of one's career and is a key driver of learning and behavior. Making it clear through policy and practice that either leadership or participation in the core group of a multifunctional team is required for promotion to a senior management position has a serious effect. In the same vein, establishing clear and rigorous criteria for attaining senior positions on the technical ladder is also valuable.

The split between individual and team-based rewards can take many shapes. Many are concerned with who writes the performance review; that is less an issue than what are the performance or promotional criteria and who makes the judgments. We have seen FCT organizations work equally well when either the function or the team handles the administrative task of actually writing the review. Exhibit 6.10 details an approach that is becoming increasingly popular.

The box at the left of the exhibit represents the amount of variable annual compensation available. In a traditional organization, it would be allocated based on individual performance as defined by the person's functional boss. In a multifunctional team organization, the distribution of the variable component is split based on the person's performance in the function *and* in the team. During the early phases of multifunctional teams, the function usually dominates, with control over as much as 70% of the discretionary compensation. As the organization becomes more ex-

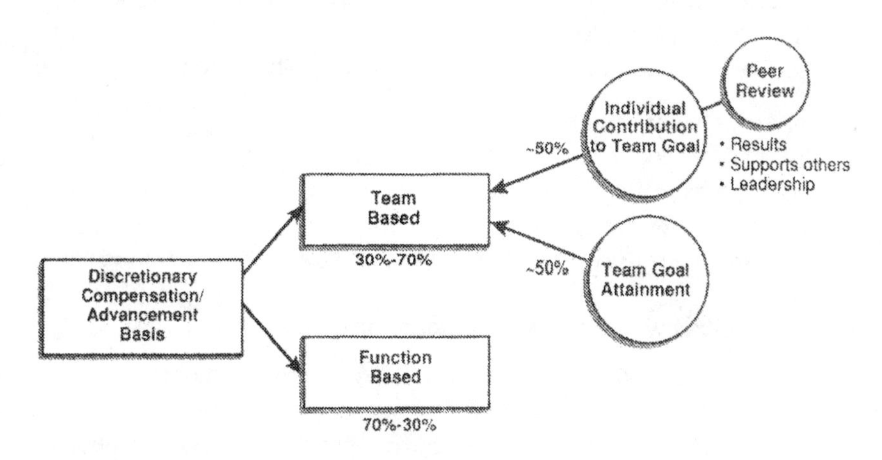


**EXHIBIT 6.10**

perienced in its use of teams, this percentage shifts, with as much as 70% driven by the teams and 30% driven by the function. Many settle at an even fifty-fifty split.

The basis for functional performance also changes. The functional manager continues to reward increases in technical capability, but functional contribution now also includes keeping the function informed about the team's learning, its needs, and how well the individual leverages the function's resources into the teams. The functional leader's role is to create a stockpile of expertise that enables the teams to maximize their value added while reducing cycle time.

The team-based component of compensation is split between two elements. The first is how successfully the team achieves its objectives. Every member of the team shares the same rating on this factor; the rating is determined by a team self-assessment with concurrence by senior management. Senior management should also ensure that there is parity across teams regarding how hard they grade themselves. Rating the teams' achievements mandates that the team and management agree to clear and measurable objectives well in advance of the rating session. A system of overall program objectives augmented by quarterly objectives works well and is familiar to most organizations.

The second element of the team component is an assessment of each individual's contribution to achieving the team objectives. This component varies from person to person and is increasingly done using peer review. Each team member rates other team members, including the team leader and often the sponsor, on their contribution to achieving team objectives. At first mention, most executives and team members are anxious, if not skeptical, about the integrity of this process. It works easily and effectively, however, if the review process is well thought out and conscientiously implemented.

Requirements for a good peer review include the following:

1. Impartial facilitation
2. Data-based feedback and judgments
3. Quarterly mini-feedback sessions for personal feedback; annually for compensation
4. Performance criteria agreed to in advance and based on observable behavior
5. Results are rewarded, as well as team process skills.

The quarterly mini-feedback sessions provide midterm corrections and, over time, reduce the anxiety regarding peer review. Teams that use quarterly mini-reviews rarely encounter surprises when the annual peer review, which defines compensation, is conducted. It is also easier to recall specific examples within the shorter review periods.

Let's leave the formal reward system and turn to the recognition system. The primary advantage of the recognition system is that it has the greatest impact on day-to-day performance and is relatively free of policy constraints when compared to the formal system. That advantage is also the primary reason recognition is vastly underutilized.

Corporate policy mandates annual performance reviews and personnel managers monitor compliance, but there are not similar policies or measurements for recognition. Recognition is left to the individual manager's predisposition and skill in using it. Most managers learn the value and use of recognition only by working for others who do it well. Because there are few superb recognition role models, combined with no policy or measurements, recognition remains underutilized. Although we read about corporate success stories such as Wal-Mart that speak to the power of recognition, on balance it has little impact on our operating practices.

Therefore, the question is not about the power of recognition, but how one can increase its use. Consider recognition as *the* method for resetting management's apparent-interest index within each employee. Does management call attention monthly to people within functions who support the new team approach? Or if a team takes initiative to serve a customer, does management have a mechanism that makes sure that it is promptly recognized with a dinner or some other acknowledgment? The recognition can be a simple face-to-face thank you, personal letter, dinner for two, FCT "behavior of the month," or whatever.

To reset the apparent-interest index, one should make sure that the importance of multifunctional teams and FCT is visible in all forms of communications. This includes staff agendas and company reporting mechanisms. For example, team reports can be made the first item on management's agenda in team-based organizations. One can also use employee newsletters, quarterly manager meetings, and the like to showcase teams. Of course, the use of team T-shirts, buttons, and all associated symbolic artifacts helps, but too often these are where recognition starts and stops.

### *Team Leader and Member Selection*

The selection of the team leader is the most critical choice management makes, followed closely by the selection of core group members. Six criteria that are applicable to team leaders and core group members are as follows:

1. Functional competence
2. Goal-driven nature
3. General management perspective
4. Change agent/learner
5. Past experience in multifunctional teams
6. Respect of other team members and the organization

*Functional competence* is critical because it is the primary basis of contribution. If leaders or core members cannot deliver their function's capabilities, they are of no value to the team. They have to have the strength and respect from their functional base to bring the required capabilities to the team. Teams will not make marginally competent people competent.

The central purpose for multifunctional teams is to provide the proper structure to add value rapidly and effectively. The people who lead these teams and their close associates must be *goal driven.* While teams certainly provide opportunity for employee involvement, that is a side benefit and not the purpose of the team.

Because multifunctional teams manage cross-functional value delivery processes, the more each member of the leadership group operates with a *general management perspective,* the more everyone who works within the team will remove their functional blinders. Often, team leaders are selected based on their leadership achievements within their specific function, but we have seen leaders who are skilled at leading their functional peers fail when asked to lead a multifunctional team. Care should be taken to assess the multifunctional leadership skills of any potential leader.

No matter how well defined the team architecture is, there will be more questions than answers during the first six months of the team's life. Those who like to have everything figured out before they start are poor candidates for team leadership or core group membership. The best people are *learners* who can quickly define a need and be willing to create answers, even if the answer needs to be modified several times before the situation is closed.

When selecting core group members, it is important that they not only be peers organizationally (within two levels), but have professional *respect* for each other. If this is not the case, the leadership group will not bond effectively. When assigning people to the team, management should ask itself if the core group members would be proud to serve with one another and if the organization at large would say this was a strong leadership group. If the answer in either case is no, stop and fix it. If the team does not start with the respect of its members and the organization at large it will be nearly impossible to gain it.

## Team Leader Requirements

In addition to the above characteristics, team leaders need to lead through influence and facilitation, seasoned with occasional daring and command. They define the structure and process that keep the team on track. They pay attention to the blending of people from different functional perspectives, and most importantly, they facilitate learning for team members and the team at large.

The team leader must embody the general management perspective. Strong functional leaders who do not have this capability will not be able to bring the team together as a whole; they will operate in what is called "hub and spoke" management. In essence, they become the center of attention and information, and decisions are made with them as the hub. This does not effectively use team resources, but even more importantly, it does not support learning. Those who gravitate to hub-and-spoke management tend to be uncomfortable with ambiguity, whereas those who work within the team have the patience to trust the team process more fully.

Team leaders should be pathfinders[5] who have the insight and courage to take action quickly when opportunities present themselves. The primary mode of operation is highly participative yet there are moments in any organization's life when opportunity and consensus processes do not match.

Opportunities to take a major leap forward are rare and fleeting. At the windmill hole in a miniature golf course, you must time your putt so that the ball passes through one hole at the bottom of the windmill when the blades are not blocking the hole. One can think of organizations as having many windmills in a row. At rare moments it is possible to putt through three windmills because of the alignment of their blades. If the leader stopped to have a classic participative decision, however, the opportunity would vanish. Effective FCT team leaders are willing to grab their team by the scruff of the neck and go. They will explain why the choice was made, but in any case, they will go! Clearly, if the leader only operates this way, the team will be ineffective; the reverse is also true. These moments are rare, and effectively seizing them is the essence of multifunctional team leadership.

## Developing the Multifunctional Team

When first formed, team members are more conscious of their differences than their similarities. In response, they rely too much on the team leader to make decisions. In the early stages it is reasonable for the team leader to make some basic decisions, but if this becomes the default for resolving all issues and conflicts within the team, the team will never live up to its potential. To become a high-performing multifunctional team takes deliberate effort on the part of the leader, combined with explicit education. The development effort has three distinct phases, which we define as *early work, middle work,* and *ongoing work* (Exhibit 6.11). Each phase benefits from an off-site working session of one to two days in length.

The development effort should be strongly biased toward early and middle work. We recommend devoting 60% of the development resource time and money to the first six months of the team's life. Ideally, a full-time facilitator should be assigned to multifunctional team implementation. Depending on the size of the team, a professional can work with three teams and have time to link with senior management. By investing in the team early, you prevent issues from becoming problems.

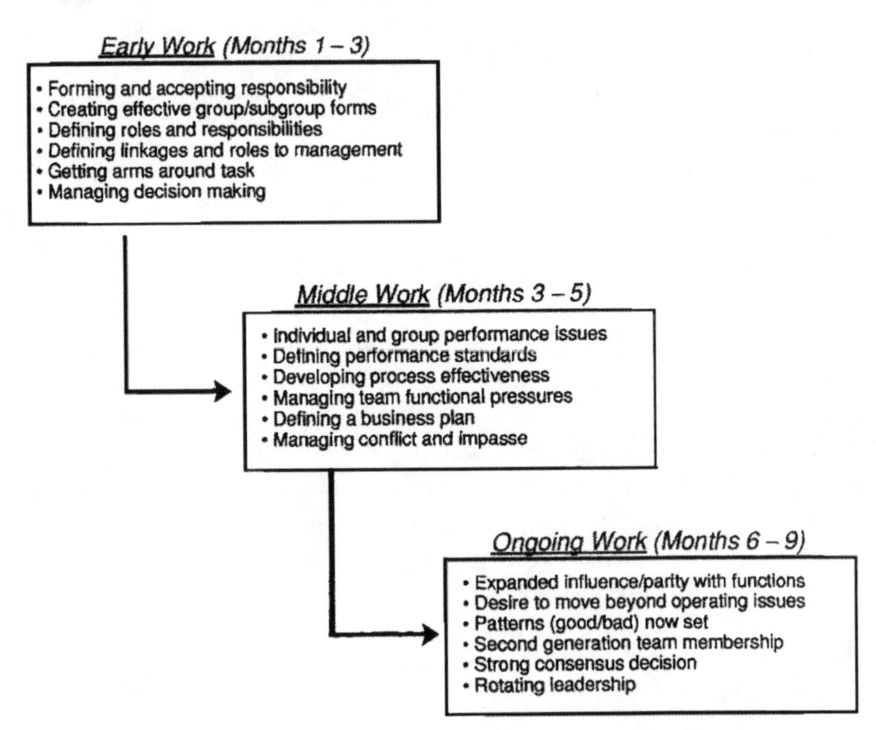


**EXHIBIT 6.11**

A word about what we mean by professional facilitation. Some facilitators are exclusively skilled at helping people learn how to work in groups. Unless the facilitator also understands FCT and the business/technological requirements, his or her usefulness is limited to helping resolve interpersonal issues. FCT requires team facilitators who understand the technical challenge required to shave ten pounds off a product or a week off a schedule. Additionally, the facilitator has to have a rich understanding of the perspectives each function brings to the team. Understanding FCT principles enables the facilitator to make sure team process itself moves as rapidly as possible.

We find that the best facilitators are those who have a business or technical background prior to developing an interest in teams. The role of the facilitator is to attend the team meetings and help the team leader and sponsor create structures (formal and informal) that accelerate the team's goal achievement. Outside the meeting, they work with subgroups and individuals to help them to learn how to work in the multifunctional team environment. The facilitator helps identify business choices and omissions the team makes as it works.

### *Early Work Issues*

Early work begins at the time that the core group is fully staffed and can continue for one to three months depending on the circumstances. It is very useful to address the following issues during a one-day meeting within a month of being fully staffed.

#### *Forming and Accepting Responsibility*

When the multifunctional team begins, it does not have a goal of its own. It has been set up by management to develop a product or execute a business strategy. The goal the team receives, until it is digested, is management's. The team must spend at least an hour chewing on the goal given to it by management until it accepts the goal as its own.

Where questions and concerns exist, the team should propose corrections to management. The discussion is typically straightforward, and since the team is very young, the leader actively leads the discussion. When the goal includes a significant cycle time decrease, it is important to state the business reasons as well as why management thinks this is achievable. The more aggressive the goal, the more responsive management must be to concerns. If the team's concerns are stonewalled by management, the members will not digest the goal and will think of FCT as work speed-up.

This is always a delicate task, because neither management nor the team has the experience or data to ensure that the goal is achievable at the time the commitment is sought. The team leader plays a critical role as he or she tries to push the team as far as possible while also honoring the issues it identifies. It is more important to have a clear goal statement that the team buys into than it is to have a tentative goal that the team intends to achieve over the next month. The latter simply does not provide a sharp focus to channel action.

### *Creating Effective Group/Subgroup Forms*

One of the biggest mistakes teams make is that they try to do too much as one large group. Effective teams use several forms, including the total team, subteams, and individual work. At the early work stage, the team must define what it will do in the total team and individually. Required subgroups will emerge naturally if these other two areas are clearly defined.

The team should explicitly choose the issues to be covered in each forum, define the respective decision processes, and establish mechanisms to integrate the forums. Co-location greatly facilitates the integration of subgroup efforts, since it creates a natural setting that enables real-time communication between subgroups and the team at large to occur. Within the parameters of the team management architecture, teams should decide how they will pursue co-location.

### *Defining Team Member Roles and Responsibilities*

A new team has to define roles within the core group and the team at large. Within the core group, it may be valuable to assign rotating administrative roles (such as recorder and facilitator) if relevant. The core group should also define its unique roles and responsibilities versus those of team members outside the core group.

Teams should avoid creating much distinction between core group members and others. This leads to hierarchy, which slows decisions and impedes information flow. At the same time, teams should be careful of overinclusion. Even though many teams use an open meeting policy, the application should be such that people attend based on need rather than inclusion or ego. The leader is ultimately responsible for managing this.

### *Defining Linkages and Roles to Management*

Management will define where the team reports, but the team has to define who should do the reporting and what should be included. In addition to the primary reporting relationship, each core group member has responsibility for linking the team to his or her function, and vice versa. It is highly useful to have a brief conversation within the core group that defines when and what team members will communicate back to their functions versus what should be reported to management at large.

When first established, the momentum within the organization and the team is toward working out most team–function conflicts through the functions. This is appropriate as long as resolution occurs. If the team has difficulty getting a response, it should escalate the issue to management. Remember, management and functional leaders must both commit to making the teams successful. If functional leaders engage in a divide-and-conquer strategy as a way to retain their traditional functional power, top management must step in. Failure to do so will quickly discredit the entire team effort.

#### *Getting Arms Around the Task*

The team not only has to digest the goal, it also must begin to detail the scope of the task before it. This includes identifying the critical roadblocks and immediate tasks that must be addressed to start the program. During early work, the focus is on identifying, prioritizing, and sequencing the major task steps required to reach the goal. This process should be conducted as a total team; each core group member will view the challenge through his or her own lens. This process is often the first time the value and difficulty of multiple perspectives comes into view for the team.

#### *Managing Decision Making*

During early work, team members are overly dependent on the leader. Leaders in time must pay careful attention to avoid creating too much dependency on themselves. The team leader is often chosen because of his or her leadership skill and knowledge, but overreliance on the leader prevents the team from accepting responsibility. This is the most difficult issue a team leader faces during early work.

### ***Middle Work Issues (Months Three to Five)***

During early work, the team defined the issues and how it wanted to operate but had little actual operating history. By middle work, the team has a short history and some issues based on the team's and individual performance. Successfully addressing the team's process problems during middle work is the heart of a multifunctional team's development. Although middle work is a phase, it is very useful to dedicate two or three days to team training early in the phase. The issues represent the progress and conflicts within the team and those the team has with its functional organization counterparts.

### *Individual and Group Performance Issues*

At this stage, individuals start to differentiate themselves by their performance. Some people are operating quite well and leading the team, while others are holding back team performance. The team as a whole has enough experience to know where it works well and where it needs help. As individuals, they must identify their strengths and weaknesses and reinforce or repair as required.

The first peer review is used to do this. This is not for compensation purposes; the purpose is to introduce the practice of giving receiving feedback. We find that asking individuals to state three things each peer is doing that help the team and two things they wish he or she would stop or start doing works well. Always ask for more positives than negatives. Each person takes a turn and listens to everyone's feedback before moving on to the next. Including a self-assessment using the same format can set a positive tone and create safety when first using peer review.

### *Implementing Performance Standards*

On the basis of its working experience, the team is beginning to develop a set of performance standards and expectations by which it measures itself. These standards are in flux and develop as the team gains more experience handling situations. The multifunctional team needs to define how it will assess its performance on three levels: as a project or business, as a team, and as individual team members. The performance measures for each should be developed and applied to the team's current operations to create a baseline assessment.

We find that an automobile dashboard serves as a marvelous model for helping teams develop a guidance tool. A car dashboard only tells you the minimal information required to drive the vehicle safely to any destination you choose. By design, it limits the information to the absolute minimum. The best dashboards have highly visible, graphic analog gauges that display the necessary information so clearly that one hardly has to take one's eyes off the road to read them.

A dashboard provides much of its information immediately—in contrast to business measures, which often lag by as much as three months. Imagine what it would be like if your speedometer told you how fast you were going three months ago! In addition, a dashboard has historical indicators (such as the odometer and warning lights) that illuminate when a switch has been activated or a condition changes. When building a team "dashboard," the goal is to have as many real-time response gauges as possible.

One builds a team dashboard by asking each core group member to draw the one or two gauges from their function that should be on the dashboard. We find that it is important to ask team members to look beyond the information already available in their own company and ask them what they would use to measure their function's performance in a competitor's organization. The gauges must be graphical; when they are done as a spreadsheet or table, our analytical reflexes take over, and soon everyone is doing an independent analysis rather than using it to reach a common goal.

Each team member the presents his or her gauges to the rest of the team and explains why he or she has selected these measures. Team members, wearing their general manager's hats, challenge why each measure is the correct one. The beauty of this process is that the ensuing discussions provide a forum wherein the functional representative discloses how his or her functional world works and is challenged by teammates who test the business relevance of that view. In the end, the team has a tool that it uses for monitoring and presenting overall performance. The dashboard in Exhibit 6.12 was developed by a team within the computer industry that was also responsible for managing the business after the product was in production.

The team should also define how it will measure its process effectiveness. This is done by reaching consensus on key qualities of an effective team and anchoring them in specific behaviors that one can observe when those qualities are present. Done well, this becomes the foundation of the peer review process, for one can assess how well each team member contributes to each quality. After agreement is reached, time should be allocated to giving feedback to each member based on the new measure. This becomes the first quarterly peer review process.

### *Developing Process Effectiveness*

The operating ground rules and processes defined during early work are now in operation. Some are effective and facilitate the further achievement of team goals; some are immature and insufficient to meet the team's objectives. The team is acutely aware of its process deficiencies, for this is where time is burned during meetings, becoming the root of many frustrations. Critical incident reviews should be held regarding the weakest process, and solutions defined.

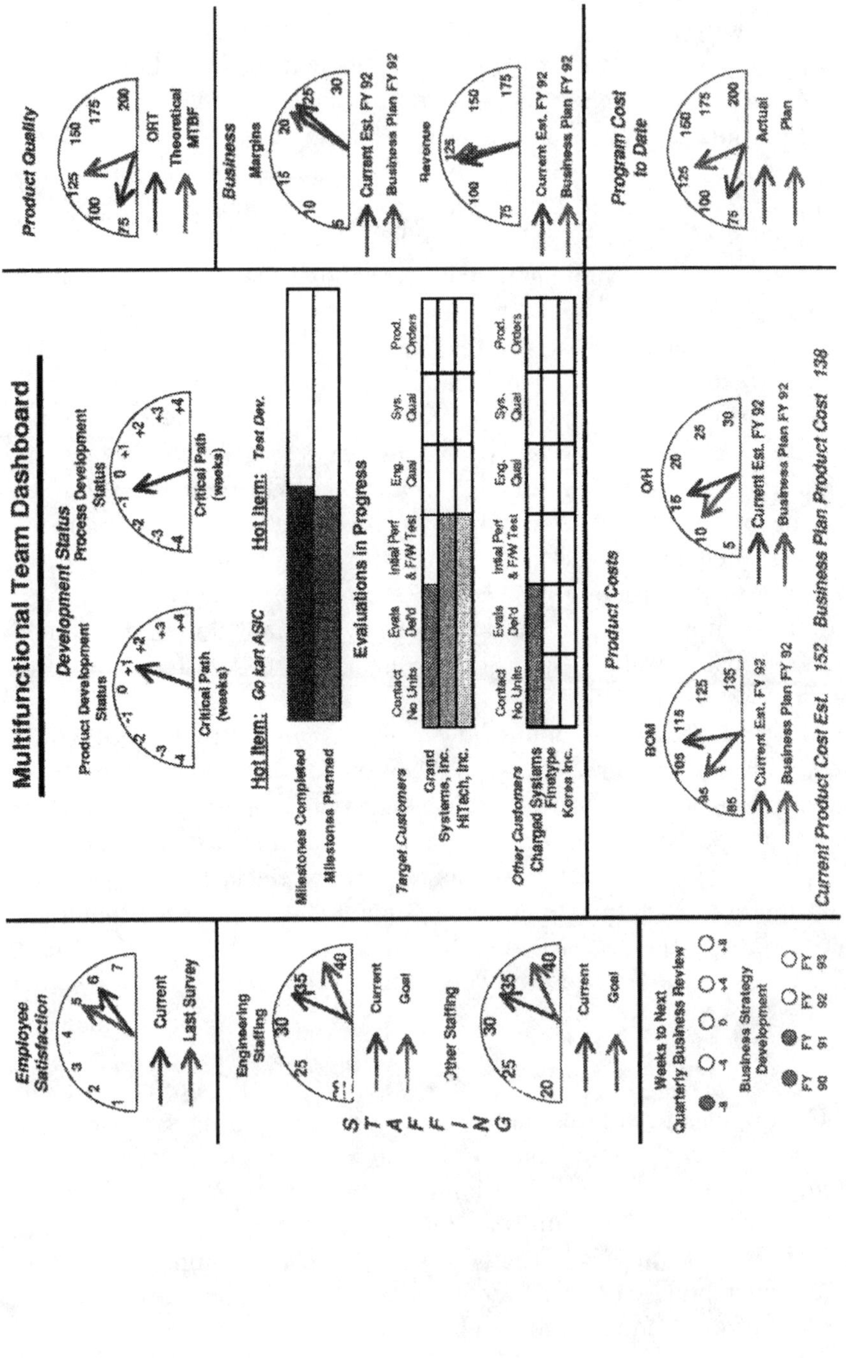

Multifunctional Team Dashboard

Employee Satisfaction
Current
Last Survey

STAFFING
Engineering Staffing
Current
Goal
Other Staffing
Current
Goal

Weeks to Next Quarterly Business Review
-8 -4 0 +4 +8
Business Strategy Development
FY 90 FY 91 FY 92 FY 93

Development Status
Product Development Status
Critical Path (weeks)
Process Development Status
Critical Path (weeks)

Hot Item: Go kart ASIC
Hot Item: Test Dev.

Milestones Completed
Milestones Planned

Evaluations in Progress

| Target Customers | Contact No Units | Evals Del'd | Initial Perf & F/W Test | Eng. Qual | Sys. Qual | Prod. Orders |
|---|---|---|---|---|---|---|
| Grand Systems, Inc. | | | | | | |
| HiTech, Inc. | | | | | | |

| Other Customers | Contact No Units | Evals Del'd | Initial Perf & F/W Test | Eng. Qual | Sys. Qual | Prod. Orders |
|---|---|---|---|---|---|---|
| Charged Systems | | | | | | |
| Finetype | | | | | | |
| Korea Inc. | | | | | | |

Product Costs
BOM
Current Est. FY 92
Business Plan FY 92
O/H
Current Est. FY 92
Business Plan FY 92
Current Product Cost Est. 152 Business Plan Product Cost 138

Product Quality
ORT
Theoretical MTBF

Business
Margins
Current Est. FY 92
Business Plan FY 92
Revenue
Current Est. FY 92
Business Plan FY 92

Program Cost to Date
Actual
Plan

EXHIBIT 6.12

Multifunctional teams take more time to develop, because the differences between each team member's background and experience is significantly greater than those within a single function team. Decision making, for example, is complicated by the fact that members do not have the same degree of technical knowledge in each other's areas of expertise. The natural tendency is to defer to the technical authority, but this must be watched.

One of the prime values of the multifunctional team is that people challenge expert thinking from a different angle. If the experts are the only source of decisions, the team is being underutilized. At the same time, every decision should not be made by the entire group. At middle work, teams should engage in problem-solving, decision-making, and conflict-resolution exercises to help each team come to its own balance of when to challenge the decision process and when to honor the functional representative's expertise. Approximately one-half of the time for team training is spent in such exercises.

*Managing Team Functional Pressures*

If there is a single element that characterizes team operation at this point in time, it is the conflict experienced with the functional organization. This is particularly true for the first generation of teams an organization implements. Now all the positive intentions designed into the team architecture are played out by the team and the functions. Even though change takes time, both parties are quick to note whenever either violates the intended contract. The team should take the lead in identifying and recommending solutions for these conflicts.

*Defining a Business Plan*

If it has not been completed by this point, the team should not leave middle work without completing its basic business plan and schedule. Because project requirements vary greatly, it is difficult to define a specific process for conducting this work. The deliverable should define the project's priorities, timing, and key interdependencies. The team needs the plan to resist managing by reaction to events instead of having a clear goal that it drives toward.

*Managing Conflict and Impasse*

The team has many more conflicts, each of which take more and more effort to resolve. Some become impasses. When impasse is reached, the team leader is torn between simply making the decision and continuing the group dialogue. The team's frustration increases as each of these conflicts takes more and more time to resolve. Training in conflict resolution and problem definition can be very helpful; the team should review critical incidents where it has reached impasse and define how these could have been prevented. Remember that transforming and testing the team's experience is the heart of organization learning.

### *Ongoing Work (Months Six to Nine)*

The last phase a multifunctional team enters is its longest. Ongoing work reflects a well-functioning team whose primary issue is renewing itself so that it does not become stagnant. The issues a multifunctional team faces during this time are as follows.

#### *Expanded Influence, Effectiveness, and Parity with Functions*

The multifunctional team is now a fully functioning work structure within the organization. Conflicts between the team's needs and the functions still occur, but these are dispatched routinely, because both sides understands how the system works. The issues move between subgroups and the total team effectively.

#### *Desire to Move Beyond Operating Issues*

The team is working so well that it has extra capacity to take new challenges. Whereas it might have been swamped trying to take on a new product in the past, the team now anticipates and seeks to be involved in strategic issues that define the next step of the business or product line. The team will initiate enhancements and small projects on its own without detracting from its core work.

#### *Patterns Are Now Set*

The multifunctional team now has an operating rhythm. For the most part, the rhythm facilitates its moving quickly and easily through its work. At times, however, the rhythm gets in the way of looking at issues with a fresh perspective. This may limit the team's peak performance. Some of the behaviors that were very appropriate earlier in its life cycle are now less so; these need to be identified and updated.

#### *Second-Generation Team Membership*

By this point, several original members of the team have moved on to the next project. Some of the comfort that comes with being able to predict how others will respond is gone. Original team founders see the original esprit de corps fading and the team becoming something less invigorating, while those who are new to the team find it exciting.

*Strong Consensus Decisions with Rotating Leadership*

If someone watched the team in action, it might be very difficult to know who the team leader was. Leadership rotates rapidly by issue, with many people taking initiative as required. The formal team leader is often free to coach other new team leaders. The team reaches consensus on most issues without much effort or driving by the team leader.

## Common Implementation Concerns

After helping multiple multifunctional team implementation efforts, we believe there are some issues that one can be sure will surface during implementation:

1. Having patience and acknowledging progress
2. Defining success exclusively based on the quality of team meetings
3. The lack of general management thinking in the organization at large
4. Viewing implementation as an event rather than a transition process
5. Developing a common language
6. Initial work overload

It is critical to acknowledge the small successes that occur during implementation and recognize that this is a dramatically new form of operating that takes time to learn and become skilled at. Our experience shows that management and team members are biased toward being overly critical about their efforts in the new structure. Both need to resize their measures of success from miles to feet in order to see progress when it happens.

Teams will often define their success based solely on their team-meeting experience. Meetings serve as a node for communication and problem solving, but they are not the exclusive forum for team activity. In fact, if a team spends all its time meeting, it is in trouble. It is especially important for the team leader to acknowledge problems solved in between meetings.

The implementation process will quickly highlight the lack of general management thinking within the organization at large. Executives are frequently astonished at how long functional thinking permeates the organization and the teams. People who are perceived to be excellent contributors in the traditional functional organization expose their narrow capabilities when placed into the team environment. The solution to this problem is to change hiring strategies and development programs. For example, functions may still do the hiring, but the criteria of what makes a candidate attractive now include their general management capabilities.

One of the most telling implementation concerns is the ability of the team and executives to view the transition to multifunctional teams as a process rather than an event. No matter how well the teams are defined at the outset, issues will surface that require additional decisions or changes in direction. Senior management in particular has to make sure that roadblocks that appear are addressed openly and quickly.

The need to develop a common language within the teams also extends to the organization at large. Although one might think the issue would fade as the teams develop more experience, in fact, the growth of the organization and inclusion of new team members makes this an ongoing issue. Organizations are changing faster than our educational institutions. People entering the organization are functionally oriented, and they have to go through the same unlearning process that employees do when teams are implemented.

Implementing multifunctional teams takes time, and initially there is an increased work load for all involved. During this time period, people become both excited and frustrated. They find that their work on the team is in addition to their functional assignments rather than replacing them. The sorting out of functional versus team responsibilities and time commitments takes approximately six months to stabilize.

## Core Products Team Implementation Experience

Once again, it is useful to view an actual working case to see the multifunctional team architecture and implementation process in action. To do so, let us return to the Core Products company and examine how it launched its multifunctional teams.

CP became interested in multifunctional teams when it investigated the implementation requirements for FCT. Concurrently, CP's growth had created confusion and delays in its own decision processes. Individuals were less sure what issues they should bring to management versus those they should resolve at a lower level. The operating practice became "if in doubt, bring it to senior management." Thus the executive team found itself increasingly becoming the prime bottleneck in the decision-making process.

Core Products first identified FCT as a potential strategy in late 1988. In February 1989, executive staff identified the barriers within CP to implementing FCT. As a result of this discussion, several executives were eager to create multifunctional teams. There were two who viewed this as a serious threat to both their power and position. Brad Worster, the CEO, elected to try and win over the holdouts.

Worster's team discussed multifunctional teams may times over the next three months but could not get the two holdouts on board. The straw that broke the camel's back was a visit to a company that was already using multifunctional teams. The CP visitors spent an entire day meeting with team members and senior management regarding how the teams worked and what it took to set them up. This meeting moved one of the holdouts from negative to neutral and, most importantly, convinced Worster to move forward.

In June, a meeting was held to define the architecture for CP's multifunctional teams. Worster used an outside consultant to help his staff complete the team architecture process. In two days, the architecture was completed, and team leaders and members selected. Within a week of the meeting, rollout began as team leaders were informed and met with their team sponsor. The consultant who facilitated the architecture session guided the implementation and development of the teams.

CP chose the business team model and made its teams responsible for product development through the end of each product's life. To do this, CP needed three teams. The teams were given responsibility to the gross margin line for their products but were asked to use a profit-and-loss mind-set when managing. The intent was to have the teams demonstrate the capability for more responsibility as soon as possible.

CP elected to create three teams, although when listing potential members, it became clear that they would have to stretch to staff three teams. CP chose to double up some core group members between teams. In retrospect, this was a serious mistake; the third team always lived with a resource gap relative to the capabilities on the other two teams. The one advantage was that team-to-team learning was greatly aided by the overlapping team members.

Within the next two months, each of the new business teams completed early work training, and by fall they were running their respective businesses. The senior management found that its involvement in day-to-day operational decisions dropped dramatically without a negative impact on the business. The speed of operating decisions increased significantly. In one case, a development issue that had been dramatically slowed due to the *perceived* need for senior management approval was resolved in three days after two months of waiting. The success of the teams enabled management to complete the strategic alignment planning process, which had frequently become delayed because of immediate operations issues.

There were several small actions that occurred before the June decision implemented teams that made these teams successful. Worster paid particular attention to working directly with the executives who were most reluctant to support the teams. During the first year, two executives left the company because of the shift to the team management system. One had fought the teams covertly, although he consistently claimed to support them in public. Worster worked with this executive in public and private, and eventually there came a parting of ways as a result of this and other circumstances.

The second executive was a more curious case. This executive served as a sponsor for one of the business teams and was acknowledged by many as the best executive sponsor. He approached Worster in the late fall of 1989 and stated that although he felt the teams were right for CP, he did not enjoy working in this environment. The situation was unusual in that this executive not only had done his utmost to support the teams but was quite effective in doing so.

Worster placed team management implementation progress on the executive staff agenda as a standing item for the first four months of the teams' life. This period was used to identify any obstacles to making the teams effective and define plans to remove these immediately. The consultant responsible for ensuring the implementation of teams and their development at CP joined the executive staff during this part of their meeting, as would team leaders on occasion.

In the first three months, conflicts between the functions and teams dominated the problem list. At the suggestion of the consultant, a group was formed composed of team leaders, sponsors, the human resources vice president, Worster, and the consultant to meet on an as-needed basis to identify and resolve fundamental operational issues between teams. This subgroup referred to themselves as "the lunch club" and would get together over lunch as required to discuss issues and find approaches that would work across the teams. This group was effective because each member had a strong investment and significant contact with the teams themselves, whereas the executive staff as a group did not have the same level of contact.

Curiously, CP's teams did not commit to sight co-location immediately. In part this was because at least one-third of each team was already within walking co-location. The other cause was resistance within the teams themselves. CP planned to move to a new facility within a year, and that was designated as the trigger for moving to sight co-location.

Eleven months after the establishment of the teams, conflicts began to rise as market shifts caused the products and customers of two of the teams to overlap. Concurrently, CP's strategic planning process identified the need to enter a new market segment, and that itself initiated a reexamination of the team management structure. In conjunction with business strategy development, the team leaders suggested a proposal for realigning the teams. After discussion by management, the teams were realigned. Two teams were combined because one had, in fact, developed the follow-on product for the other team. A new team was created to address the new market segment CP decided to enter. There were other minor adjustments of team membership and sponsorship, as well as a continuing effort to improve the capability of CP's lagging third team.

As is usually the case, when an organization converts to multifunctional teams, it has to convert existing developments with their current schedules into the team model. Thus, when CP established its teams, each one already had an established development schedule that predated the company's discussions of FCT. The newly established team was the first team to start a brand-new development since CP had started its quest for FCT. As part of that effort, the new team asked for the resources to be sight co-located. Since temporary quarters were rented for them to begin with, this was fairly easy to do.

Between the initial establishment of the teams in June 1989 and the restructuring in February 1990, CP's executives focused on increasing the capabilities of the teams by hiring more senior-level managers. These new managers were selected based on their ability to eliminate the team members serving double duty. It was partially based on these hires that CP could redefine and expand its team structure.

## Summary of CP's Team Experience

The CP case once again demonstrates that the implementation template presented earlier in this chapter must be adjusted and tuned on a regular basis for it to be effective. The hallmarks of CP's success with its team management program can be attributed to the up-front definitional architecture it did, Worster's commitment to identifying and removing obstacles, and each executive's actions to shift the support of his functional entity to the teams. The actual success of their teams is indisputable. Much of the work formerly done by the executive staff was, within the space of three months, competently and capably undertaken by the teams. In fact, during the first five months of the team management program, the team responsible for CP's primary product (accounting for over 90% of revenues) handled a major product problem—that historically would have been handled by the executive staff. Though the team did not manage it perfectly, upon a joint postmortem review with the executives it was agreed that the executive staff would not have done any better.

# 7

# FCT Process Redesign

Every result a business achieves is the output of a process. In order to change substantially the timeliness, cost, or quality of any output, one must change the process that creates it. Simply increasing the speed of an existing process will usually cause damage to quality or cost. The result is similar to what race car drivers experience when they ignore the red line on their tachometers. An engine tolerates a short burst of stress, but if it is over-taxed for a long period of time, it will disintegrate. The organizational analogue of an overstressed engine is that quality degrades, costs soar, and people burn out.

FCT is dependent on rapid *and* flawless execution of the key value delivery processes within the corporation. To increase speed, one must clearly understand the key deliverables, dynamics, and ingredients of the process one is trying to accelerate. In this regard, U.S. firms operate very differently from their Japanese counterparts. Two-thirds of the average U.S. firm's R & D dollars are dedicated to *product* development, with one-third targeted at *process* development. In Japan, the numbers are reversed. Their devotion to process development enables them to gain speed that in turn spurs more new product opportunities.[1]

Still, most managers resist taking time for process management and redesign. We'll begin this chapter by understanding why that is and prescribing steps to make both more attractive. The rest of the chapter will detail how to implement the FCT redesign process.

## Why Managers Resist Process Management and Redesign

We rarely encounter an executive who argues that understanding and improving core work process is not important. At the same time, we rarely find that the time executives devote to understanding and improving their work process is congruent with the importance they attribute to it. There are five primary reasons for this seemingly contradictory behavior.

### *Organizational Processes Are Intangible*

It is much easier to examine a company's product than the process that generated it. As one moves upstream away from the visible equipment and work of manufacturing and into the realm of knowledge work, the situation gets worse. Because process is not easy to see, process problems do not capture our attention. And since they are difficult to see, it is even more difficult to develop a common understanding of each problem, because everyone carries a different picture of the problem and what the underlying process looks like.

At the same time, everyone who has created a product development schedule or PERT chart has made the invisible development process visible. We find that people possess more capability to understand and examine process than they give themselves credit for. Too frequently, understanding process is equated with "touchy-feely" personnel work, when the human dimension is only one aspect of process. The technical and administrative processes are equally important and not nearly as emotionally charged.

The FCT redesign methodology provides an easy to use method that stays focused on cycle time. As part of the redesign, a modified version of Rummler's Is/Should[2] mapping process makes processes visible and therefore creates a common figure that a group of people can focus on and improve. Constructing Is and Should maps creates a learning forum where people disclose and clarify each other's picture of the process as they construct the collective map.

### *Most Organizational Performance Measures Are Results Oriented*

There is no question that organizations need results measures. Our concern is that exclusively using such measures does not tell one much about what caused the poor results. In addition, the longer a problem takes to detect and correct, the more rework and cost are associated with it. Therefore, the longer a process's cycle time is, the more dangerous it is to operate using only results measures, since you will not know if there is a problem until the cycle is completed.

The issue is more difficult upstream. Through the use of statistical process control, manufacturing has become relatively skilled at designing and using predictive process measures such as statistical sampling to control repetitive processes. In the design process, the work is not as repetitive, and companies have not been nearly as successful in designing repeatable process measures.

We find value in tracking the number of engineering change orders, value-added versus non-value-added time, engineering deployment relative to schedule and need, and counting projects started versus projects open and projects shipped. Other measures will be covered in Chapter 8. Clearly, this is a new territory for which there are no silver bullets. We see a potential contribution in "design for experiments" as practiced by quality experts, but even that has had relatively little upstream exposure.

### *Process Improvement Is Incremental, Not Revolutionary*

Nearly every week, one can find another new article describing the speed of Japanese new product development. In selected high-profile industries such as consumer electronics or automobiles, the Japanese have demonstrated their ability to speed successive generations of new products to market. Although we know intellectually that "made in Japan" did not lose its negative connotation overnight, we emotionally want (and too often expect) our own organizations to turn around on a dime. A firm or industry does not lose *or* regain its competitive edge overnight.

Increasing your organization's speed results from an iterative process of identifying obstacles, designing a new process that eliminates them, and then most importantly, ensuring that the new way is accepted and implemented by those who do the work. Removing the first layer of obstacles is required to see the second layer. If your organization has not examined its core value delivery processes for some time, there may be plenty of low-hanging fruit in the first layer. We have seen first-time FCT redesign efforts result in as much as a 50% cycle time reduction, and individual tasks within the process can have increases well in excess of 100%. This energizes the organization, but it can also set expectations too high for each FCT process analysis.

Without question, consistent cycle time improvements come from iterative, highly focused FCT process analysis as opposed to large-scale improvement efforts. We strongly believe that using a pragmatic style, combined with reasonably sized redesign projects, gets people sufficiently excited about the results to undertake another redesign effort. We

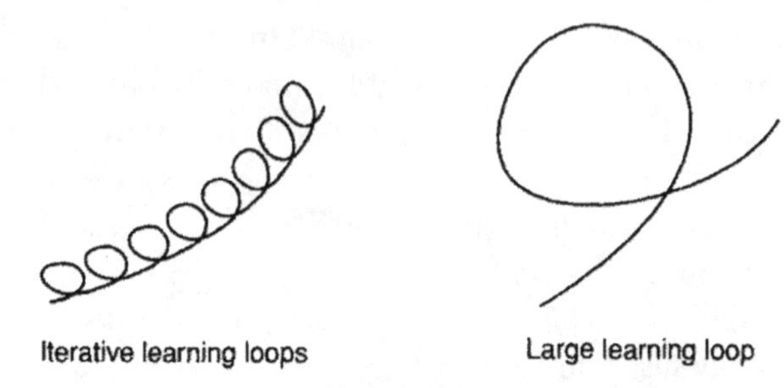


**EXHIBIT 7.1**

think of it as a series of many small learning cycles rather than one large loop, as shown in Exhibit 7.1.

### *Time Devoted to Process Analysis Slows Down Productive Work*

The difficulty with this objection is that in the short term, those who object are right. If you take a multifunctional design team away for two days to analyze the product development process, its members are not designing new products during that time. But just like the mechanic in the oil filter commercial who touts the cheap cost of an oil change compared to a major engine overhaul, the two days may end up saving fifteen if taken early enough in the project.

Another reason process improvement efforts are not considered productive is that they take too long. In many cases we agree. *Process improvement methodology itself is in need of FCT process improvement.* Additionally, a disturbing number of process improvement specialists become zealots who treat process improvement as an end in itself rather than as a tool to improve the firm's competitive standing. We find that resistance drops dramatically when the process improvement methodology itself is crisp and efficient. The FCT redesign methodology presented herein is flexible enough to be used by a dedicated team or "live" with the people who run the process under study. We have conducted a complete first-pass redesign in two days using this process.

### *People Confuse the Act of Analyzing a Process with Achieving FCT Results*

The goal of FCT process redesign is to accelerate the speed of the process under study. The process analysis component of the redesign process is a critical step, but the redesign is not done until those who use the process have changed their behavior to meet the new design's speed targets and quality specifications. People become frustrated with the time spent analyzing a process because they often see lots of plans but not much implementation.

*In order to achieve successful implementation and results, the goal of FCT process redesign must be behavior change, not analysis.* This has significant implications for how one conducts FCT process analysis. Just as designers should "design for manufacturability and assembly," one ought to "design for implementation" when doing an FCT redesign. Conducting the most thorough analysis has no value if the organization cannot implement the recommended changes. For example, who should be involved in the redesign effort changes significantly when behavior change becomes the target. Rather than staffing the effort exclusively with those who possess the best analytical skills, one ought to include key opinion leaders whose buy-in will be required to make any new process work.

## Making Process Improvement Attractive: Leverage

The most compelling reason we can offer for managing processes and using FCT process redesign is the leverage these offer compared to just focusing on results. When one focuses predominantly on results, it is easy to slip into a "find and fix" mentality. Each poor result initiates an independent investigation and, therefore, an independent solution. After that problem is solved, the next problem is attacked as a totally fresh situation. The leverage in find-and-fix systems is a random function based on how and when the problems present themselves. Find-and-fix is conventional thinking, as discussed in Chapter 2, applied to problem solving.

Alternatively, the process redesign mind-set causes one to step back and view individual problems as part of a larger system. One gains significant leverage by moving beyond the event orientation of find-and-fix. By looking for patterns and structures that cut across an entire process such as product development, improvement efforts can influence current and future products at once.

For example, specification setting always plays a critical role in FCT product development. Consider the case of the Millard Products Company. Management noticed that most projects suffered delays during the specification-setting phase. When it asked the development teams what the problem was, each team gave a different answer in each case. One felt management provided poor leadership during the specification-setting process. Another attributed the delay to a constantly shifting, immature market. A third did not acknowledge there was a problem, saying it always took a long time to do things right.

Millard's team leaders got together to see if there was more to the problem, and very quickly a different story emerged. The leadership and market issues were real, but they were relatively minor, project-specific issues. The real answer was that each team created its own definition of what should go into a specification, who should provide the data, how long that process should take, and who approved the specification once you had it. Additionally, the definitions changed from project to project, even within the same team.

The lack of leadership and vacillating market issues turned out to be intervening variables rather than causal variables as once thought. The team leaders established a "specification for specifications" along with responsibilities and proposed it to management. It was quickly approved with minor changes. Specification setting on the next set of projects took 60% less time, across all teams. When you fix a root cause, the fix is leveraged across multiple projects. The leverage available from fixing processes, particularly those directly tied to the organization's value proposition, cuts across the entire system.

## Implementing the FCT Redesign Process

There are seven steps to the FCT redesign process, as depicted in Exhibit 7.2. The first step is to select a target process, after which one creates a multifunctional team to conduct the process analysis *and* implement the recommended changes. The team creates a map of how the process works today (the "Is" map), which they analyze to remove non-value-added time and activities. Next, it creates a new process architecture, which is detailed by building a "Should" map. The process is not over until structures are defined and implemented that reinforce the Should map requirements. The Should map becomes the new Is map, and the process starts again.

The FCT redesign process requires a facilitator to guide it. The facilitator's role is to teach the FCT redesign process to the team, challenge current beliefs, facilitate conflict resolution, and keep the process moving at a steady pace. He or she should understand FCT principles and apply them to the redesign process itself so it does not bog down. He or she should also have a baseline understanding of the target process's goals. Internal teams are usually too invested or close to today's process, so they do not propose or explore enough alternatives without a gentle nudge. A major role for the facilitator is to expose historical practices that may no longer be useful while guiding the process forward.

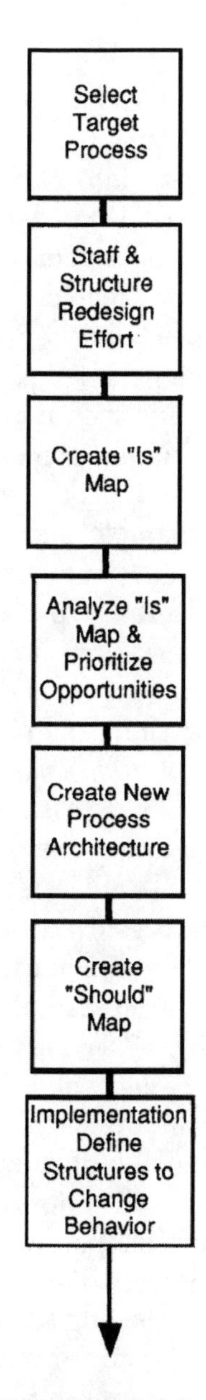


**EXHIBIT 7.2**

We will now walk through each of the steps and detail what the focus of the step is, who should be involved, and how it should be conducted. We'll offer practical tips and try to forewarn you of the typical problems one encounters along the way.

### *Select the Target Process*

The first step in any FCT redesign is to decide what process to attack. We segment organization processes into two basic camps: value delivery processes and support processes. Value delivery processes are processes that *directly* deliver the value defined in the firm's mission and strategy to the customer. Typical examples include the new product development process, the order-to-fulfillment process (including manufacturing and distribution), and the customer service process. Support processes include traditional support activities such as human resources development and financial administration. Support processes also include tasks that are currently required to support a value delivery process but do not directly add value themselves. For example, most testing processes support a value delivery process such as development or manufacturing, but in and of themselves, they confirm the value's presence rather than add to it. *For maximum competitive impact, we recommend selecting value delivery processes for redesign. Focusing on value delivery processes will also illuminate the most important support process impediments and do so within the context of meeting customer needs.*

Identifying value delivery processes is easy *if* you have previously created strategic alignment. Guided by the definitions of the mission and business strategy, one selects the processes that deliver the defined values to the customer. When the organization mission and strategy are fuzzy or out of alignment, this is very difficult to do. Some executives find it useful to list or create a high-level map of their business to identify the value delivery processes. Exhibit 7.3 is an example of such a map; the map serves as a reference point to select value delivery processes.[3]

The other considerations are of secondary importance. The redesign process goes much more smoothly if the process selected is currently under control. If the process itself varies dramatically with each repetition, the redesign team has to work harder during the analysis phase, because there is no common process. Paradoxically, one could argue that this is the perfect reason for selecting such a process to work on if it is critical to the overall business; a process out of control is unlikely to generate a quality output reliably or quickly.

The next task is to establish the scope of the redesign process. The larger and more complex the process, the more time and involvement it will take to redesign. A parallel consideration is whether the process cuts across several functions or is within the control of a single function. If the process is within a single function, it will typically be easier to redesign. The primary advantage of choosing a process within a function is that one has more direct control over implementation. On the downside, redesign

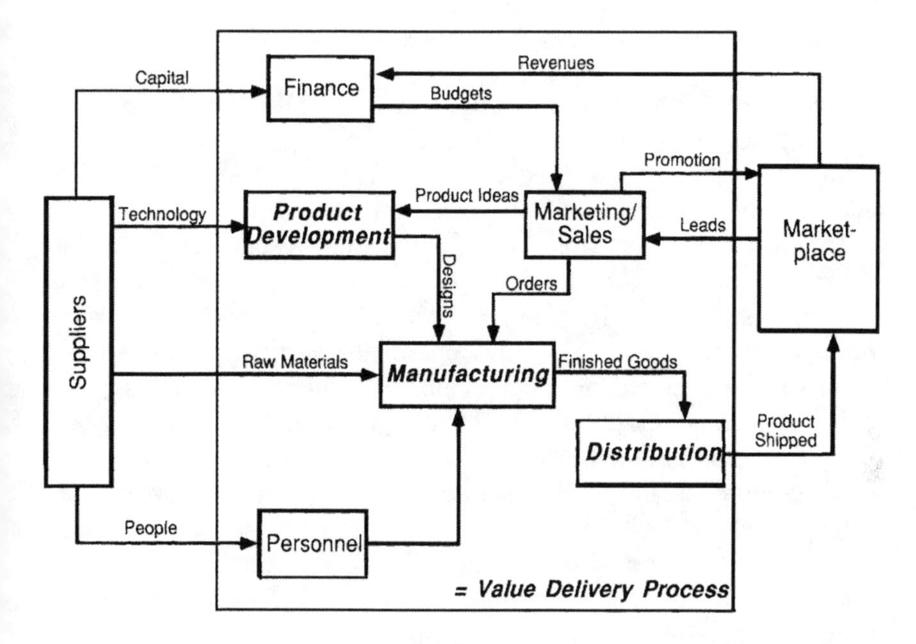


**EXHIBIT 7.3**

efforts on cross-functional processes illuminate opportunities in the cracks between functional entities that are not visible otherwise. As we have seen so often with quality problems, the major value delivery and FCT improvement opportunities are usually cross-functional.

Just as executive leverage in new product development is up and to the left, so is it in the FCT redesign process. Executives ought to make the target process selections based on the business's strategy and mission. Because the targets selected send a signal to the rest of the organization, it is important to choose with this in mind. The more important the process under analysis, the stronger the signal sent regarding the importance of FCT.

Executive should clearly define any assumptions within which the redesign team must work before the effort begins. The list should be as short as possible. We strongly recommend appointing an executive sponsor for each redesign effort to keep management aware of progress and to provide an avenue for support if required. Typically, the sponsor is the executive closest to being what might be called the process owner on the management team.

It is a judgment call whether to begin with a smaller, discrete process in order to establish a beachhead for FCT or to take on a larger cross-functional process. Pilot efforts are easy to conduct, but they often are too small or not visible enough to spark the interest that is hoped for.

### *Staff and Structure the Redesign Effort*

This phase establishes the FCT redesign team and develops the plan for the complete effort from analysis through implementation. The primary responsibility for this stage begins with management and then transfers quickly to the redesign team with management support.

The selection of the team is management's first responsibility. *We cannot recommend strongly enough that the redesign team be multifunctional in composition and chartered to complete the entire process from analysis through implementation.* When the responsibility is split, typically between analysis and implementation, implementation suffers tremendously. The multifunctional composition ensures that those who either supply, conduct, or use the outputs of the process are actively and directly involved.

Management should use the team architecture, design, and development concepts outlined in Chapter 5 to form this multifunctional team. Although shorter in tenure, most of the elements apply. One additional membership requirement is that redesign team members should have as much direct knowledge as possible of the process being redesigned. A rule of thumb for selection is that the more involved and knowledgeable the team is about the target process, the more effective the redesign effort will be. This will not be possible in all cases; where it is not, the team member must be familiar enough with the process to know who to call on for direct experience.

Management should charter the team with an overall goal expressed as a cycle time reduction target. For example, the goal could be to define and implement a new development process that reduces by six months the cycle time from concept approval to first revenue shipment. In this example, the goal defines the improvement target as well as defines the beginning and end points of the process. The cycle must be defined before data collection can meaningfully begin. As is the case with permanent multifunctional teams, the team has to review and internalize the goal.

Next, the team should use its early work period to outline the team structure and define the tasks required to complete the redesign process. This includes deciding who should be involved in the data collection and the mapping effort and how much of that work will be done by the redesign team versus others. For example, the design team could build the Is and Should maps themselves based on interview data or in direct connection with others. Once the tasks are identified, a task time line should be developed that defines the tasks, sequencing, timing, and implementation responsibility within the team.

The team should also identify the key stakeholders in the current process, plus those required to implement any changes crafted during the redesign. Stakeholders are those who have direct input, have approval re-

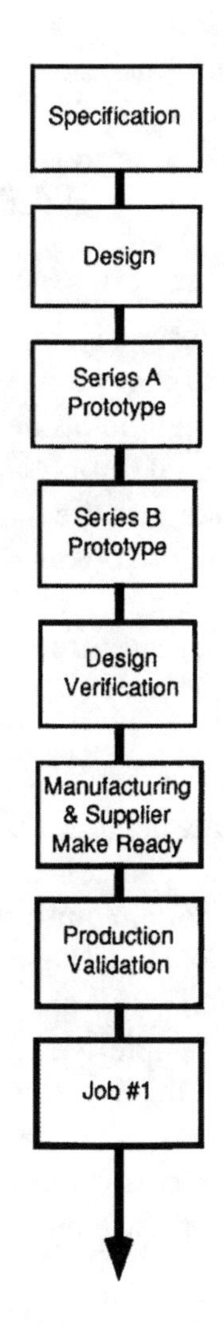


**EXHIBIT 7.4**

sponsibilities, or receive the output of the process. Stakeholders can be internal to the organization or external, such as suppliers or customers. The primary stakeholders should be represented on the redesign team. By thinking ahead to those required to implement changes, one can involve stakeholders early in the redesign process and thus incorporate their knowledge while lowering their resistance to change.

It is usually helpful to have a high-level model of the process under study at this point. Such a model is typically a six- to eight-box diagram that defines the major project phases. One can usually get this from the team sponsor. For example, the model in Exhibit 7.4 represents the major phases in an engine design process.

The most common problems we see during the scoping period concern starting the team and planning the work. The team should undertake the early work set of tasks as soon as possible after it is formed. Minimally, the team needs a crisp goal definition for its project, as well as defined roles, operating procedures, and schedule. Without question, it is to your advantage to co-locate the redesign team. There is inherent pressure in a temporary task force to jump right into the task because of its short tenure. Those groups that do not take a day to structure their team and block out a work schedule (as described above) usually spend five times that amount in later confusion and rework.

This is also the time to make sure the team has the right players or access to the necessary information to conduct the analysis and make the change. *The scope of the team's authority must be clearly agreed to by team and management.* Implementation suffers greatly when this is not done.

### *Create an Is Map*

Creating the Is map is the next major task. The mapping process is critical, because it provides a tangible collective picture that shows how a process works. Although we work in our organizations every day, each of us has very little knowledge about all the tasks and transactions required to make a complex cross-functional process work. We also fool ourselves about how much we know. People typically know what their own responsibilities are, but they do not know the consequences of their actions on others or what it takes to prepare an input they receive. People make assumptions about how the processes work based on past experience, incomplete information, or company policies that define how the process *should* work.

In addition to finding problems, the Is map also captures fixes that are in use but are not documented. For example, although a phased review model approved by the corporation may suggest a certain sequence of steps, the product development community may have found that a different sequence works even more effectively. If one does not construct an Is map, these learnings are lost.

Last, the process of building the Is map provides a forum for unlearning that builds momentum for change. Unlearning takes time, and the Is map development process uses time efficiently. As people participate in mapping the current process, they begin to understand what is wrong with it and let go of their attachment to it. The greatest difficulty facing most organizations is not deciding what to do differently, but developing the critical mass of energy required to change today's behavior.

The Is map should portray the process as it *actually* occurs today. The Is map is a snapshot from an anthropologist's point of view. It encompasses success, failure, waste, and efficiencies where they exist. In contrast, the Should map defines how the redesigned process should work.

Both Is and Should maps use the same multifunctional flowchart format (Exhibit 7.5). A time line runs along the top or bottom of the map, along with the labels for each phase of the process. The y-axis of the map lists the process's critical stakeholders. These can include functional groups, cross-functional groups, customers, suppliers, and any other stakeholder that has a significant role in the process. The tasks each stakeholder undertakes are placed in boxes from left to right within the row; these are referred to as *stakeholder streams*. Traditional flowcharting conventions are frequently used, such as diamonds for decision points, rectangles for tasks, ovals for results, and "pianos" for documentation.

The multifunctional flowchart methodology works well for defining the key steps but does not do as good a job in illustrating process dynamics, particularly as one moves upstream. For example, rework and iterative learning loops do not distinguish themselves easily. These patterns show up as "pipelines" of prototype, test, analyze, and fix, each followed by a similar pipeline. When one sees a series of tasks repeating themselves, that indicates such a pattern. When the map is completed, go back and number each step from front to back; these numbers serve as mapping coordinates to facilitate tracking what item is being talked about during group discussion. The numbers do not indicate priority or exact sequencing.

The internally developed Is map approach contrasts strongly with using outside experts to analyze the current process and present a series of recommendations including a new process design. Outside experts present recommendations to a management group that is much smaller than the group that will ultimately implement them. Although the analysis may be fundamentally accurate and more detailed than an internal group might put together, it does not create the same learning forum and, therefore, does not generate the same commitment to change that developing an Is map does.

In the interest of saving time, many want to know if they can skip the Is map and go straight to the preparing the Should map. Our experience is that this is rarely a good idea. The Is map provides a vehicle to understand the current process so that when changes are proposed, one does not have to answer questions such as "Didn't you know we do that now?" or "Why are you changing that?" Furthermore, until the Is map is built, one does not know if there is collective agreement about how the process *actually* works as opposed to how each one of us thinks it works in our own minds.

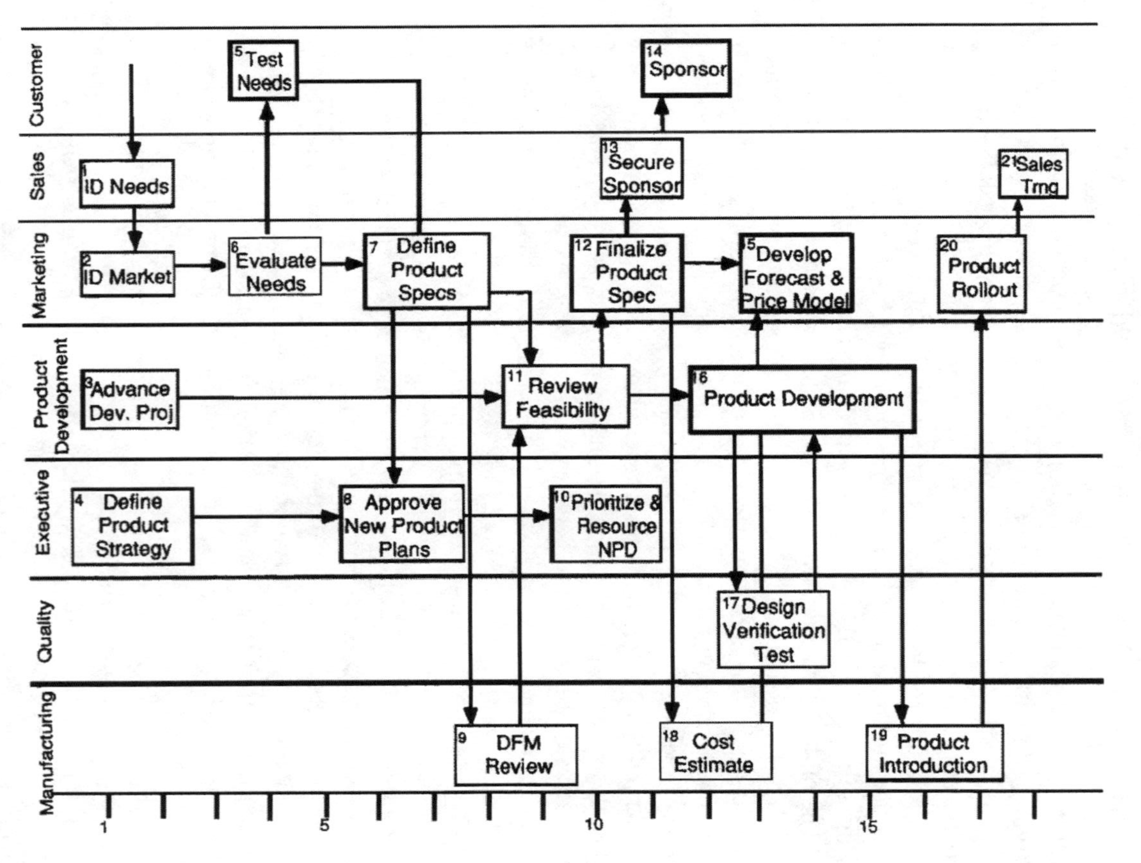
Customer
Sales
Marketing
Product Development
Executive
Quality
Manufacturing
1 ID Needs
2 ID Market
3 Advance Dev. Proj
4 Define Product Strategy
5 Test Needs
6 Evaluate Needs
7 Define Product Specs
8 Approve New Product Plans
9 DFM Review
10 Prioritize & Resource NPD
11 Review Feasibility
12 Finalize Product Spec
13 Secure Sponsor
14 Sponsor
15 Develop Forecast & Price Model
16 Product Development
17 Design Verification Test
18 Cost Estimate
19 Product Introduction
20 Product Rollout
21 Sales Trng
1
5
10
15

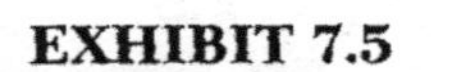

**EXHIBIT 7.5**

The Is map construction process creates a learning forum for those who ultimately must change their behavior. They test and engage each other regarding problems in the process. For people to change their behavior, they usually need more than a simply analytic reason. Although there is no single key to facilitating behavior change, we do know that the more individuals are involved and chartered to define change for themselves, the more likely it is that the change will eventually take place. It would be to the organization's advantage to have a less than perfect analysis of a process if it achieved the buy-in and commitment of the key players to fundamentally change their behavior. We are against sloppy analysis; rather, we are suggesting that with guidance and support, one can build an Is map that accurately provides the data necessary for analysis.

### *Is Map Construction Mechanics*

The Is map provides the springboard for the entire redesign process, because it creates a common, tangible picture of the process. Every time we either hand one out after interviews or build one live, the excitement and interest soar as people recognize the process and the problems they have experienced. The Is map must replicate the process, but the map itself has no long-term value. It is used for diagnostic purposes to shape a new process architecture and to detail the Should map that follows. Accuracy is defined by asking whether the map replicates how the process is conducted today with 80% or greater accuracy. One should not strive for 100% accuracy; as one moves upstream, there is increasing variability between the ways different products are developed. One wants the map accurate enough to use as a basis of the process.

A popular method for building the Is map is for a small group to interview a broad cross section of people who conduct the process currently and to construct a map based on their input. This information is augmented by interviews with those who must live with the process's outputs. The interviewing and map building can be done by a subset of the mapping team or subcontracted to a third party.

Done properly, contracting the Is map preparation does not disenfranchise the team from the map. Creating the Is map, in many respects, is a mechanical process. The critical ingredient for an effective Is map is the input of the key players. As long as the confirmation of the map's accuracy and subsequent analysis remains squarely within the organization, companies can successfully use third parties to produce the Is map. The primary deterrent is that organization members do not gain as great an appreciation for fixed process interdependencies or the experience of building an Is map.

The preferred method is to build the Is map in a single meeting. Here the mapping team, either as an entity or expanded with representation from key stakeholders, constructs the map itself. Many of the techniques for doing this are applicable to the interview approach. The first step is to define the stakeholders and major project phases; these are used to create a blank Is map, as shown in Exhibit 7.6.

The design team should agree ahead of time to the level of detail it wants. This is a judgment call that depends on the people and the process. Too little detail and the map does not offer enough understanding for redesign; too much detail and it becomes too cluttered to be helpful. We prefer to keep maps to less than 100 tasks for the first pass and do another map if required to detail a particular subprocess. Our experience is that the confidence gained by more detail is outweighed by the clutter and confusion. Major cycle time barriers will quickly show themselves at the described level.

Once the template is defined, one needs a stakeholder who can detail the task steps within each horizontal stream. Each stakeholder starts at the end of the process and works backward by identifying the tasks required from the final deliverable to the first task undertaken. Working backward keeps the stakeholder grounded in facts, because one leg is always anchored in a tangible output.

Each stakeholder works as an anthropologist and constantly asks "intelligent stupid questions" about each step in the process. The basic questions are as follows:

1. What is the final deliverable of this task?
2. What do you need to begin this task?
3. How do you know you are finished?
4. To whom do you give the final deliverable?
5. How long does it take to complete this task?

If one is using the interview method, it is frequently useful to ask why individuals do what they do. This provides insight that enables the mapper to better understand the process. When using the real-time approach, the "why" issue comes later during the analysis phase.

Keep the map to the detail level set by fixing a limit on the maximum number of tasks per stakeholder stream per phase. We use self-stick notes for *each* task step when mapping in real time, because they are easy to shift around. For each task, use a new self-stick note that has the task name and its duration on it. Starting from the end, place the notes on the template in order within the appropriate stream.

At this point, all the tasks are identified in all the streams, but they have not been tied together. Beginning at the end and working backward, con-

| | Specification | Design | Series A Prototype | Series B Prototype | Design Verification | Manufacturing & Supplier Make Ready | Production Validation | Job #1 |
|---|---|---|---|---|---|---|---|---|
| Engine Division | | | | | | | | |
| Material Control | | | | | | | | |
| Purchasing | | | | | | | | |
| Manufacturing | | | | | | | | |
| Testing | | | | | | | | |
| Powertrain | | | | | | | | |
| Vehicle Office | | | | | | | | |
| Other | | | | | | | | |

Time

**EXHIBIT 7.6**

nect the appropriate inputs and outputs for each task, one phase at a time. Undoubtedly there will be inputs that are missing or outputs without a place to go; these will require discussion. *Use these conversations as an opportunity to better understand the process.* Be very careful not to get so absorbed in the map-building task that it becomes the focus rather than understanding the process. As issues emerge, capture them on a flip chart, but resolve them. Work backward until all tasks have been connected.

Determine the worst-case cycle time by tracing the process from front to back. This is done by following the critical path taken by the tasks with the longest durations. Then complete the time line at the top or bottom of the map and align the self-stick notes as required to the time line.

The final step in the Is map process is to reproduce the map itself. Flowcharting software is commercially available that offers sufficient flexibility to build such maps and can speed up the mechanics significantly. One should produce a wall-sized map for the analysis phase, as well as personal-sized maps. The wall-sized map becomes a graphical reference point, whereas the personal maps are usually easier to read and handle.

The major Is map problems are resolving conflicts between different perspectives and the "every project is different" syndrome. Resolving conflicts is best done by always asking people to ground their discussions in an actual event. In some cases, agreement will be reached quickly, while in other situations, one has to accept that the process was different for each project. Rather than getting into a rat hole trying to make the map perfect, capture the importance of the difference. Is one way becoming the trend? Is this step critical to overall process? *Do not resolve the problem at this point. The job of the Is map is to portray the issue, not to resolve it.*

Regarding the differences between projects, every project *is* different, and at the same time, every project addresses many of the same steps and themes, though at slightly different times. The role of the mapping process is to capture a useful snapshot of the process, with the recognition that the map will never equal the territory being mapped.

There are several approaches to handle these differences. For example, products developed for manufacture at location A may go through a different process than products designed for manufacture at location B. In such cases, one can use a separate stakeholder stream for each of the manufacturing facilities. When conflicts arise between participants, get a third and fourth perspective.

### *Analyze the Map and Prioritize Opportunities*

Before process analysis can begin, the Is map's accuracy must be confirmed and errors fixed. This is done by the mapping team and includes key stakeholders as appropriate. *The purpose is to identify major corrections and clarify the content rather than make the map perfect.* It helps to have people review the map before they discuss it. One will find some managers want to add a step they perceive as missing, while those who do the work will say that same task is not being done in practice. When a box is not represented on the map, test whether that task actually takes place. If it passes this test, draw it on the map if important. Keep the group centered on using the map as a springboard to better understand the process as opposed to making the map perfect. *One rarely has a problem with map accuracy if the people who were interviewed or built the map had in-depth knowledge of the process.*

The focus of the process analysis is to identify non-value-added time and activities so they can be reduced and ultimately eliminated. To do this, the working group needs an operating definition of value-added and non-value-added work. This is always a sensitive discussion, as everyone believes they are adding value. Common sense suggests that people do not come to work with the intent of doing anything other than adding value.

Value added, however, is always defined by the end customer. We are aware that many organizations have adopted the term *internal customer* to promote teamwork and accountability. We strongly believe that this language creates more problems than benefits. If your organization has adopted this language and believes that now is not the time to change, then call revenue paying customers "end customers."

End customers pay for the product and are the only ones who can appropriately determine what is value added or is not. When you are a patron at a restaurant, you determine whether you received the value you expected. The proprietor, maître d', waiter, or chef has no role in that judgment. Although they may have more restaurant and culinary experience, it is only the judgment of yourself and other patrons that determines the success or failure of the restaurant.

One could argue that internal purchasers from other divisions are end customers. This is true, but treating them as equal to revenue-paying customers is misleading. Transfer pricing can become a game in itself. Additionally, revenue-paying customers demand an integrated solution, whereas internal products transferred are usually components.

Internal customers engage in activities that are valued by other internal customers but produce no value for end customers. Suppose a parts-and-service organization launches a two-day training program to educate parts managers in the use of a new computer system. The program may have value for parts managers as an internal customer, but the training offers little direct value for the end customer. Equating the parts managers' needs to those of the end customer would be a serious mistake.

Obviously, one would be foolish to eliminate any element of non-value-added work until one has redesigned the process to eliminate the need or substitute something in its place. In the above example, it would be foolish to eliminate the parts management training program until there was another way to educate people about the new system's requirements. FCT thinking would lead one to think about how the parts system could be designed so that the training could be done in half a day, or so that help was on-line or not even required.

Our point is that one cannot simply will non-value-added work away. Some experts suggest that more than 95% of the time spent in organizations is non-value added,[4] and manufacturing operations we know are delighted when value-added time exceeds 10%! One could get tied up in the semantics and techniques of measurement and miss the point: *when we do not fully understand the processes and technology used to produce a product and service, we must include many non-value-added steps to make up for our lack of understanding.* What the customer wants and what is currently required to produce it are two different discussions. Just because something is required does not make it value added.

We use two definitions of value added as departure points for the team's discussion. The first states that value added is anything for which the end customer is willing to pay. A car buyer, for example, will certainly pay for the wheels being on the vehicle. We like to use a hypothetical window-sticker invoice as a way to test and focus the value-added discussion. For example, if he or she wanted special racing wheels on the car, a customer would not object to an additional cost on the window sticker. At the same time, it is quite likely he or she would object to a $5 wheelhandling cost for transporting the wheel from the receiving dock to the assembly line.

Our second definition states that any action that directly leads to meeting customer requirements is value added. *Directly* is defined as a single, direct step: the fifth attempt that finally gets it right is value added, but the first four are not. Building a component in a larger form than will be used in the final product does not directly meet customer requirements, whereas designing the actual size does.

*Requirements* refers to what the customer actually requires, as opposed to what is technically achievable. In technology-driven products, we find many features that the customer does not require or use but which excited the technologists. Obviously there is a gray area with new technologies, where a customer has no experience to determine whether he or she desires them or not. New technologies will always present this dilemma, but it is important not to overestimate it. This definition of value added moves upstream reasonably well. It is often difficult to define whether an end customer would pay for a certain design step; it is somewhat easier to ascertain whether that step does directly go toward customer requirements.

In all cases, one cannot define value added until senior management has clearly defined the mission and business strategy, especially the firm's value proposition. The value vector is always internally grounded by where and how the company chooses to add value. When this is not clear, process analysis is reduced to simply cleaning up the current process; one cannot challenge or eliminate the added value of any step.

Value added can never be answered permanently, since the customer determines it. It changes as new technologies emerge and competitors introduce new products. Therefore, defining value added requires ongoing discussion.

Do not expect your organization to identify or attack non-value-added activities quickly. Initially, most find it much easier to identify items that are out of sequence or poorly handled. Singling out an item that is well done but not value added is more difficult. In the course of process analysis, our experience is understanding and eliminating non-value-added tasks occurs as the organization becomes more experienced with process analysis. One's expectation should be that there will still remain a great deal of non-value-added tasks. From the competitive standpoint, however, the firm that is able to increase value-added steps from 10% of the process to 11% achieves a 10% productivity improvement in that process.

The second and much easier item to look for is what we call *disconnects.* Disconnects represent items that are out of sequence, inadequately performed, or missing entirely from the map. A disconnect can be a value-added task or a non-value-added task out of sequence. The term *disconnect* suggests something that is not connected as it should be, without consideration of its ultimate value to the end customer. This category attracts more attention during a first iteration through FCT process analysis because it is inherently less rigorous and easier to identify.

Now, walk through the Is map from front to back and identify disconnects and non-value-added tasks. Balance the discussion between understanding what the individual is saying and reaching agreement whether the item is indeed a non-value-added step or disconnect. List each item chronologically on a flip chart, with a bias toward including an item if there is a debate. Note the task number that each item relates to on the Is map.

After the entire map has been examined, the disconnects and non-value-added items should be prioritized. Many find it useful to prioritize items a phase at a time rather than all at once. In that case, a final prioritization step is required to select the issues. Reduce a long list by requiring individuals to vote only for the top three issues. Expect to have nearly as many issues as there are steps in the process. The voting method enables the facilitator to be generous in listing issues during discussion, for they will be sorted in the final voting.

Before conducting the final prioritizing, ask the working group to step back and examine the process as a whole. Whereas the previous analysis happened on a micro basis, it is also very important to identify major themes and patterns that repeat themselves throughout the process under study. Conduct a step-back review that works at a figurative altitude of 50,000 feet and ask the group to generate a list of no more than ten items that are key issues across the process. The balance between micro and macro perspectives during the analysis is absolutely vital; neither one by itself is sufficient.

The phase is complete when the list of disconnects and non-value-added improvement opportunities have been reduced to a short list. Rather than fix every issue identified, it is highly preferable to work two or three major issues to implementation with a new process design and follow this with a second FCT redesign effort.

### *Defining a New Process Architecture*

Leverage in process redesign comes from making a major change in the overall process architecture. Replacing a complete prototype cycle with electronic simulation has significantly more leverage than executing a prototype faster. Removing inefficiencies between current tasks can generate a significant one-time improvement in cycle time, but a new architecture provides the framework for substantial breakthroughs that continue to improve over the years.

Once again, we use the term *architecture* to define the organization of the tangible and intangible structures of the system that cause it to behave in a unique manner. Adopting concurrent development and implementing multifunctional teams are examples of changes in the product development architecture. To some, adopting a new architecture is quite threatening, because the change is more revolutionary than evolutionary.

When one is working with those who are uneasy, it is important to distinguish between defining the new architecture and the path one follows to implement it. As competitive pragmatists, we always consider the consequences of not making a revolutionary change, as well as the cost involved in making it. The difficulty is that one is more familiar with what will be lost than what may be gained. Our experience in high-technology companies contrasts with more traditional firms, which tend to overestimate the losses and underestimate the gains.

After prioritizing non-value-added opportunities, the team wants to move directly to constructing the Should map. If one does that, the Should map usually becomes a "shrink" of the existing process. A shrink is a process made shorter primarily by squeezing out the waste between major steps but not fundamentally changing the process itself. *To avoid this, the team should dedicate a separate session to creating a new process architecture.* Ideally, this session should be held off-site, or at least in an environment different from where the team normally meets. The process redesign team is the primary participant, with an occasional sprinkling of outsiders. The basis for broader inclusion is to add creativity and spark rather than inclusion to support implementation buy-in. The architecture session is aimed more at idea generation than implementation.

To even see a new architecture, one must distance oneself from the current one. Once again, we see the role of learning and unlearning in FCT. The ability to develop a new architecture is directly dependent on one's willingness to see beyond and let go of the current one. This pushes people to the edge of their understanding: creating a new architecture requires one to let go of the old *without* having a replacement to grab hold of. The task is to create that replacement.

Letting go of a familiar process requires time and a willingness to experiment and play. It took time to learn the old ways, and it will take time to let go of them. Play is being willing to create alternatives and different combinations without concern for what someone else might think. The critical beliefs and injunctions people hold about learning can quickly sap the joy out of any creative process.

Facilitators are essential for this work. Their contribution is to design a process that will stimulate creativity. They know how to unfreeze a group and generate ideas in a progressive manner that loosens people up yet maintains a sense of safety. We have been successful starting meetings at one venue to stimulate ideas and then moving to a more traditional setting to sort through them. Starting the meeting at a beach, zoo, or even a shopping center might be appropriate. The point is to create an environment that is significantly different from the norm to help open minds.

A creative environment is one where suggestions can be increasingly radical and free from judgment. We find that engineering organizations are typically very skilled at brainstorming product features, but find brainstorming process innovations much more difficult. By definition, new ideas rarely are free of warts; as soon as the team starts to "fix" new ideas, the flow shuts down. We find asking team members to begin each idea with the words "I wish" has significant value in opening up the subconscious to partial ideas that would be highly desirable but are not fully thought through. Small conventions like this have a great deal of power.

Use a 50% or greater cycle time reduction target as a bogey to drive the new architecture and the "I wish" session. This helps people think beyond their current process paradigm and examine new methods. The "I wish" session works best when it is conducted intensely for about ten minutes, followed by a break and a second pass. After the second pass, the group should revisit the list and select items that either individually or combined have some potential for creating a new architecture.

A specific approach is to take the value-added tasks identified during the Is map process and experiment without regard to current stakeholders or sequencing. As a team, assume you were starting from scratch and could define the resource groupings, tasks, and sequence. Have each person think of it as "My Product Company" and define how he or she would deliver the value from a blank slate. This facilitates a very clean look and a redefinition of resource grouping within the organization that is based on your value proposition.

Another method is to set a cycle time target for the new process that pushes the edge of reality. For example, if a process currently takes eighteen months, one might ask what would be done if the continued existence of the company depended on our getting a product out in three months. Such radical approaches often stimulate thinking and suggestions that would not normally come out during traditional brainstorming. A key is to have fun during this process. Sacred cows, such as never outsourcing component development, are exposed and challenged when this approach is used.

The final deliverable of this step is a new, large block model (Exhibit 7.7) similar to the blank Is map. The architecture should identify how much time is allocated to each phase, define the main inputs and deliverables for each phase, and specify new elements or philosophies such as multifunctional teams.

There is a clear pattern to the FCT architectures we see evolve from redesign efforts. First, firms strive for as much parallel processing as possible—sequential activities use more time. Second, they move away from

| *Phase* | *Target Cycle Time* | *Phase Inputs* | *Phase Outputs* |
|---|---|---|---|
| Advanced Development<br>*Ongoing evaluation of product and process architecture/building blocks* | Continuous | • **Product customer selected**<br>• **Corporate strategy**<br>Product plan<br>Technology roadmap<br>Process/technology development<br>Plan<br>Advanced manufacturing strategy<br>• Vendor strategy<br>• Manufacturing strategy | • **Solution for customer**<br>• **Trained development staff**<br>Product champion plus 2-3<br>• **Base business analysis**<br>• **Long-term product architecture**<br>• **Long-term Process Architecture**<br>• **Staffing**<br>Business team (100%)<br>Critical engineering mass (80%) |
| Product Definition | 1 month | • **Solution for customer**<br>• **Trained development staff**<br>Product champion plus 2-3<br>• **Base business analysis**<br>• **Long-term product architecture**<br>• **Long-term process architecture**<br>• **Staffing**<br>Business team (100%)<br>Critical engineering mass (80%) | • **Customer signed up & their product milestones defined**<br>• Product architecture & specification<br>• Process architecture<br>• Management approval<br>• Business plan completed<br>• Engineering PERT signed off |
| Product Development<br>*Phase 1* | 4 months | • **Customer signed up & their product milestones defined**<br>• Product architecture & specification<br>• Process architecture<br>• Management approval<br>• Business plan completed<br>• Engineering PERT signed off | • **Customer deliverable**—<br>Meets all functions except:<br>Simulated ASICS<br>• Defined problem list<br>• Manufacturing & test process design<br>• **PCB**<br>PCB assembly not in form factor<br>PCB fab within form factor<br>• ASIC's simulations complete<br>• Vendors identified |
| Product Development<br>*Phase 2* | 3 months | • **Customer deliverable**—<br>Meets all functions except:<br>Simulated ASICS<br>• Defined problem list<br>• Manufacturing & test process design<br>• PCB<br>PCB assembly not in form factor<br>PCB fab within form factor<br>• ASIC's simulations complete<br>• Vendors identified | • **Customer deliverable**—<br>Meets all functions except:<br>Error rate<br>Defined problem list<br>• All product build on production line<br>• ASIC in house<br>• BOM released<br>• PCB assembly in final form factor<br>• Testing begun on customer's systems |
| Product Development<br>*Phase 3* | 3 months | • **Customer deliverable**—<br>Meets all functions except:<br>Error rate<br>Defined problem list<br>• All product build on production line<br>• ASIC in house<br>• BOM released<br>• PCB assembly in final form factor<br>• Testing begun on customer's systems | • **Customer deliverable**—<br>Full spec unit<br>• Full EC control with full document release<br>• Manufacturing capacity & capability<br>• Test results documented & released<br>• Agency approvals<br>• Final pricing<br>• Product launch plan |
| Product Development<br>*Phase 4* | 2 months | • **Customer deliverable**—<br>Full spec unit<br>• Full EC control with full document release<br>• Manufacturing capacity & capability<br>• Test results documented & released<br>• Agency approvals<br>• Final pricing<br>• Product launch plan | • **Customer deliverable**—<br>Product meets specification with no waivers<br>• Mass production line yield = 80% overall |

**EXHIBIT 7.7**
**Product Development Architecture**

find-and-fix maturity development. Find-and-fix is an undisciplined process of testing product maturation at every point in the process. Instead, more robust testing and simulation are used earlier to define weak spots. Third, control and risk management become a development team responsibility, and external approval reviews occur early during the concept and specification phases. For example, phase-gate review models can stifle rapid product development when too much time is spent explaining what has occurred to approving groups that lie outside the process. Gates can be created within the process that are administered by the team; outsiders provide an audit function to ensure that gate standards are upheld. Last, use simulation whenever possible to reduce the time from detection to correction in product design. Simulation alone is responsible for the vast majority of the cycle time improvements in the electronic circuit arena. We will discuss these and more approaches in the next chapter.

### *Construct a Should Map*

The Should map adds the detail to the new architecture. The Should map uses the exact same format as the Is map. The mechanics of developing the Should map are essentially the same as the Is map, with the exception that working front to back is optional. The Should map is built by the redesign team, frequently with broader involvement and testing by others. The definition of who should be involved in the Should map's development is driven by two factors: knowledge of the process, and role in implementation.

Those who know the technological and other process capabilities required need to be involved so that the Should map is aggressive but achievable. A common mistake is building a Should map that looks great on paper but is unrealistic. Be wary of adding elements such as electronic simulation without assessing how one is going to get there. Non-value-added work cannot be replaced by the stroke of a pen!

Involving those who will implement the changes is also absolutely critical. If those who develop the Should map are the ones who will implement it, one does not need to sell them on its viability. *In the case of product development, one would ideally have the entire FCT process redesign effort conducted by the multifunctional team who was going to staff the next development effort. They would redesign the process and then implement it on the next project.*

Assuming the architecture was developed using a goal of 50% cycle time improvement, the Should map should continue along this path. The final cycle time reduction is determined when one completes the Should map. We find that you should not let go of the 50% target until very late in the Should map development, because once it is let go, it cannot be reclaimed.

The amount of detail required within the Should map varies depending on the tangibility of the process. Detailing downstream repetitive processes (such as order-processing procedures) is important, whereas it is less so in upstream processes (such as development). The key differentiator is based on how much the process is a repetitive, mechanistic process versus a nonroutine, creative process. The more mechanistic, the more it lends itself toward detail.

For product development, one takes the architecture with the phases defined, along with the key deliverables, and selectively details additional steps only as required. The danger in detailing too much is that people might institutionalize the new process. For example, by detailing each step in a product development process, it can become a "cookbook" wherein people check off each step as they complete it rather than constantly rethink and shape the process to meet their unique development's needs.

Once again, be careful about becoming consumed by the Should map mechanics and do not lose sight of the overall FCT process redesign goals. This often manifests in assumptions the team creates to support its Should map. To resolve a timing mismatch between carry-forward and new hardware developments, a redesign team declared that its Should map would apply only to those products using a carry-forward hardware. Later discussions revealed that few of the products in the new product plan used carry-forward hardware. Although the Should map made sense under the specified conditions, the conditions did not match the business requirements.

When using a new architecture, it is important to keep the detail in line with the assumptions of the new architecture. If multifunctional teams are to be used for the first time, then the tasks within each stakeholder stream should reflect the new role and power shift that accompanies the implementation of teams.

### *Implementation Map*

Whereas the traditional rule of thumb for success in real estate investing is described as "location, location, location," the corresponding rule of thumb for FCT process redesign is implementation, implementation, implementation. Success equals achieving target cycle time reductions through the implementation of new behaviors without distorting quality and other defined parameters.

We have illustrated how implementation must be in the forefront of one's thinking throughout the redesign process, from the moment one chooses the target process through the end. If implementation is not addressed until the end, it becomes extremely troublesome. When addressed from the start, many of the most difficult aspects take care of themselves due to the commitment generated within the redesign learning forum.

The team must now take the Should map and, using nearly the same format, create an implementation road map (Exhibit 7.8). This time the stakeholder streams are used for *implementation activities* required to make the Should map come alive. The phases at the top should be replaced with implementation phases: approval, rollout, and so forth. Instead of reflective process timing, the time line establishes the timing of implementation activities. The self-stick notes define the implementation tasks and their duration. Initials should be added to the self-stick notes to define the team member responsible for ensuring that the task is completed. This implementation map creates a common implementation

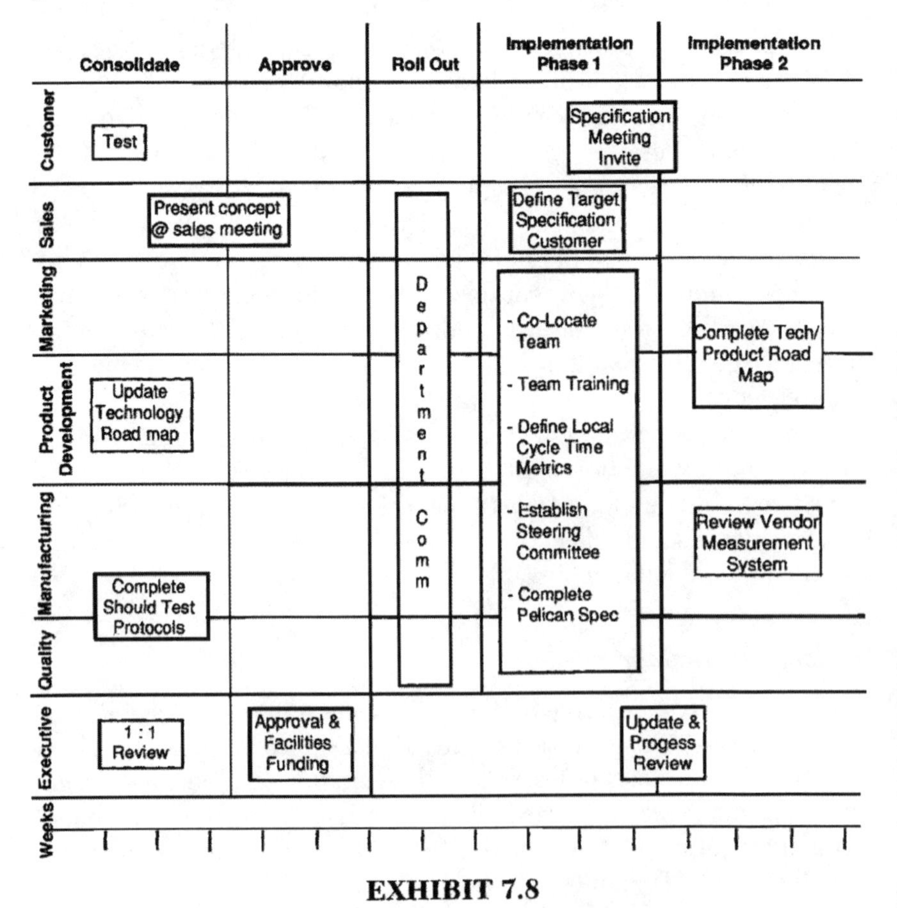


**EXHIBIT 7.8**

**FCT Implementation Map**

plan that makes the intangible change process tangible. To build such a road map, one has to identify the elements listed below.

### *Structural Changes Required to Support Architecture*

The current process is supported by many tangible and intangible structures. *In order for the Should map to become real, new structures have to be designed that make following the process it outlines the path of least resistance.* To do this, one has to walk through the major architecture and process changes defined in the Should map and ask what has to be done to make these changes easier than the old way. For example, co-location makes communication within the multifunctional team the path of least resistance. Do not make the time additive to the existing work in the organization: the golden rule of implementation is always to ask yourself what you are going to stop doing in order to get started with the new process outlined in the Should map.

### *Stakeholders Affected*

Some stakeholders will face major change. The greater the degree of change required, the more attention should be focused on planning and getting buy-in from that stakeholder. The rule is to start earlier than you think is needed. The earlier the affected stakeholder is involved in detailing how the change should be accomplished, the better off you will be. Senior management's encouragement, along with selected recognition, can be very reinforcing.

Where the impact is not as great, the issue is primarily ensuring that people understand the importance of the Should map relative to other company goals and current priorities. The key is to see who is affected and to define what is required to enlist their emotional and organizational support.

### *Anticipated Resistance*

No matter how you cut it, change is a political issue. The redesign team should step back and ask itself: Who could blow this new process out of the water, and who could significantly increase our ability to implement it? Both lists should be reviewed and a strategy developed to address the resisters and to leverage support. Every firm has several opinion leaders that must be wired into a change effort. Believing that the rational benefits of the change speak for themselves is irrational. The good news is that if you encounter resistance, you are definitely making change.

*Approvals Required*

The FCT redesign team will usually have to get blessing and support for implementation. Like implementation, the approval process itself should not be addressed for the first time at this point. It is far better to keep key decision makers aware of the trends and directions that redesign is taking as it moves forward. How and when to get the approvals should be defined.

*Timing Priorities*

There are never enough resources to do all the things we want to do when we want to do them. Implementation priorities should be established based on the impact a change can have on the business and the leverage it offers to enable other changes. For example, if creating bookshelf technology components is a prerequisite for many other elements in the Should map, it should receive early attention. As a rule, the more one has made changes up and to the left, the more important it is to start as early as possible on implementing the structures required to support the change.

One should balance this by aiming for some near-term successes. These successes help build momentum and demonstrate the value of the Should process. Focusing all one's resources on the highly leveraged long-term items may make intellectual sense, but it is not realistic and does not build early momentum.

*Technological Requirements*

Where new technologies are required such as CAD tools, they must be specified and planned for. Typically, the new technology included in the Should map is underdefined. The requirement definitions should be sharpened and incorporated within the firm's technology road map from the strategic alignment process. Too frequently companies cite new technologies as an FCT enabler in the Should map but do not adequately detail the requirements to make them real.

*Cost Implications*

The beauty of FCT compared to many other strategies is that cost is frequently the smallest component of the change. With the exception of facility changes for co-location and limited design equipment expenses, FCT is not capital intensive. To be sure, though, there are few companies where approvals will be forthcoming if the Should map's cost implications are not defined and agreed to. When doing this, one should also attach a pro forma summary that demonstrates the benefits inherent in the change. Although is it never possible to have the same accuracy on missed opportunity as it is actual cost, using reasonable assumptions, the case should be made.

*Process Measures*

The Should map will require new process measures to guide its operation. The design team should provide a set of high-level results and process measures to be used with the new process. The Should map timing is used to define the new cycle time targets and should be supported by quality and cost measures as appropriate. The redesign team uses the implementation road map to monitor implementation.

Implementation progress should be reviewed monthly by organization leadership, or at least by the executive sponsor of the FCT redesign team. The focus of the review is to identify obstacles to implementation and define strategies to remove them. If greater senior management involvement is required, it should be sought immediately. One should not wait for the monthly meeting if a major obstacle appears. The redesign team provides the drive behind the implementation, and problems need to be resolved in as close to real time as possible. When the organization sees implementation moving quickly, they see the FCT message in action and respond positively.

A final caution: most redesign teams are disbanded too early. There is a great temptation to dissolve the team once the planning is complete. The team should be kept in place during the initial period of implementation, and when it is disbanded, responsibility for completing the implementation has to have a clear and important home within the organization. The FCT redesign team often meets monthly as a steering committee even after it is disbanded.

## Summary

The heart of FCT process redesign implementation is understanding which activities are value added and which are not. Those that are not become lifelong targets for elimination, even though many will not be done away with overnight. By far the most important thought one can keep in mind during the redesign effort is this: what will help implement this change? Although process thinking is new to many, we do not find that is the barrier to significant cycle time improvement. Success comes to those who think implementation, implementation, implementation.

# 8

# Tools and Tactics to Speed Product Development

One speeds up the rate of new product development by leveraging the knowledge that already exists within the corporation and increasing the creation of new knowledge. In product development, the learning cycle has four elements that repeat themselves throughout the development process: *design*, *fabricate*, *assemble*, and *test*.[1] The learning cycle operates within a constantly narrowing range of options over the life of the development (Exhibit 8.1).

For each phase of the development process, there are tools and tactics one can implement to leverage existing learning or to increase the rate of new learning. Companies are often attracted to taking the tools and tactics that were used successfully to reduce cycle time in manufacturing and apply them to development. Although manufacturing has learned more about process management than other functions, its tools yield mixed results in product development. Although many of the manufacturing principles have analogues in product development, we have found the transfer is not as easy or as effective as one might think.

The reason is that there are intrinsic differences between the two processes. Mistakes are essential to learning and are an expected part of the development process, whereas manufacturing seeks to eliminate errors. In manufacturing there is one right way, whereas development has many right ways. Last, although there are certainly areas of product de-

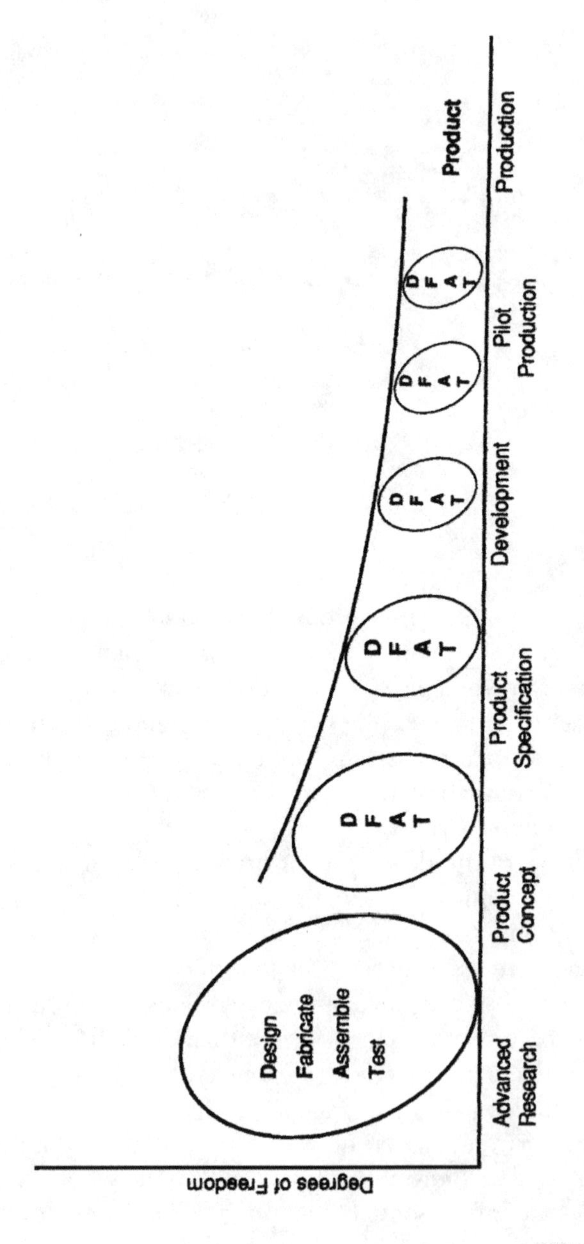
Degrees of Freedom
Design
Fabricate
Assemble
Test
D
F
A
T
Advanced Research
Product Concept
Product Specification
Development
Pilot Production
Production
Product

**EXHIBIT 8.1**

velopment that are routine and execution oriented (such as engineering services), many are not. The product development process *creates* new knowledge, whereas the manufacturing process uses existing knowledge and *executes* it, albeit seeking continuous refinement.

This chapter will survey the FCT tools and tactics for speeding up new product development. We will continue our process orientation and focus on tools and tactics that speed up critical subprocesses within product development. We will shy away from detailing specific technologies, such as computer-aided design, for several reasons. First, we rarely see a firm attain and sustain FCT leadership through a specific technology tool, although we have seen the reverse. We do know several companies that dramatically reduced their cycle time by redesigning their product specification process or by creating a common architecture that is leveraged across product families. Second, there is not sufficient space to do justice to individual technologies. Third, the underlying technology changes rapidly, and our comments would be quickly outdated.

We will follow the development model illustrated in Exhibit 8.2, focusing our suggestions on the first four phases. This follows our experience that pushing for cycle time improvements in the later phases of development encourages time compression rather than substantive and sustainable improvement. We will delve a little deeper into tactics that we have used the most and find particularly effective.

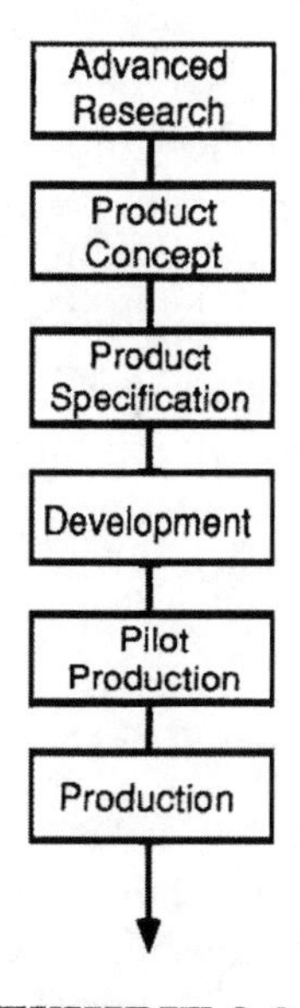


**EXHIBIT 8.2**

## Advanced Research

Advanced research distinguishes itself from product development by the degree of raw invention. FCT companies try to remove invention from the development cycle and move it upstream into research. Additionally, FCT competitors recognize that a technological advantage no longer lasts as long as it used to. Today's products depend on an increasing number of technologies, such that a significant improvement in any one of them can move a competitor to the front of the pack. Additionally, technology development and dissemination occurs at an ever-increasing pace, and customer preferences shift rapidly in constantly fragmenting markets.[2] Although FCT cannot speed up the rate of raw invention, FCT philosophy and operating principles channel how this expensive resource is deployed. In this regard, FCT competitors employ four strategies, which are detailed below.

### *Establish Strong Links Between R & D and the Business at Large*

FCT firms limit the amount of central funding to their research units to force closer working ties with operating units. The last ten years have seen such established icons of pure research as Bell Laboratories devote an increasing amount of their resources to middle- and near-term efforts defined by operating business units. Similarly, Hitachi allocates approximately 70% of its research resources to work directed by the business units and an additional 23% to one- to two-year corporate projects. Only 10% of the resources are allocated to "North Star" research, which is defined as having a ten-year-plus horizon.[3]

A major implication of this trend is the increased role that business leaders play in identifying core technologies required for ongoing success. Historically, R & D has defined the critical technologies required, based on technological expertise. The FCT company uses customer feedback and value delivery process requirements to define core technologies that it requires research to develop. In turn, research plays a growing role in defining new product and process *architectures;* they also define and lead the migration to these new architectures.

### *Increase Process Development R & D*

FCT competitors recognize that process technology is growing as complex as product technology, and they devote an increasingly large percentage of their dollars to it. Over the past five years, Intel has devoted 20% of its R & D dollars to developing CAD tools to speed the development of increasingly complex circuits.[4] Toyota increased R & D spending between 1984 and 1989 from $750 million to $2.2 billion. Rather than focus on developing flashy items such as four-wheel steering, the firm concentrates on practical manufacturing process technology, such as new ways to stamp sheet metal.[5]

### *Increase Focus on Incremental Development and Technology Fusion*

New technology to an FCT competitor often means the incremental development of an existing technology or joining two seemingly disparate technologies to create a third. The United States has historically been strong at major breakthroughs or "home run" technology development. Increasingly, the glamour of such success is being frayed by the lack of reward. Research demonstrates there is a negative correlation between economic growth rate and the number of Nobel prizes won.[6]

FCT firms devote a larger percentage of their research dollars to incremental research. This leverages existing knowledge within the firm regarding the markets and processes used to develop products, as well as the products themselves. Incremental research and products provide quicker market feedback, which enables one to target future products more accurately to meet customer needs.

Because incremental research is built around the existing product, the research effort is more cross-functional than the technologist-dominated home-run effort. Those who build the product know it best and help define technology improvement requirements. Sales, manufacturing, customer service, and repair provide insight that can yield successful new products requiring minimal investment.

This does not suggest that home-run products and base research should be abandoned. The issue is balance. Just as one would not manage a baseball team by asking everyone to swing for the fences, neither should one base a development strategy heavily on revolutionary developments. One client described the PERT chart from a home-run project by saying that it was so large, it could block the sun's rays from reaching the city he worked in. Once again, our point is to focus, learn, refocus, and learn again. Development speed comes from taking many rapid small steps.

### *Use Others' Technology in Combination with One's Own*

FCT competitors do not try to invent everything themselves. They recognize that it is impossible for any competitor to keep up with all the technology requirements in a given industry. FCT firms use a variety of frameworks, from university partnerships to joint ventures, to access product and process technology. Cross-licensing agreements are increasingly becoming the substitute for patent infringement cases. These firms are noted for looking around the world for partners; for example, Quantum Corporation's success in the disk-drive industry is tightly linked to the success of its partnership with Japanese manufacturing giant Matsushita's MKE.

## Product Concept

The product concept phase includes product planning, platform definition, and product and process architecture. FCT executives spend their time defining and addressing the issues within the product concept phase, because this is where much of the "up and to the left" leverage is. There are five themes that characterize the FCT approach during this phase.

### *Increase the Visibility of the "Fuzzy Front End"*

FCT competitors make the "fuzzy front end" of product development much more visible than traditional firms.[7] The visibility of a product and management's attention to it in traditional firm occurs once the product is deep into development. In the early stages, staffing is at its lowest point, and there are no tooling or lab expenses to attract management's attention. Financially driven firms are particularly subject to this, because there are few expenditures to signal attention at this stage.

Paradoxically, up and to the left is where the leverage for future spending resides (Exhibitt 8.3). When management commits to a major project, it implicitly commits to spend the required money. Only the signing of the check is deferred until the money is actually spent.

FCT firms create visibility by regularly auditing their product and technology road maps relative to market windows. For example, one firm uses

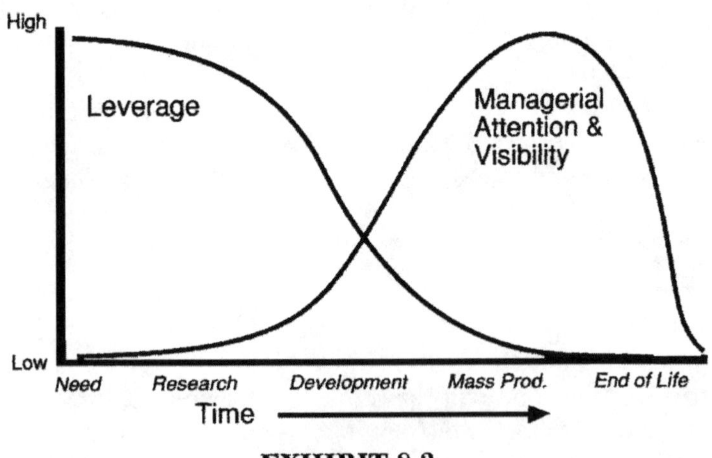


**EXHIBIT 8.3**

its FCT steering committee to monitor every project that has not completed specification setting. Another uses their executive staff to do the same thing. They both watch to make sure products do not get stalled during the concept phase for any reason. *FCT firms quickly learn that rapid development is a function of crisp, clean starts.* Hewlett-Packard uses a planning metric called break-even time (BET), which measures time-to-market trade-offs as part of the planning basis. We will discuss the BET metric in the following chapter.

### *Inject the "Voice of the Customer" in Concept Creation*

FCT firms try to get their customers *directly* involved in the product concept phase. This occurs through site visits, sponsorship, and Quality Function Deployment (QFD).

#### *Site Visits*

Site visits are conducted by the multifunctional design team. For example, when Silicon Graphics Computer Systems designed its first low-cost, 3-D computer, it sent a multifunctional team to meet directly with customers in each of its key markets to learn the most important requirements for a low-cost machine. The face-to-face contact between the team and the customer underscored the needs in a way that an individual marketing specialist simply cannot. Additionally, the time spent in hotel rooms and airplanes during the two weeks of travel allowed the team to test the ideas and created a natural forum for the members to get to know each other.

#### *Sponsorship*

Sponsorship is a concept that is particularly powerful for suppliers to original equipment manufacturers, such as those in computers, automobiles, and aerospace. It recently gained visibility through the success of Conner Peripherals. Conner designs and manufactures disk drives using a philosophy of "sell, design, build." It strives to always have a customer for its development efforts before they begin. Conner targets leading-edge companies so it can leverage their success with other customers later. Besides the obvious advantages for revenue, the sponsorship approach can also lock out competitors.

The most powerful impact we have seen from companies that use sponsorship is the clarity it brings to resolving product development problems. Development never goes exactly to plan, so there are several times during every effort when one must go back to the customer(s) to get direction regarding key choices. When you have a sponsor, you go to one customer and do what they want; only if their choice is wildly out of line with your expectations and the market would you even try to negotiate with them. When one does not have a sponsor, marketing has to contact several customers and create an answer that is often rightfully challenged by other members of the team as a compromise. The advantage of sponsorship is it pulls you through this "knothole" that is part of every development.

To make sponsorship work requires current technology or similar value-adding capability, multilevel selling, and a willingness to create a viable partnership. Without having something to offer in terms of technology or other value, sponsorship is not attractive to a buyer. You have got to have something to offer that makes it worthwhile to partner with you rather than stay with the open market. In this era of shrinking supplier lists and increasing partnership, this is increasingly possible.

Sponsorship cannot succeed without an executive to sell it, because the risk for both firms is significant. If the supplier is late, the buyer's chances of securing an alternate component are slim and extremely costly. If the buyer slips, the supplier has to scramble to broaden its product to meet others' needs. The risk is mutually significant, such that sponsorship only works when the working levels on both sides participate with a spirit of cooperation and support. A sponsorship arrangement is more involved than a traditional supplier and often includes joint responsibility for product definition, testing, and integration. Co-location at the buyer's facility is also common.

Sponsorship requires both sides to be significantly more open about their respective success and failures during development. As we discussed, being open about problems is not natural within a company and even less so between two companies. When using sponsorship, mistakes and fixes that would normally be invisible to the customer are now visible. One develops confidence in one's partner not by finding fewer problems, but by seeing the ones you find attacked and resolved quickly.

### *Quality Function Deployment (QFD)*

There is a significant difference between product specifications and customer requirements. Product specifications are an outgrowth of understanding customer requirements but are expressed in technical language. Customer requirements are rarely expressed as explicitly as the design team would like. Therefore, tools and techniques that facilitate the clear expression of customer requirements and translate them into design parameters can greatly speed up the development process.

Quality Function Deployment is a product of Mitsubishi's Kobe shipyards that more recently was popularized by Toyota.[8] QFD is a disciplined analysis and planning tool for translating customer requirements into robust product designs, from product definition through quality control processes. The process is built on a foundation of four matrices:

1. Use customer requirements to define product characteristics
2. Use the product characteristics to define the part characteristics
3. Use the part characteristics to define the required process characteristics
4. Use the process characteristics to define the quality control process

The power of QFD is that it provides a comprehensive framework that channels customer requirements into the design process, making choices explicit. In the first matrix, forcing the distinction between customer requirements and product characteristics ensures that technology is applied appropriately. Exhibit 8.4 illustrates the first QFD matrix for a bilge pump for recreational boaters.

The rows in Exhibit 8.4 define what the customer's requirements are and their relative priority. The columns define how those requirements will be achieved. The intersection of the main rows and columns illuminates where a "how" might positively or negatively affect more than one

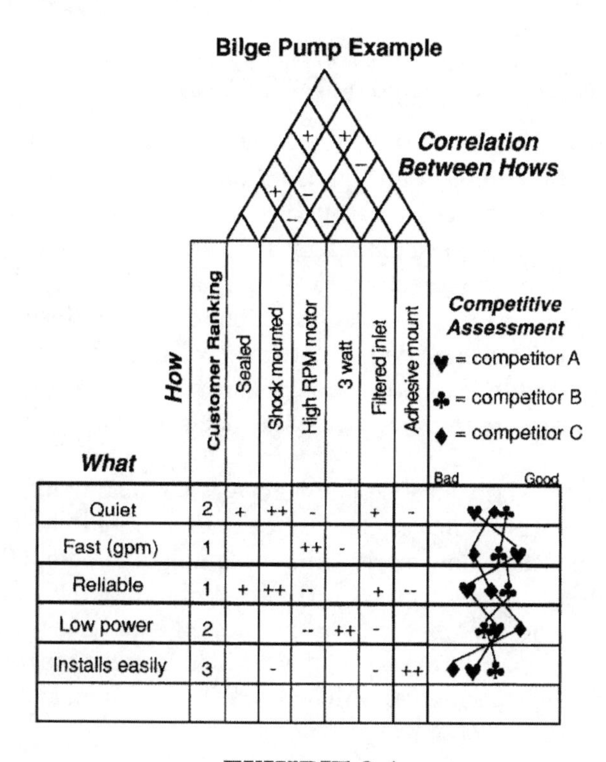


| What | Customer Ranking | Sealed | Shock mounted | High RPM motor | 3 watt | Filtered inlet | Adhesive mount |
|---|---|---|---|---|---|---|---|
| Quiet | 2 | + | ++ | - | | + | - |
| Fast (gpm) | 1 | | | ++ | - | | |
| Reliable | 1 | + | ++ | -- | | + | -- |
| Low power | 2 | | | -- | ++ | - | |
| Installs easily | 3 | | - | | | - | ++ |

**EXHIBIT 8.4**

"what": high RPM motors move water quickly, but at the cost of reliability and power. The "roof" of the matrix shows the correlation between the design choices. A positive correlation occurs when design choices support each other, such as when shock mounting increases the life of the adhesive bonding. The competitive assessment compares others' ability to deliver the defined customer requirements.

QFD's comprehensive power is also its greatest problem. Regrettably, one hears of more QFD efforts started than completed. The weight of the QFD process itself can be enormous as one moves into complex products; we have seen matrices with over fifty rows and columns for a single component! We have encountered only a couple of companies that have even tried to get beyond the first matrix. The methodology is also less applicable to brand-new technologies, because customers have difficulty defining requirements for products they have not used before.

We believe we will see more of QFD, rather than less of it. The basic premises make significant sense for translating customer needs into concepts and ultimately products. The matrix approach offers the potential of providing a structure to surface potential problems early in the development process. The key will be targeting its use and simplifying the methodology.

### *Make Decisions Quickly and with Real-Time Data*

The underlying dynamic during the early stages of development is managing the risk inherent in making decisions without complete information. The truism that causes so much of the procrastination at this stage is that one will always have more knowledge tomorrow; therefore, delaying a decision is a rational action. FCT companies understand that no decision does not mean no cost. As one client described during a product concept debate, "Once we decide, the team will make either choice work. And until we decide, they won't work on anything." Decisions made early affect the entire development, whereas decisions made later have less leverage.

Research by Kathleen Eisenhardt reveals fascinating differences between rapid decision makers and others.[9] First, rapid decision makers maintain a constant flow of real-time operating and competitive information. Research suggests that the tap root of intuition is experience. A study of the microcomputer industry showed that the executives who were described as intuitive were most attuned to real-time data. By constantly refreshing themselves with real-time information, FCT executives develop their intuitive skills.

They also rely on fast comparative analysis of multiple alternatives as a way of speeding decision making. Decisions are made by consensus with qualification. In those few circumstances where a decision is required before consensus is reached, the leader makes the call. Otherwise, a consensus process is used. In contrast, slow-moving firms become bogged down in an endless search for more information, which is used to generate excessively detailed alternatives. Whereas fast decision makers rely on real-time information, slow decision makers rely on planning and futuristic information.

We have paraphrased Eisenhardt's suggestions, because they match our experience of FCT leaders.

1. Be ready before the decision is needed by tracking real-time information
2. Once in the decision process, rapidly generate alternatives
3. Ask everyone for advice, but have one or two familiar anchors who know you over time and whom you can trust
4. At decision time, involve others and try for consensus, but make the decision in any event
5. Think systemically and integrate your choice with prior decisions.

### *Define and Migrate to Product Architecture(s) That Leverage and Allocate Resource Capabilities*

FCT companies leverage product and process developments through the use of product families that maximize common product and process architectures. Doing so enables these firms to save as much as 50% of development time. Using product families leverages existing technology across multiple products, minimizes multiple development of low-value technology (such as power supplies), and helps separate invention from the development process. Predefined families and common architectures accelerate the specification-setting process, because one does not start with a clean sheet of paper for each individual product. To implement product families, FCT companies move up and to the left in order to define each family's primary platform, the derivatives, components that should be common within and between families, and a transition plan.

The product, technology, and supplier road maps developed during the strategic alignment planning process are absolutely essential to define product families and to create a common product/process architecture. If these do not exist, one has to create them before proceeding. This illustrates the dependence and synergy between the strategic alignment process and fast cycle time. With these in hand, FCT companies then address the following:

1. Confirm market timing of future product requirements
2. Group products in families based on common product and process technologies
3. Aggressively identify common product and process opportunities within each family
4. Create options that increase the amount of common parts and processes through integration, elimination, and so forth
5. Define common architecture development needs, especially components and processes
6. Develop migration plan to product family
7. Define development responsibility

Using common parts and architecture requires increased attention to the design of modules and their interfaces.[10] Once developed, standard interfaces reduce design and test time. To be long-lasting, the interfaces have to have sufficient margin to enable (rather than confuse) problem isolation during testing. When designing the modules themselves, one should be careful not to put all the risk in one module, as well as to isolate stable versus changing technologies in different modules. Last, too many modules will slow down performance. One has to achieve a balance of cost, performance, and flexibility; this should be measured over time and must include revenue gains due to the time-to-market advantage.

The goal is to design a platform that is sustainable in the marketplace, maximizes the number of common parts and processes, and can support several derivative products. Some opportunities for common components identified can be implemented by individual development teams in service of the company, but one should carefully avoid adding invention to the development process.

Exhibit 8.5 introduces the wall of invention. *FCT companies try to keep all invention to the left of the wall.* When invention occurs to the right, development slows down due to technical challenge and its lack of predictability. This means being careful of seemingly small changes, such as increasing the number of features from five to six. The number of new interactions approximately doubles with the addition of each new feature. Development teams are biased to recognize only the positive outcomes rather than the unintended consequences of adding a feature.

The wall of invention applies to more than product technology development. FCT companies find that every function requires an advance de-

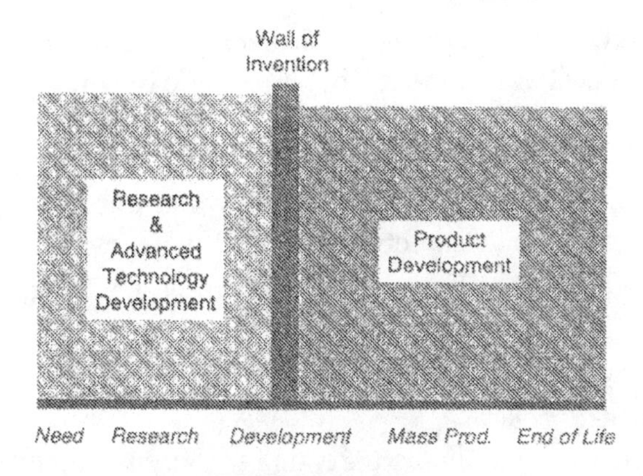


**EXHIBIT 8.5**

velopment component in order to move "up and to the left" and to support common architecture. For example, advanced manufacturing development is required to develop manufacturing processes that have greater flexibility; advanced marketing is required to create product families that meet market segment needs; advanced quality and reliability processes are needed to design robustness into products; and advanced human resources planning is required to forecast capabilities required for FCT.

Developing a migration plan to a common architecture is also critical. Common architecture does not eliminate custom parts; defining which parts must be customized to meet different customer requirements in complex products is not easy. Designers want as much safety margin as they can, so the pressure is to select the highest performance part for the specific need. *The fundamental issue faced when defining a common architecture is deciding where to put the development risk.*

There is a human issue that surfaces with a company's transition to product families and common architecture. As one develops increasingly robust platforms and architectures, the nature of development work becomes increasingly narrow (although potentially deeper). Development engineers sometimes interpret this as narrowing their job scope and limiting creativity opportunities. These worries are best addressed by involving key engineering leaders in the design and development of the product and technology road maps as well as the architecture. Left unattended, one may find the biggest obstacle to product platforms and common architecture is not technical but human concerns.

Another issue is identifying those elements that will be developed internally and those that will be developed outside or jointly with key suppliers. Internally developed elements should fit clearly within the organization's core competency requirements to compete with their particular business. Those elements that lie outside the firm's required competencies should be resourced either by outsiders or in conjunction with them.

Tactics that FCT competitors employ when implementing product families and common architecture include the following:

1. Avoid having more than one new platform under development at any one time
2. Start platform development with the easiest technically and learn from customer feedback
3. Use commercially available parts unless there is a compelling advantage for doing otherwise
4. Don't develop every new technology yourself
5. Bet on future trends happening so your platform can sustain itself
6. Be willing to make your products obsolete before your competitors do
7. Keep a watchful eye on process technology; increasingly, it is the limiting factor for volume production
8. Don't underestimate the total resource requirements for each variant in the product family

***Resource Allocation***

FCT competitors do not start more programs than they can staff effectively. They would rather staff one program fully to ensure a fast development cycle than split the resources between two with the hope that they will be able to squeeze two products out with only a slight time penalty. FCT companies are brutally honest with themselves about what it takes to complete a program, and they staff their development teams accordingly. This is illustrated by the model in Exhibit 8.6.

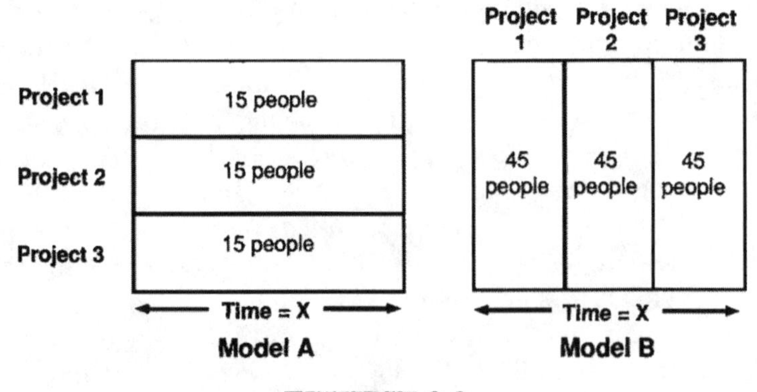


**EXHIBIT 8.6**

Models A and B in the exhibit represent opposite product development resource allocation models. Both models assume that you have forty-five engineers and three projects to complete within the same time period. Model A allocates fifteen engineers to each project and executes them in parallel, whereas model B completes projects serially by allocating all forty-five people to the first project, completing it, and rolling the engineers on to the second and then the third. In practice, adding more people rarely yields a one-for-one productivity improvement; for explanatory reasons, however, assume for the moment that all forty-five people can be fully utilized in model B.

When we ask new product development executives which model they think is most effective within the given assumptions, one-half to two-thirds select Model A. Reasons for selecting model A include the following:

1. Smaller team size is more effective
2. One can move people between projects if one runs into trouble
3. People have broader jobs
4. Manages risk should one or two projects fail

The ability and effectiveness of a smaller group to work together is difficult to debate. The other issues supporting model A can be challenged. The resource flexibility in model A is not usually considered positive by the person being moved from one project to another, nor is it cost free. At best, each must hand off his or her work on project 1 to another individual, as well as learn from someone on project 2. Project 1 is now understaffed, and it takes time for workers to come up to speed on project 2. The bottom line is that one pays a price for flexibility.

The assertion that there is broader job opportunity in model A assumes only a single project, whereas it is possible for someone in model B to hold three completely different positions within three different projects. The ability to manage risk is not limited to model A. Model B will find out about problems earlier than model A; in model B, one could stop project 1, start project 2, and still have a product on the market before model A. Our argument is that model A's advantages are rarely clear-cut or cost free.

Model B operates in fast cycle time. The first two products are generating revenue and, more importantly, customer feedback before any product in model A. The customer feedback from project 1 can influence projects 2 and 3. Although the team is larger in model B, once developed it stays intact over three projects, whereas in model A, three teams must be developed into effective working units. Perhaps the most important reason behind model B is that each participant has three *complete* learning cycles, whereas model A participants have only one.

Noting that both models represent extremes, we ask executives which model reflects the way their company usually operates. Nearly all cite model A. When asked why, the answers boil down to risk management. When we probe how the risk management works, we find risk is not actually managed but evolves through a Darwinian survival-of-the-fittest process. Projects weed themselves out for a variety of reasons. Political factors govern survival as much as deliberate decisions regarding economic return or strategic importance. Just as transferring a person in model A from one project to another has an invisible cost, so does the Darwinian selection process. Resources are spent on efforts that we know will not make it to market.

FCT companies regard product development as a very expensive undertaking. They know there are always more ideas available than can be successfully developed. They use product planning as a process to define and select the short list of critical projects rather than entering into more efforts than they know they can fully support. The golden rule is never to commit fewer resources than are required to do the job quickly and completely; resources allocated to projects that are not completed do not pay for themselves. FCT companies will use model A when the technical and market risks require but do so knowing the "tax" they are paying in the process. Their preference is to use model B as much as possible.

## Product Specification

If there is a critical phase to a fast cycle development, it is specification setting. The product specification phase sets the development in motion. During this phase, the team develops critical mass and becomes the locus of program-related decisions. The project typically receives its code name and becomes a visible entity within the corporation. The primary activities are as detailed below.

### *Setting Specifications*

Every year a new graduate student conducts a study to identify the major barriers to fast product development, and every year the top rated item remains the same—poorly defined and/or unstable definition of product specifications. Poorly defined and unstable specifications are primarily the result of each party trying to minimize its risk in new product development. Manufacturing will always know more about its ability to build the product at the target cost a month from now. Design engineering will know more about the technology required to produce the product, and marketing can guarantee it will have better insight into customer needs. The specification-setting process discusses technical alternatives, but the underlying issue is the requirement to make an expensive decision without complete information.

Ironically, the longer the development cycle time, the more motivation there is to delay specification setting. For example, if the product development cycle is thirty-six months, it is extremely difficult to assess accurately what customers will want in three years. Delaying specification setting feels productive, since customers can define their needs better a little later. In fact, customer requirements are constantly moving and continue to do so during the development effort. Six months spent defining specifications is six months that cannot be used to overcome a major technology problem.

FCT companies differentiate themselves by "latching" key decisions, such as specifications, during the development process. Latching describes the premium FCT leaders attach to reaching commitment rather than simply agreement. A latched decision is one that *people work to make work* and is not reopened except under extraordinary circumstances. The energy saved by latching decisions is significant and extends through all those involved in or influenced by the development effort.

Achieving the commitment required to latch a decision such as specifications is a function of how open the decision process is. Openness includes content and involvement. *A latched specification is the result of multifunctional participation sufficiently early in the process to raise substantive issues and influence their outcome.* The smaller the group setting the specification, the easier it is to do; conversely, the smaller the group, the harder it is to latch.

The specification-setting decision should involve anyone whose commitment is essential to make the project successful. In addition to the project team, this includes those whose opinions would influence the commitment of others. For example, if a senior technologist's opinion carries a great deal of weight in hallway conversations, one should be sure he or she is involved so that he or she understands and supports the specification. The same is true for senior executives.

In traditional firms, decisions such as specification setting are often pursued using a hub-and-spoke process (Exhibit 8.7). The development team serves as the hub, and it meets with individual stakeholders in the home organization, customers, and suppliers to reach agreement on the specification. Just as the functional organization minimizes contact between functional groups, hub-and-spoke development minimizes contact

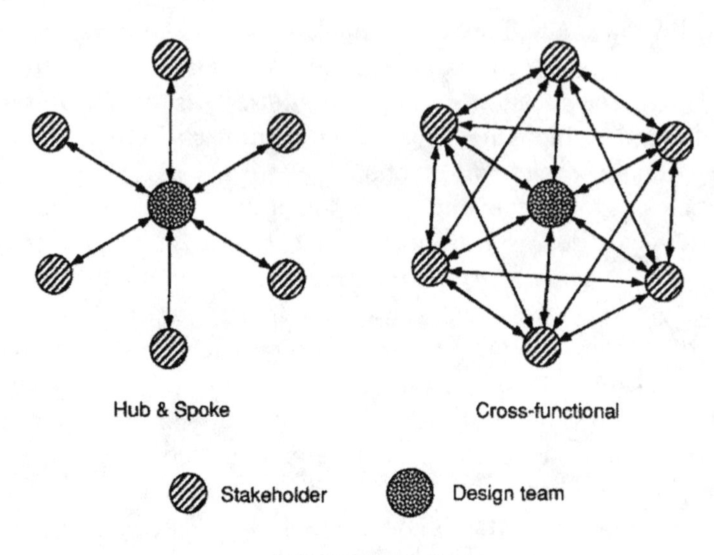


**EXHIBIT 8.7**

between the various stakeholders. The ugly head of conventional thinking is raised again, because the agreements reached with each stakeholder focus primarily on those elements that affect them directly. The team aggregates these agreements into a specification that is presented to management for approval. The stated goal of this process is to set the best specification possible; that goal is often subverted by an implicit goal to get a specification *approved*. The hub and spoke process is attractive to many because it keeps specification setting under control, but the result is actually a collection of semi-independent functional agreements.

The strength of the hub-and-spoke method is its liability. The hub generates agreement by serving as arbitrator of stakeholder concerns. As a consequence, it does not provide an open forum where stakeholders can directly engage and challenge each other early enough in the process. Because the hub resolves the conflict, the stakeholders have little ownership in the solution. Thus, we achieve agreement at the expense of commitment.

Commitment to a specification requires a forum early in the decision process to encourage cross-functional discussion that engages differences as much as agreements. When one does so, the decision process becomes messy because broader involvement occurs earlier in the process, when there are more degrees of freedom. Additionally, conflicting stakeholder needs are publicly exposed in a large group. Rather than detracting from the process, the messiness adds value by creating an active and open discussion forum for choices instead of passive listening to a development team's polished presentation of conclusions. It enables commitment to grow between each stakeholder as well as to the program itself. It is real and honest.

Once again, we need a structure that facilitates rapid, cross-functional learning and decision making. To this end, we have created a specification-setting process called "messy meetings." This is a structured approach for developing specifications that can be used for resolving major cross-functional issues. We will detail it here and include an outline agenda we use with our clients.

### *Messy Meeting Overview*

Messy meetings are one or two large, multifunctional specification-setting meetings where issues are identified and decisions made in real time. The final deliverable is a durable commitment to a specification that is typically accompanied by a high-level definition of the project requirements, including market timing. The detail level varies from industry to industry, but it typically includes the essential product and process parameters. *The second messy meeting does not end until there is agreement among the stakeholders.* When agreement is reached, everyone signs the agreed-to specification before leaving.

### *Messy Meeting Preparation and Ownership*

The meeting is owned by the development team. It is responsible for preparing and conducting the messy meeting. The team should come to the meeting with a business rationale and straw-man product specification. The business rationale defines the market need and timing; for several reasons, it should not be a full-blown business plan. First, preparing a business plan is a time-consuming activity. If one waits until the business plan is developed, many of the program/product elements will become set prematurely. Second, issues raised during the messy meeting can guide the plan's developmental focus.

The business rationale should define the market opportunity, the time-to-market window, key potential customers, and cost/performance requirements. Based on this, the specification should identify the critical performance features that address these requirements: performance, power requirements, technology, and so forth. This is similar to the high-level specification most customers see during the early development phase. A first-pass schedule is extremely useful, since some specification choices will influence development cycle time.

It is important to think of cost or performance targets as points in time.

For example, higher costs may be acceptable if the product is available six months earlier. Similarly, lower performance may be acceptable if it significantly precedes other competitors to market. Schedule trade-offs should reflect this.

The team should highlight critical choices made or pending within the business rationale and straw-man specification. Note again that development team agreement is not required or even desired on every element. The purpose of the presentation is to provide information and context for the attendees.

### *How Many Messy Meetings Are Required?*

Our experience is that two messy meetings are frequently required. The first introduces the program to a broad cross section of people for the first time. At this meeting, the development team should establish the broad parameters of the program and identify the major decisions made to date, plus those pending but yet to be made. The second meeting covers the same material and is held no later than seven to ten days after the first. For any question that cannot be answered in that time, one should ask, is waiting for the information more important than making a decision and getting started?

The second meeting, while covering the same general ground as the first, has a greater focus on key issues. Issues that were resolved in the first meeting are noted during the program review but not reopened unless required. There is increased focus on the remaining open issues; additionally, the second meeting will present resolution to many issues identified during the first meeting.

### *How Should the Meetings Be Structured?*

A suggested agenda is detailed below.

**I. Welcome and Introduction of Development Team**

- Introduce team
- Review messy meeting intent/purpose
- Present meeting ground rules
  - Don't be bashful; ask if you don't understand
  - Participate positively; look to improve as well as criticize
  - Use of flip charts to capture items
  - Decisions remain within development team
- Review agenda

**II. Market Review**

- Market opportunity

Key customers/partner potential
Market requirements
Time to market
Cost
Performance
Competitive overview
Open issues
Q & A

**III. Product Specification and Program Definition**

Review specification
Highlight key choices made and pending
Review key program elements
Schedule
Staffing requirements
Other
Q & A

**IV. Discussion and Agreement**

Reach agreement on product requirements
Reach agreement on product specifications to meet requirements
Identify unresolved issues and establish process and near-term time frame for resolution.

**V. Closure**

Thank participants
Big hand for development team!!

### *Who Should Be Invited to the Meeting?*

Ideally, the meeting should be attended by anyone whose efforts or resistance could influence the program's success. Obviously, judgment has to be exercised in order to keep the group to a reasonable number; thirty-five to fifty people is a good rule of thumb. A larger group can be managed, but it requires using subgroups for discussions. It is better to be discriminating about who could help or hinder the program's success. For example, issuing knee-jerk invitations to all senior managers does not make sense.

### *Closing Advice for Successful Messy Meetings*

A messy meeting exposes many people to the program in its earliest form. At that time, there are typically as many legitimate answers as there are legitimate questions. It is important to set the expectations of participants to this fact. If this is not done, participants, program members, or presenters may walk away feeling disappointed that they did not hear or present the "right" answer. The fact of the matter is that it is within the *process* of messy meetings that we expect the right answer to emerge.

The messiness of the meetings themselves is not easy for people to tolerate. In development organizations, most people seem to be more comfortable after a decision is made than they are before. Therefore there is a great desire to get to the answer—in fact, any answer—as quickly as possible. We recommend that an individual who is trained in designing and conducting large meetings serve as facilitator to ensure that decisions are made.

The messy meeting concept can be thought of as a platform for exposing trade-offs and alternatives regarding product specifications and program timing. The focus is to create a forum and a pressure to make the risk assessment and decision crisply and early. While it is impossible to ever know all the answers one would like, experience demonstrates that by the time a messy meeting process is completed, all the basic knowledge available to make the decision is visible. The issue is not finding better information; the issue is making the decision.

### *DFx: Design for Manufacturability, Assembly, Serviceability, Localizability, Etc.*

Moving up and to the left also has to happen during the specification phase. Increasingly, FCT companies are incorporating more than product performance attributes in the specification phase, if not the specification itself. Criteria such as part count, use of fasteners, and speed of assembly are determined during this period. Traditional competitors leave these items to be addressed downstream, where there is little leverage to make substantial improvement.

We use the term *DFx* because the list is endless. For example, as local regulations continue to fragment and change, the cost in time and money of localizing a product for sale in the United States, Europe, and Asia can become a significant impediment to market success. Designing flexibility into the product such that the final configuration can be postponed until the product reaches its final destination without creating cost or difficulty offers tremendous advantages.

An area that has received significant attention because of its impact on product cost and repair/warranty costs is design for manufacturability (DFM). The overall goal is to design the product with the manufacturing process in mind. There are four primary rules to DFM:

1. *Eliminate.* Parts that are left out of the product never break
2. *Simplify.* The less complex, the lower the cost and higher the yield
3. *Group.* Reduce tooling and assembly
4. *Decouple.* Separate manual from machine processes

DFM is common sense, but it is rarely uppermost in the product designer or marketing manager's mind. One can read the list below (which details many of the most popular DFM techniques) and attend workshops, but the real secret to DFM is co-location. When manufacturing representatives are "in the face" of the designer, they can see, react to, and collaborate on the design in real time. That is much more potent than attending a design review meeting. DFM techniques include the following:

1. Minimize the number of parts
2. Robust design; avoid close tolerances wherever possible
3. Eliminate/reduce fasteners
4. Use rigid parts
5. Strive for "auto-alignment"
6. Eliminate processing surfaces
7. Process in full view
8. Provide handling surfaces
9. Single-sided assembly
10. No use of adhesives or cure time
11. No tape
12. No blind holes
13. Design out part nesting
14. Provide assemble nesting
15. Maximize part symmetry and compliance
16. Provide clear access and view for assembly
17. Design for vertical assembly

### *Staffing the Development Team*

If there is a problem that plagues many companies, including FCT competitors, it is getting a crisp start to staffing development programs. When a development effort ramps human resources slowly, certain technical issues are deferred or ignored until a person with the required expertise joins the team. The later the resource joins the team, the more rework and disruption accompanies the eventual discovery and resolution of a problem.

As we have dug into what causes slow staffing, we frequently find that the staffing problem is due not to the lack of resource planning but to the quality of it. FCT firms use their product and technology road maps as a basis for human resource planning, combined with assumptions about staffing and cycle time. In their planning, FCT firms use the actual cycle time as a basis for planning, whereas traditional firms often use an overly optimistic cycle time assumption.

Common sense suggests that using shorter than actual cycle time assumptions creates a roll-off problem. One plans to start a program before resources from the last program are available. FCT firms maintain a clear distinction between cycle time goals and planning assumptions. Simply turning a goal into a planning assumption not only does not make it come true; worse than that, it actually increases cycle time.

An additional problem is caused by one's initial success with FCT. For example, a health care company dramatically improved its product development cycle time. Its products attracted many new customers, each of whom demanded support services. This far exceeded the company's existing support resources, causing it to call on anyone and everyone to meet the support demands; those who would normally have rolled off to the next program had to stay to provide support. This caused the start of the next program to slip. One could accurately say that the company's initial FCT success created a cycle time problem on its next effort. As we have studied this phenomena, it becomes increasingly clear that in product development, *crisp beginnings are a function of crisp endings*.

We have learned several lessons about the roll-off dilemma. First, nothing replaces doing the product right the first time. And doing the product right is a function of how quickly one gains knowledge about the new product and process limits. Second, once knowledge is gained, it must be distributed beyond the initial development team to those who will sustain the product. As long as the information is confined to the development team members, they cannot be released. Third, in order to transfer the knowledge, there must be resources capable of receiving the knowledge. All too often we find that design engineering is robustly staffed while sustaining, continuation, commodity, quality, product, and manufacturing engineering departments are understaffed. This sets up a dependence that quickly grows into an addiction to the original development resources. The solution to the addiction is to buttress the capacity and capabilities of these other resources.

This requires breaking some long-standing taboos. Classically the pay, status, and hiring requirements for a design engineer are greater than for a manufacturing engineer. This makes getting into design engineering the goal for many, regardless of where they begin. Design engineering looks around at other engineering resources and plucks the best, which further deteriorates the support resources and increases the dependence on design.

FCT firms work to bring pay and status into a more appropriate balance. Until that is done, the addiction will continue, because the firm will be unable to attract the quality or quantity of talent to offload development engineers. During the transition, FCT firms involve the downstream groups as early as possible in the development effort. By using other tactics, such as generic job titles like "member of technical staff" and co-location, they also reduce the status issue.

### Co-Locating the Development Team

The golden rule of co-location is to align the relationships and equipment within the physical environment to the support multifunctional work teams. Bluntly stated, does the physical environment put those who need to work together physically in the same place? The advantages from co-location are many, including the following:

1. Real-time discussions that go to decision are now possible
2. Less time is wasted in transit; this is particularly true with large projects and large companies
3. Enables parallel problem solving and simultaneous engineering
4. Better understanding of colleagues' mutual needs and dependencies; you *see* what happens when commitments are not met
5. "Hallway" conversations reduce the requirement for non-value-added administrative and project procedures
6. Reduces hierarchy and status barriers; senior management sees everyone's work
7. More face-to-face contact creates better personal bonds and relationships

Implementing co-location begins with senior management. Although most people prefer co-location after they have done it, few support it immediately. Because space is usually limited, the transition to co-location requires that management match the need to near-term facility requirements and availability. The transition process is like a puzzle in that one moves one group and then consolidates the freed space for the next group. The logistical issues are not insignificant; the extent of co-location is usually limited by current facilities and locations. Our experience suggests that co-location is not just for development teams but a mind-set one should use throughout the organization.

There are several elements to consider during advance planning:

1. *Involve the team in the facility design.* One can take much of the edge off the move by involving group leaders and team members in lab design and office mapping. This can alleviate the intense personal concerns people have over their only private space inside the company walls.
2. *Size the facility accurately.* Co-location requires more conference rooms than traditional environments.
3. *Include vendors as appropriate.* Co-locating vendors very quickly increases their integration and commitment to the project. It also encourages greater value added as they better understand the role their component plays. Their performance is also more visible.
4. *Size and fund the total facility requirements.* This includes support equipment such as computers, laboratories, networks, coffee makers, phones, and copiers. Co-locating people without their tools is not co-location!
5. *Make sure the facility is ready.* If the space does not support the group's needs, co-location becomes a liability and creates a first impression that is tough to overcome. The cycle time performance measure for a co-location move is time from first move date to full team productivity.
6. *Make the move painless.* If this means using a professional mover, then do it. FCT firms usually pack on Friday, move over the weekend, and have every phone and computer up and running in the new location on Monday morning.
7. *Orient people to the building and new operating philosophy.* Place maps with office, rest room, exit, and food locations throughout the facility. Before the move, define behavioral expectations for the new environment around issues such as community responsibilities, privacy, and conference room usage. Co-location creates a community that must be cooperatively managed to work.

Of all the different approaches we have seen to co-location, some themes and tactics of success repeat themselves:

1. *Distinguish the environment.* Through color or decor, teams like to create their own identity. This is particularly useful during the early stages when they are first coming together.
2. *Keep space flexible.* Use movable walls and avoid permanent furniture and fixtures. Change the space and configurations during the development to bring the people who need to work together at that point in time closer. Prepare people to move as required.

3. *Create a "bump" environment.* Co-located offices can become institutionalized, with people only talking to those directly next to them. Be creative about placing subgroups and common facilities such as coffee and copiers to force movement throughout the facility.
4. *Use information kiosks and "war rooms" to share information.* Visual displays are much more accessible and leverage the multifunctional grouping.
5. *Seat interdependent groups together.* For example, placing firmware engineers right next to the servo engineers facilitates both being successful.

Co-location also has downsides. The most important one is that the stronger the co-located group becomes, the more it distances itself from those outside the team, perhaps including experts or resources from functional organizations that support the team. At the same time, people on the team may feel cut off from their home location. Typical coping tactics include holding meetings at the functional organization, rotating participation on co-located teams, and increasing the number of people co-located such that moving one's office to meet a specific need becomes a way of life.

Co-location makes organizational inconsistencies such as title differences and varying overtime policies plainly visible. In this respect, co-location is like multifunctional teams: it does not create more problems, but it exposes the ones you have. The only tactic is to address each issue directly as it appears.

Sometimes co-location requirements can reduce the size of the home organization below the critical mass required for support. In part, this is a planing and transition issue. Since the value-added work is done in multifunctional teams, one could argue that the issue is a resource problem made visible by location, rather than a co-location problem.

Co-location is not required for everyone. Firms can get overzealous in co-location as the solution to everything. One should always use the requirement to work together on an ongoing basis as the primary rationale for co-location.

### Controlling and Scheduling the Effort

A primary benefit of reducing development cycle time is that it reduces the need for scheduling and control mechanisms. The shorter a project takes, the less need there is for a project control system. Conversely, when a project takes a long time, a control system helps keep track of everything. Control systems do not add value to the end customer; their input and maintenance sap energy and take time from development tasks. Therefore, FCT companies keep control overhead to a minimum.

In traditional serial development, phase-gate review systems ensure that the development meets certain performance and maturity criteria before the handoff from one functional entity to another takes place. Although the primary focus is to guarantee product maturity, when gate reviews are used in serial development structures, they are often manipulated by each function as a way to limit its liability for the other functions' mistakes. The focus can shift totally from assessing product maturity and become a game that manages accountability between the upstream and downstream entities. A powerful advantage FCT multifunctional development teams have over serial development is that they eliminate this misuse of phase reviews.

FCT projects *appear* more difficult to control. This is especially true for those outside the team. A co-located, multifunctional team uses informal communication and control mechanisms that are invisible to the outsider. For example, it is common to have morning operations meetings during critical times that take half an hour and only touch integration or problem areas. The purpose of such meetings is to make sure that problems are surfaced and ownership identified, but little is discussed about problem resolution specifics. That happens afterward in hallway conversations and ad hoc meetings. Because everyone required to resolve a problem is often within sight, impromptu conversations raise and resolve many issues that are not reported, because those that need to know are present at the impromptu meeting. This process is both impossible and wasteful to try and report.

Imposing external controls and approvals on a multifunctional team requires the team to bring the outsiders up to speed on both the content and context of their issues and decisions. Because of the intensity that colocation and multifunctional teams bring to development, one cannot do this in a way that satisfies those who are used to traditional reviews. Our experience is that neither party is satisfied by the process. On the one hand, the team finds the time preparing for the review is non-value added and questions the value it receives from the reviewers. On the other hand, the reviewers feel as though the information and issues blow pass them as though they are standing in a NASA wind tunnel. Things are moving so fast that it is hard to know whether one should intervene or not. The issue is not whether there should be controls on the project, but where they should be administered and what they should focus on.

FCT companies keep as much as possible of the responsibility for administering controls within the multifunctional team. This greatly increases the ownership for achieving the results the controls are intended to ensure. Whenever control of a person or a system is external to the individual or the system, there is a lower degree of ownership and an increase in delay responding to the controller. For example, asking people to introduce themselves to a group in less than thirty seconds requires a timekeeper who typically will have to interrupt one or two people to tell them their time is up. A different approach is to ask each person to strike and hold a lit match before he or she begins speaking. When the match burns out, the time is up. In the case of the match, the control is within the system; you can literally see people speed up as the flame reaches their fingertips, as opposed to the timekeeper having to fight people saying, "I'm almost done."

Once again, the *architecture of the total control system* is where FCT leaders focus their attention. They identify the minimum set of decision gates they need to be directly involved in and define the criteria for other gates but leave the administrative of these to the team itself. FCT companies strongly bias their executives' involvement toward the product concept and specification phases. Once the end product has been clearly defined, the executives stay out, with the exception of auditing major gates and expenditures.

Auditing means that the team is responsible for administering the gate, and the executives audit the team's process to make sure the responsibility is accepted and acted upon. Our overall experience is that FCT companies exercise executive control through business strategy and product planning and avoid gates. Motorola uses contracts with its development teams and eliminates gates entirely.

What is audited changes in an FCT company. For example, development costs are not looked at in isolation but are treated with the time-to-market context. As noted in the McKinsey study mentioned earlier, a cost overrun of 50% only reduced total profits over the life of a product by 3.5%. Certainly million-dollar tooling or prototyping decisions may require external approval, but these are the exceptions rather than the rule.

Based on the McKinsey study, one could argue that the most important cost-control element in an FCT company is schedule adherence. FCT companies use the scheduling process as a way to challenge the team and the development process itself. Scheduling is done by the multifunctional team using a methodology similar to Is mapping. Once the end item of the project is decided during the specification process, the team creates a PERT or similar planning chart. It identifies and sequences tasks and key milestones. Using self-stick notes, each team member lists the key tasks, time required for completion, and critical inputs required to start. It is not uncommon to involve a critical vendor in the scheduling meeting. Like the "messy meeting" results, team members sign the final schedule when it is complete. The team arranges the tasks with the following FCT principles in mind:

1. Work in parallel whenever possible
2. Schedule in days, not weeks or months
3. Schedule with a "do it, test it, fix it" bias; get testable, incremental items fast
4. Build final components; avoid building components just for prototypes
5. Push as much value added upstream on suppliers as possible within the confines of business strategy
6. Avoid dual efforts for the same component using competing technologies; choose one approach early and make it work
7. Use realistic roll-off and staffing assumptions for all functions
8. Prototype by calendar (see next section)

FCT companies construct a *multifunctional* PERT that includes all the tasks required to be successful. A multifunctional PERT would include market introduction press conferences as well as manufacturing process development. The multifunctional PERT exposes interdependencies that a pure engineering PERT will not. The PERT is posted and updated in as close to real time as possible. Status is determined through negotiation rather than declaration. In other words, team members use the PERT review process as a way of honestly raising issues and resolving them rather than reporting a yes/no answer to bury problems.

The PERT is the road map for the project. When it is not accurate, speed is lost. There is nothing that hurts an FCT development more than the lack of truthfulness in a PERT. This underlines the importance of using ongoing updates and keeping the process within the team itself. Involvement of outside management in updating invites too much positioning on the part of individual team members. Keep the nomenclature regarding status to three categories: on time, in trouble, and missed (requiring a catch-up strategy).

Several FCT competitors use FCT reviews early in the schedule development. The role of the FCT review is to challenge the basic assumptions within the schedule. The FCT review is held with an experienced group of cross-functional colleagues who are outside the project. Oftentimes, members of the firm's FCT steering committee participate in the review as a way to transfer learnings from one project to another. The ownership of the schedule remains with the team, and it can reject or accept any suggestion from the review. The reviewers examine key assumptions concerning the product and development process. Some typical issues that arise include the following:

1. Is the team making maximum use of existing parts?
2. Is there an aggressive part count target?
3. Is process development synchronized with product development?
4. Are components or time being unduly added to for design margins unrelated to the specification's requirements?
5. Is company experience with specific component development reflected in the schedule assumptions?
6. Are vendors leveraged as much as possible?
7. Are major risks clearly identified and managed?

## Focusing the Development Effort

As one moves through each successive phase in the development effort, leverage is lost. Each learning cycle of design, fabricate, assemble, and test (DFAT) occurs within a narrower field. Development speed at this point depends on how fast DFAT cycles can be completed and integrated so that a new DFAT can begin. Time is measured in half days and days during this phase.

Just as visitors to Japanese companies are surprised to see how similar their basic operations are, visitors to FCT companies find there is little that is visibly different during this phase. In both cases, the difference is in *how* the task is done rather than *what* is done. For example, prototyping continues to be a central theme of the development process, but an FCT company has a broader purpose for it and behaves differently. The focus remains on leveraging current knowledge and speeding up the acquisition of new knowledge. To that end, we will discuss new tools for prototyping and supplier involvement.

### *Prototyping*

Traditionally, prototyping is used to verify product performance and to assess maturity. Each industry has its own labels for phases within the prototyping process. The model in Exhibit 8.8 uses terminology from the computer industry. The three prototypes assure basic functionality, design reliability, and manufacturability, respectively. Each build is followed by testing to identify problems. Problems are assessed and fixed throughout the process.

The focus of traditional prototyping is narrowly focused on assuring product maturity. The basis for initiating a prototype build is believing

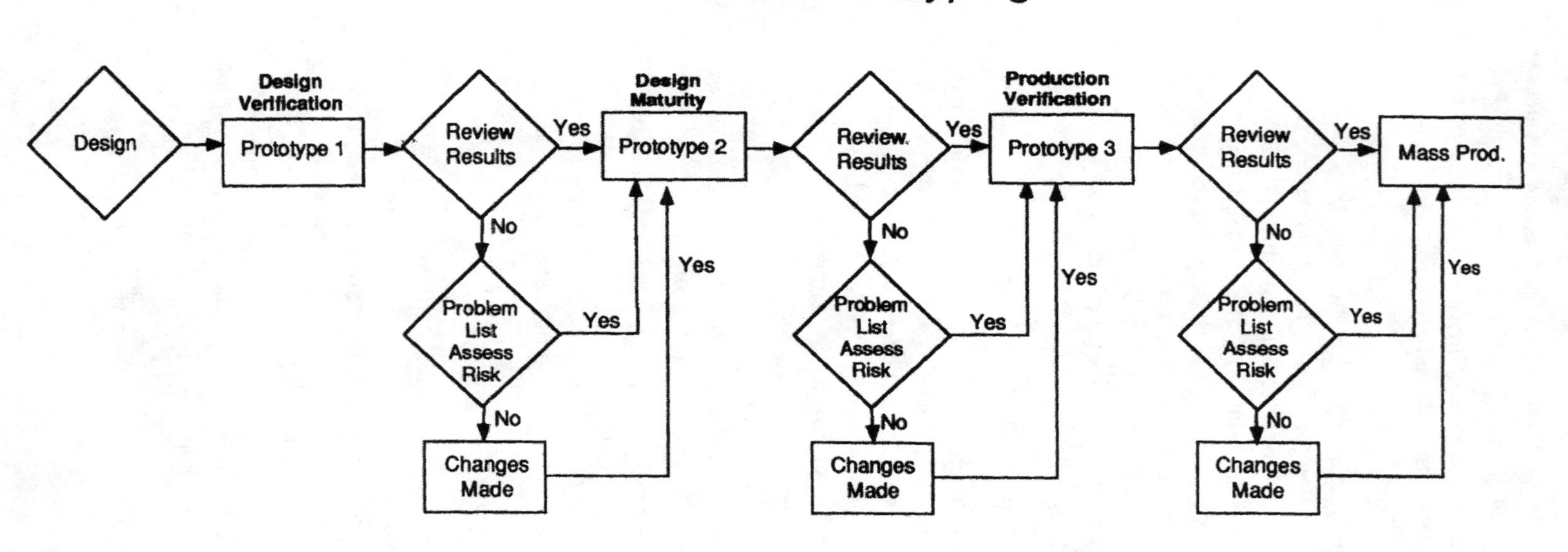
Traditional Prototyping
Design
Design Verification
Prototype 1
Review Results
Yes
No
Design Maturity
Prototype 2
Problem List Assess Risk
Yes
No
Changes Made
Yes
Review Results
Yes
No
Production Verification
Prototype 3
Problem List Assess Risk
Yes
No
Changes Made
Yes
Review Results
Yes
No
Mass Prod.
Problem List Assess Risk
Yes
No
Changes Made
Yes

**EXHIBIT 8.8**

the product can pass the tests that follow each build. Build dates are targeted in the schedule but are frequently moved depending on progress. Each build has an owner who controls the build. In traditionally structured organizations, ownership shifts to the function that leads that stage of development. Early prototypes are owned by engineering, and later prototypes are owned by manufacturing.[11]

Prototypes have tremendous impact because they are an integrated, tangible embodiment of the collective knowledge developed during a primarily intangible process. One can show a drawing of a component to a colleague, but that does not compare to seeing the component integrated with others in a working prototype. The power of the prototype is that it becomes a common figure that everyone in the group can see, poke, prod, and test. Until a prototype is produced, most conversations are about ideas and components; the birth of a prototype brings everyone in the team together.

FCT companies do not limit their use of prototypes to within the company. The lack of tangibility causes the same problems for suppliers and customers. Customer design needs such as form factor and "look and feel" can be tested very early using technologies such as stereo lithography[12] to produce a three-dimensional model. Suppliers see firsthand what their challenge is or how they have succeeded.

FCT firms, within reason, do not scrimp on the number of prototypes they build. Obviously there is a significant difference between prototyping a computer and a space shuttle, but $500,000 expended on computer prototypes is well spent if it can significantly accelerate learning and shorten the development cycle. Spreading prototypes around increases the opportunity for testing, which in turn increases the amount of knowledge gained per prototype. If prototypes are hoarded, the purpose behind prototyping is defeated.

Periodic prototyping (Exhibit 8.9) is an alternative to the traditional maturity-based model. As described by Wheelwright & Clark, prototypes are built according to a predetermined calendar-based pace.[13] The fundamental difference is that periodic prototyping is conducted as a learn-

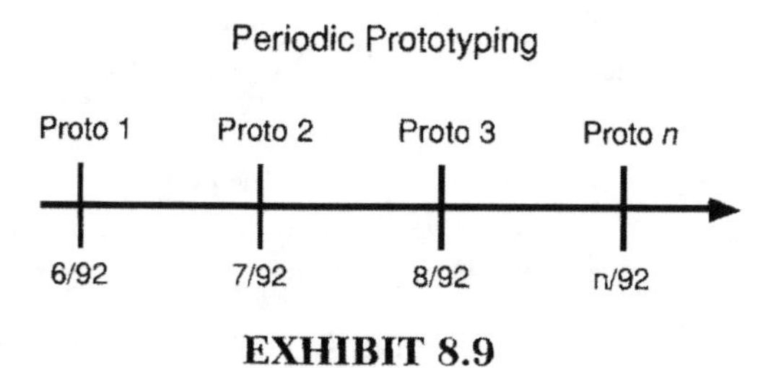


**EXHIBIT 8.9**

ing process, rather than a maturity-testing process. The goal of each prototype is to maximize learning so the development can process as fast as possible. Prototype iterations continue until they are no longer needed.

Each prototype build begins on an established date. As the date approaches, people adjust their tasks to maximize the learning from each build. Thus, a mechanical engineering group may design a component earlier than planned, because that would enable the software team to test its servo logic. Rapidly pacing prototype builds can present a problem for test and quality groups; they must be cued up and ready to go as soon as the prototypes emerge, because their cycle time will determine what learning gets integrated into the next build.

We witnessed a fascinating success story when a client scheduled the intervals between periodic prototypes such that it only had time to identify major problems before the next build but could not always design or implement a fix for each one. Thus, a fix for some problems found in the first prototype were incorporated in the third build rather than the second. The process worked extremely well and by itself represented a 5% cycle time reduction in the *total* product development process.

The rate one chooses for periodic prototyping establishes the pace and rhythm of the development. Using the calendar also minimizes the impact that a delay in one area can cause. In practice, an area might miss one prototype build, but rarely will it miss two. The embarrassment factor created by the visibility (combined with team support) simply does not allow that to happen.

***Supplier Involvement***

FCT competitors leverage the value added that suppliers contribute by creating a *codeveloper relationship* instead of the traditional lowest-bid supplier role. To do this, the FCT firm treats the supplier as a part of its organization rather than an outside entity. Exhibit 8.10 illustrates how the operating boundary of the FCT organization changes. Just as the FCT firm tries to bring the customer in as a sponsor, the supplier is asked to become a codeveloper. The buyer moves selected value-added develop-

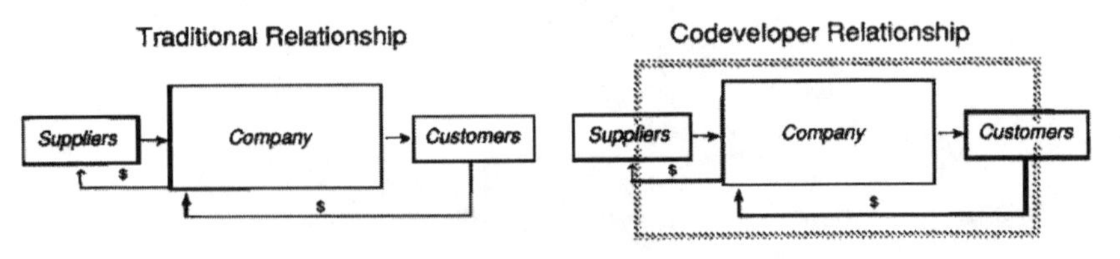


**EXHIBIT 8.10**

ment tasks upstream to the supplier. Once again, the change is less visible, because the shift is in how work is done.

The most fundamental change is the sharing of information. Traditional competitors provide their suppliers with a specification and look for low bids that can meet quality, schedule, and volume requirements. With few exceptions, the specification is the only substantive information that is shared. In the codeveloper model, specification development is a joint effort beginning with a description of product concept and high-level requirements from the buyer. The business strategies of the supplier and the buyer are shared in order to ensure that the flow of technology continues over time. As described by Cyril Yansouni, CEO of Read-Rite (which supplies thin film recording heads to the rapidly changing disk-drive industry), "We have an open-kimono relationship with our customers. They know our plans, and we know theirs."[14]

In the Japanese auto industry, the practice is extended further.[15] Toyota defines a market price for the vehicle and, based on that, determines what each component can cost in order to meet the cost and profit margin targets. The supplier and Toyota then look at what the supplier's costs have to be in order to meet the target and make their own margins. A starting price and planned cost reductions are mutually agreed to at the beginning of the contract. Both work to achieve the cost reductions; any cost reduction achieved in excess of the plan is retained by the supplier.

This market-minus-price orientation is in stark contrast to the Detroit supplier-plus-cost approach, where a company takes the best price it can get and adds its margin. To use the Japanese approach one must understand value engineering and analysis, but more importantly, one has to build a relationship where both parties are invested in each other's success. Once that investment exists, exposing margin information is much less formidable. Critics argue that the interlocking ownership of Japan's auto companies with their suppliers is the only reason this is possible. Our experience is that this is an intervening but not a causal variable.

A visible manifestation of the tighter relationship is co-location. Internally, purchasing representatives are part of the co-located multifunctional team. This is particularly true during the early planning phases, when product cost and getting engineering samples is critical. The purchasing representative has responsibility for all material tracking and reports to the team. Externally, FCT companies ask their suppliers to co-locate their people with the development team at the customer's site. This increases the supplier's understanding and participation in the overall effort. One would have a hard time distinguishing who was an employee and who was a contractor at a program meeting.

## Summary

The tools and tactics used by FCT competitors share the same goal of speeding up the rate of new learning and leveraging what is already present in the corporation. Be it through "messy meetings" or periodic prototyping, FCT competitors establish a clear goal quickly, make the development highly visible, and then focus on speeding up the rate of learning within each cycle of design, fabricate, assemble, and test.

# 9
# Implementation Dynamics and Measures

The endless discussion about how formidable it is to change organizations concern us. Our experience is that once a problem becomes serious enough to gain everyone's attention, the chances that it will be resolved are extremely high. When people focus on a problem and decide to change it, change happens. The difficulty is getting people at all levels to focus.

Consider the all-too-familiar case of the soon-to-be-shuttered manufacturing facility. The story always reads the same. It begins with a lengthy treatise about how the once industry-leading Riverway Plant of the XYZ Corporation has eroded into a living hell of poor productivity, dismal labor relations, and high operations costs. In a last-ditch effort, XYZ's CEO puts in a new plant manager with a one-year ultimatum to either turn the plant around or see it closed. The plant manager is often a maverick that management does not really understand or appreciate, but at this point, it is willing to try anything.

The maverick starts by defining the gravity of the situation in no uncertain terms to management and labor. The hurdle for continued existence is crisply and simply defined. Next, the manager makes it clear to everyone, "We've got to do this as a team, and anything and everything about how the plant operates is up for grabs." A year later, the plant is the most productive and lowest-cost facility in the corporation while still using most of the original capital equipment. Grievance levels are the lowest in years, and the word *miracle* is used often enough to suggest that sainthood may not be out of the realm of possibility. What happened? First, nothing helps people change more than crisis and pain. Dramatic improvement was not merely a choice. Second, there is no place for dishonesty, positioning, or turf protection when you've got to get something done. Third and most important, turning around the plant became the sustained focus of everyone's energy and attention.

We have never seen an organization fail to implement FCT successfully when it attached the same importance to implementation that it did to insufficient operating margins or profits. The constant dilemma is, where does the time to implement fast cycle time come from? The honest answer is that management has to believe in the value of managing this way and make FCT implementation a priority. *Organizations can change anything they want to, but they cannot change everything they want to at the same time.* If implementing FCT is the seventh or eighth priority, then wait until it moves into the top three.

FCT changes the paradigm one uses to manage the business. FCT changes how one approaches long-term strategy, organization architecture, product development process, daily operations, and the performance measures one uses. The shift from a traditional functional perspective to a time-driven, value delivery process orientation is not insignificant. This does not mean the transition is overwhelmingly complicated or more difficult than any other change; one simply should not underestimate the scope of the change. It goes far beyond simply adding cycle time to the existing list of things to watch.

With any major change, it is important to calibrate one's measures and expectations regarding the pace and assessment of the implementation process. Success should initially be measured in inches rather than feet. Most U.S. firms look for home runs in organizational change, just as they do in product development. The reality is that it took you and your organization several years to develop today's mode of operation; it will take at least half that time to change it fundamentally. FCT has an advantage in that early success stories of significant magnitude are common.

This chapter will present a template for systemwide implementation of FCT. After a brief discussion of general implementation dynamics, we will discuss how to use performance measures to support FCT implementation. Then we will track implementation through four critical phases: problem recognition, strategy development and goal setting, launch, and ongoing change management. For each phase, we will define the tasks and present the performance measures that support that phase. Before concluding, we will return to see how Core Products, Inc., staged its FCT implementation.

**Implementation Dynamics**

FCT implementation usually follows a pattern of education followed by successes that eventually become plateaus of "midlife crisis," as depicted in Exhibit 9.1. Midlife crisis comes after the low-hanging fruit is picked.

The first wave of successes are created by a small but enthusiastic group of early adopters. Early adopters are unique because they take action based on belief in themselves and the logic of FCT, whereas middle and late adopters take a "show me" perspective. The bulk of adopters are split evenly between middle and late adopters. To spur implementation, one should make sure that early adopters have significant contact with potential middle adopters as they start achieving success.

The midlife crisis period is a difficult one. It follows a period of dramatic improvement and can cause people to think they have made all the advances they can. This is not true. Use the plateau to consolidate and institutionalize gains; make sure the work that has been done is wired into the operating system of the organization. Frequently, one development team has a significant success, but other teams struggling with the same basic issue do not know about it. Next, take another pass at FCT process redesign, specifically the Is/Should mapping process. Typically, the low-hanging fruit that was exposed in the first Is map has been picked. At this

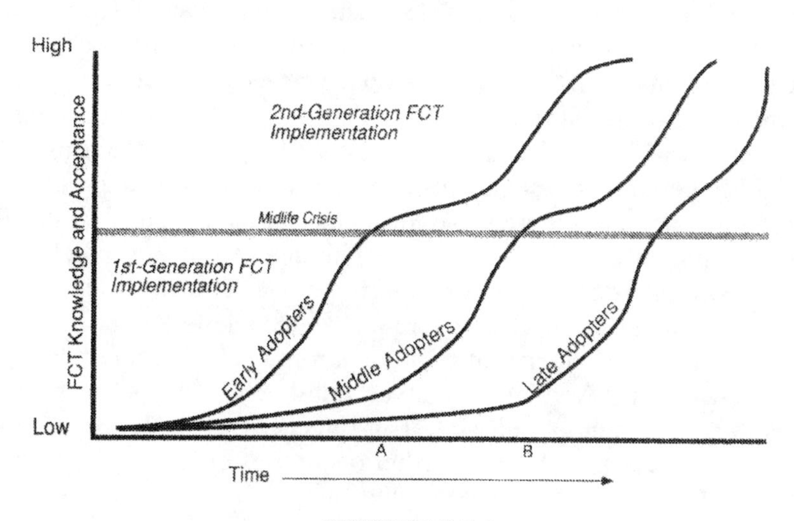


**EXHIBIT 9.1**

point, the original Is map is no longer accurate. Initiating a second Is map will illuminate new opportunities and rekindle people's energy.

## The Role of Measurement in Implementation

Before one reviews each implementation phase and the associated measures, it is important to understand the purpose behind measurement. When executives are asked why measurements are important, many will respond that they tell you where you are relative to some goal. This is true, but simply knowing one's status is not a complete answer. As a human system, an organization's performance does not change until people change their behavior about the condition indicated in the measure. We really don't measure just to know where we are; we measure in order to know when we should change our behavior and (hopefully) how. For example, a race car does not contain a speedometer, whereas a passenger car does. A passenger-car driver needs a speedometer to monitor speed relative to posted limits. If he or she is traveling too fast, the passenger-car driver reduces speed. A race car driver wants to go faster than the other cars, regardless of their speed. Putting a speedometer in a race car is irrelevant, because it would not change the driver's behavior.

*The fundamental reason we measure anything in an organization is to change behavior.* If there are any measures currently within your organization that can vary dramatically without causing anyone to change their behavior, the measure is a waste and should be eliminated.

Most organization measurement systems have lost sight of this perspective. First, results measures dominate organizations. Results measures tell if one has achieved a desired outcome but say little of why the outcome was or was not achieved. Second, most measures serve top management, the firm's auditors, and the Securities and Exchange Commission while providing very little that helps operating managers to run their businesses better. The vast majority of performance measures serve those outside the local area responsible for the performance. Third, costs are overly emphasized relative to revenues, because it is easier to get hard data on costs than on lost revenue opportunities. Fourth, the data on costs are not as complete or hard as we would like to believe. We measure incurred costs and rarely measure the opportunity cost of such things as delayed decisions. Even more pointedly, most organizations have five to ten times the amount of indirect versus direct costs, yet 75% of the cost data relate to direct costs. The further one moves upstream in an organization, the more problematic this becomes.

A purchasing manager told of a case that demonstrates how these perspectives blend together to reinforce each other negatively. During a car development "face-lift" of an existing model, the team designed a new exterior door handle that would blend with the exterior changes much better than the company's existing part. When the new design was brought to purchasing, the engineer was asked to do a cost analysis comparative to the existing part. The manager reported that it took the engineer twice as long to estimate the cost than it did to design the part in the first place; the analysis showed the cost was roughly equal. Then purchasing asked the engineer to estimate the warranty cost of the new part, since they had historical data on the old part. At this point, the engineer gave up in frustration and returned to using the old part. Common sense also suggests that processes such as this lengthen cycle time and, more importantly, constrain people from building the best products they know how.

The dominance of the cost ethos presents a challenge during FCT implementation. Cost results are treated as substantive facts, whereas costs not measured or lost revenue opportunities are not. It is much easier to show how much a project overran its budget than to show how much revenue was lost by being late four months. Furthermore, those who establish and run the organization's measurement system are invested in past practices and habits. Their clout is often grossly disproportional to their value added to the end customer. We respectfully suggest that an additional advantage of FCT is that it moves measurement back to serving the local operating manager so that the drivers of cost, cycle times and defects, can be addressed properly. FCT companies do not eliminate results measures; they augment them with a combination of process and results measures that focus on cycle time and learning via defect reductions. A good FCT measurement system is based on four principles, which are detailed below.

### *Clear and Graphical Information*

Cycle time measures lend themselves to graphics. Whether in the form of miniature clocks, line charts, or bar graphs, graphical information is much quicker for people to absorb. Rather than depending on cognitive understanding, charts can visually demonstrate complex relationships. The multifunctional team dashboard presented in Chapter 5 is an illustration of this.

### *Timeliness*

Timeliness means that the measures should be as close to real time as possible in order to reduce the time to detect and correct errors.

An undetected problem continues to spawn such destructive offspring as waste, customer dissatisfaction, and rework. One should also eliminate "information float" wherever possible. Information float occurs when information is in the system but is not accessible by those needing it.

### *Illuminates Process Drivers*

FCT companies constantly try to improve the percentage of value-added time within their value delivery processes. To identify opportunities, they create process measures that differentiate special causes from common causes. Common causes are inherent variables in the system that will always cause fluctuations; special causes are specific variables that cause the system to respond uniquely. If one treats a common cause as though it were a special cause, there is a high probability that the situation will get worse or (at best) merely remain the same.

FCT companies develop complete rather than comprehensive measures of process drivers. Complete systems measure the minimum elements required to control the business. For example, top management at one FCT firm measures only three processes using three measures. They track cycle time, defects, and people capability within the product development, order-to-fulfillment, and customer technical problem resolution processes. Each team and functional group uses the same measures. In support areas such as finance, the company will also use cycle time, defects, and people capability to measure unique finance processes, but it is understood that the three value delivery processes are the central focus for the business at large.

Comprehensive measurement systems can be overbearing in that they measure so much that it is difficult to know what is important. They are the equivalent of putting the cockpit instruments from a 747 into a compact car. Comprehensive measurement systems take on a life of their own, and people spend more time feeding information into them than they do getting usable information from them. When one encounters a comprehensive measurement system, be wary. Too many measures are a warning sign that the firm has not focused its strategy or operations on value-added tasks.

### *Easy-to-Use Elegance*

The hallmark of any powerful measurement system is that it creates the maximum insight with the minimum data. Elegant FCT measurement systems measure the few right things. You know when your system is easy to use by how widely it is used. Developing a complete measurement system takes four steps:

1. Define the behaviors you want (cycle time, defect reduction, and so forth)
2. Define measures for each behavior
3. Test a prototype
   a. Watch for adverse impacts
   b. Did you get the behavior you wanted?
4. If there is a match, implement the measure

The critical element of designing the measuring system is keeping it as simple as possible while avoiding adverse impacts. A classical example of adverse impacts occurred when productivity experts measured secretarial productivity by counting typing keystrokes per hour. Secretaries very quickly found that their productivity soared if they rested their thumb on the space bar! FCT companies typically measure cycle time and defects for two reasons: defect generation and correction slows down cycle time, and speeding up cycle time without altering the process increases defects.

## FCT Implementation

FCT implementation has four phases, as shown in Exhibit 9.2. We will walk through each of the phases, describing the tasks, measures, and issues one should expect to occur during that phase. Whenever possible, we will give tips and suggestions for dealing with these issues.

### *Phase 1: Problem Recognition*

Until senior management believes there is a significant performance gap between the firm's performance and either customer requirements or

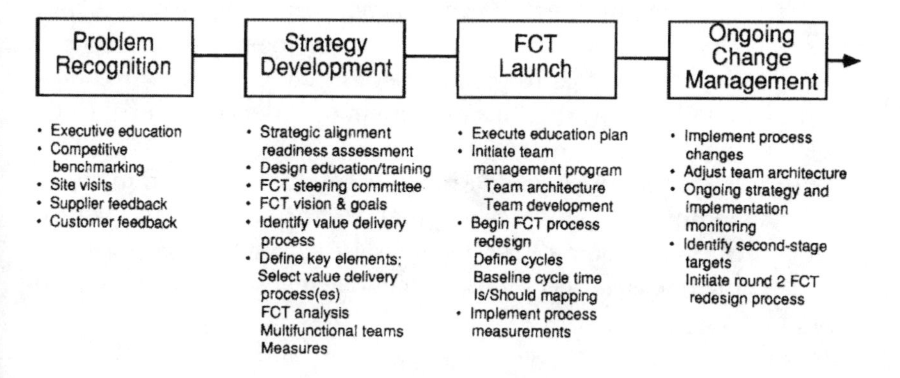


**EXHIBIT 9.2**

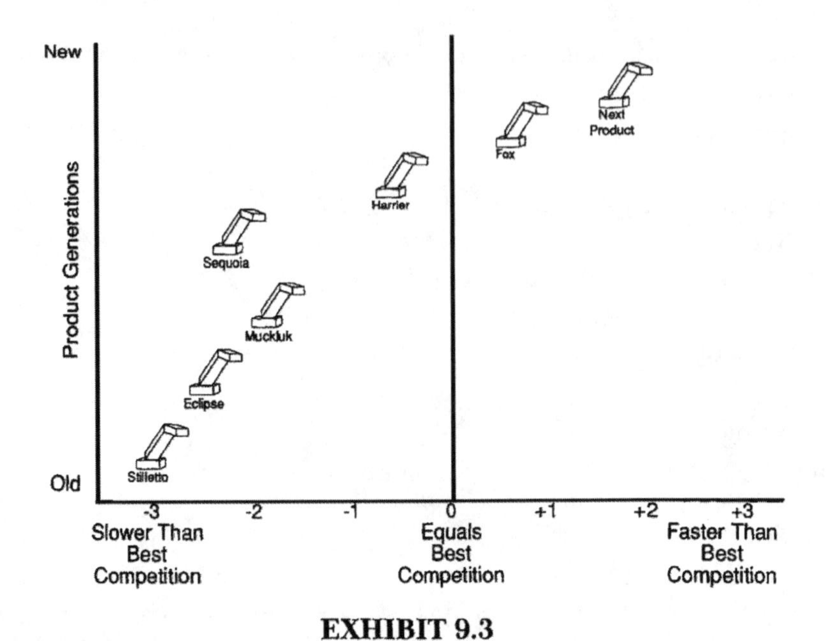


**EXHIBIT 9.3**

competitors' performance, it is impossible to consider FCT implementation seriously. The performance gap can show up in many places: the most obvious indicator in product development is being late to market. Exhibit 9.3 illustrates how one company tracked its products relative to the competition over time.

Other measures that can indicate a performance gap include reduced market share, increased customer complaints, or growing cycle times in the sales cycle, repair cycle, and order-to-fulfillment cycle. Industry suppliers can also provide useful insight regarding performance relative to the competition. There is a high correlation between organizational growth and lengthening cycle times. The larger an organization gets, the more its cycle time increases if action is not taken. One firm we know measured its average cycle times and compared them with its fast-track cycle times. They saw that they could be fast, but only on an exception basis. The good news is that this gave them confidence to pursue FCT implementation.

Once recognized, one should expect the performance gap to widen, since competitors who are attacking their cycle time problems will get even faster through their efforts. Obviously, the larger the performance gap, the more one can expect the leadership team to be motivated to implement FCT.

Assuming the gap is recognized and is sufficiently large for the company to pursue FCT further, the next step is to educate executives on what FCT is and what it takes to get there. Executives are much more familiar with the results FCT can bring than they are about how to do it. They often view FCT as a tactic reminiscent of personal time management carried to the organizational level. They underestimate how much their involvement is required in the strategic alignment process, defining value delivery processes for FCT redesign, creating the architecture for multifunctional teams, and establishing new measures for managing the business. Without education, the tendency is to initiate inadequately defined cycle time improvement efforts and throw together multifunctional development teams without creating an architecture or training. In the worst cases, they continue to operate as before but now add cycle time improvement to a list of priorities that is already too long.

A critical subject for discussion at this stage is understanding and committing to the power shift that FCT requires. Speed is a function of making decisions in real time, which means making them locally to the greatest degree possible. The executives should openly discuss their hopes and concerns regarding this shift. They can be sure the organization will test their sincerity throughout implementation.

By engaging in self-education first, executives develop a common language that enables strategy development and a rollout that is backed by commitment. Education alternatives that exist include external and internal seminars, reading, and site visits. The preferred approach is to use an internal seminar that combines education with plenty of time to test its application internally, followed by a site visit. The education session should be led by an outsider experienced in cycle time implementation alternatives, who can save a great deal of time by directing the executives to the most important issues. He or she also can use his or her role as an outsider to surface sacred cows and unfreeze some of the "not invented here" attitudes one always runs into.

Site visits are difficult to set up, because many companies consider their FCT capability a competitive advantage and are unwilling to allow visits. We encourage such visits as long as the companies are not direct competitors, because it is quite difficult to copy a firm's capability just by observing it. This phase ends with a go or no-go decision from the organization's leaders.

### *Problem Recognition Measures*

The primary focus at this stage is internal and external benchmarking. Possible areas to benchmark include the following:

1. Time from idea to market
2. Time from project start to first customer ship
3. Inventory turns and levels
4. Cycle time for major production runs
5. Decision cycle time
6. Time lost waiting for decisions
7. Percentage of deliveries on time
8. Time to repair
9. Quoted lead time versus customer request
10. Work in process

An additional measure is vintage charting. A vintage chart (Exhibit 9.4) illustrates the contribution to revenue or profits made by products based on their year of introduction. Companies such as Hewlett-Packard set targets to have at least 50% of their current year's revenue come from products introduced in the last three years. A vintage chart provides a quick snapshot of the productivity of R & D investments to revenue or profits. One can reasonably infer that profit and revenue contribution is a function of development cycle time.

***Phase 2: Strategy Development***

Strategy development is where "up and to the left" is during FCT implementation. Decisions made here set up every action that follows. A critical issue is ensuring that people commit to the strategy rather than just agreeing to it.

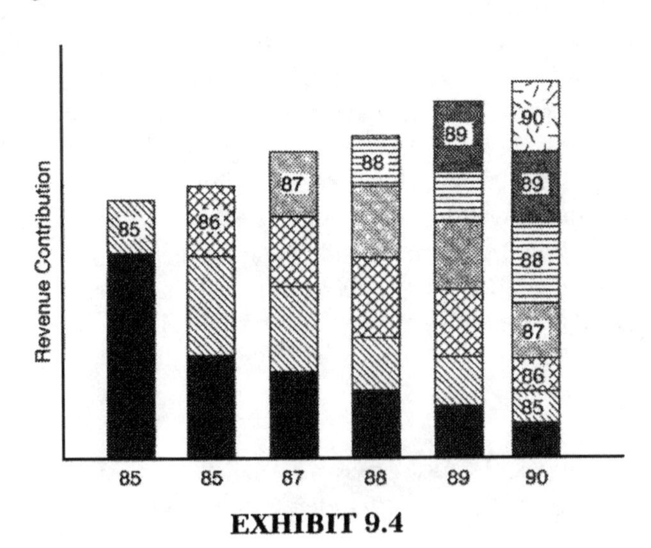


**EXHIBIT 9.4**

Many firms work with an external change agent to provide a fresh set of trained eyes that can illuminate improvement opportunities and obstacles that the internal leadership either does not see or is not willing to discuss. Such outsiders help establish an open and honest discussion forum that is critical at this time. In many respects, the ability of senior management to work openly determines the level of commitment it can generate. The change agent also structures the conversation, which enables all to concentrate fully on participating in it.

Having confirmed the need for FCT, the leadership team examines the organization's readiness for implementation. A common concern is how to fit FCT with all the other initiatives already under way, particularly any quality initiatives. Practically, FCT and quality initiatives mutually support each other. As described in Chapter 2, FCT provides a better umbrella strategy that helps implement quality. In many cases, however, a company learns about FCT after it already has begun implementation of a quality improvement effort. In these cases, one can fold the added dimensions of cycle time and its value-added focus into the quality implementation effort.

A more important question is, does the organization and its leadership have the ability to focus on making FCT implementation successful? This is the key implementation question. It is fair to say that many underestimate the paradigm shift FCT entails. The good news is that once it is set in motion, FCT can snowball rather rapidly. If management is not ready to dedicate time and energy to implementation, it will be negatively perceived as the major obstacle by most employees. Better to delay implementation by a month or whatever it takes than to start with a bang and have FCT fizzle in three months.

Another consideration is whether the firm has its purpose, strategy, and structure defined and aligned. Until the firm's leaders can clearly articulate what the value proposition of the firm is, asking people to speed up existing processes invites turbocharging your worst mistakes. Those that start without this work completed find that it is quickly flagged as one of the major barriers to FCT. If it is a known gap, fill it first.

Implementation responsibility rests with executive management. In smaller firms, the role is played by the executive staff; in larger organizations, a steering committee is often used to oversee implementation. If a steering committee is used, the membership should be multifunctional, and its composition should reflect the importance of FCT to top management. Who is chosen for membership will send a quick signal to the organization about how important FCT really is. The role and charter of the steering committee should be defined at this stage.

Steering committees are most effective when their role is to facilitate implementation rather than push it. Because of the built-in potential for people mistakenly to consider FCT as management's way of getting people to work faster, the more direct power the steering committee exercises, the more it evokes this response. A typical steering committee charter includes the following:

1. Insuring that FCT successes and learnings are shared
2. Selecting and coordinating implementation targets
3. Identifying opportunities to reduce cycle time
4. Educating itself and being a resource to others

The fastest and most effective implementations occur when the leadership acts in accordance with the FCT operating philosophy, organization architecture, leadership, and business practices outlined in Chapter 2 *as though they were already in place.* Much of what we have described regarding effective multifunctional teams and fast product development applies to the leadership group during the strategy phase. The leadership group is a multifunctional team creating a new product called the FCT organization.

The core of the strategy development can be summarized in five actions that have to be taken at this time. We will review the key considerations involved in each decision and conclude by suggesting a balanced approach that works in most cases.

### *Creating an Overall FCT Vision*

The FCT vision sets a stake in the ground that establishes the focus and magnitude that others will use as a first-pass target for action. Several years ago, John Young, former CEO of Hewlett-Packard, selected a 50% cycle time reduction in new product development to be achieved in three years as the goal. Young's aggressive target made the dimensions of the improvement sought clear to everyone. As they moved forward, each business within Hewlett-Packard tuned their particular situation to this target.

A common question that arises regarding the vision is, should the improvement target be set based on internal baselines and competitive benchmarking, or can one use an arbitrary number (as Young did)? The time required to do the baselining and benchmarking usually does not add significant value as long as one focuses on the overall magnitude of the change.

Most of the concerns regarding using a number without baselining are concerns not about the number itself but about what will happen to people's performance ratings and careers if the number is not met. This is more an issue about how the number is used than it is about the number itself. Such concerns ought to be addressed directly, for they are symptomatic of broader issues that will surface as either decision-making delays during mapping or empowerment issues during the creation of multifunctional teams.

It is useful to define the financial impact that achieving the vision can have for the business. For example, one can make reasonable revenue estimates based on price and volume assumptions had a product been available six months earlier. Show the impact this would have on profits and earnings per share. The same can be done for the cost savings that accompany a more rapid development process.

### *Select the Critical Value Delivery Processes That Need to Be Redesigned*

The leadership group next defines the critical value delivery processes to focus on. A common question that emerges is, should the company focus on cycle time reductions across the board or focus only on value delivery processes? The advantage to attacking every process in the organization is that everyone in the organization has a clear and familiar place to get involved. A major disadvantage is that this lacks focus and leverage. Additionally, it creates a large training and implementation support requirement. With rare exceptions, speeding up the rate of the monthly financial close does not have the impact on the business that speeding up the product development process has. Focusing on the value delivery processes and significantly improving them teaches people about FCT and what is critical to the firm's customers. Both lessons are important. How many value delivery processes one should attack initially is a question of resources. Again, focus is important, and only take on as many as you can do extraordinarily well.

### *Sequencing FCT Process Redesign and Multifunctional Team Implementation*

The leadership has to decide the order in which it will implement the major elements of FCT. In every case, FCT redesign and multifunctional teams will be required, but the question is in what order one will implement them. There are three primary choices, as shown in Exhibit 9.5.

Exhibit 9.6 highlights the advantages and disadvantages of each option. In general, option A has the greatest impact but requires the most planning, resources, and management. Option B is frequently preferred for new product development, because one does not need to analyze the de-

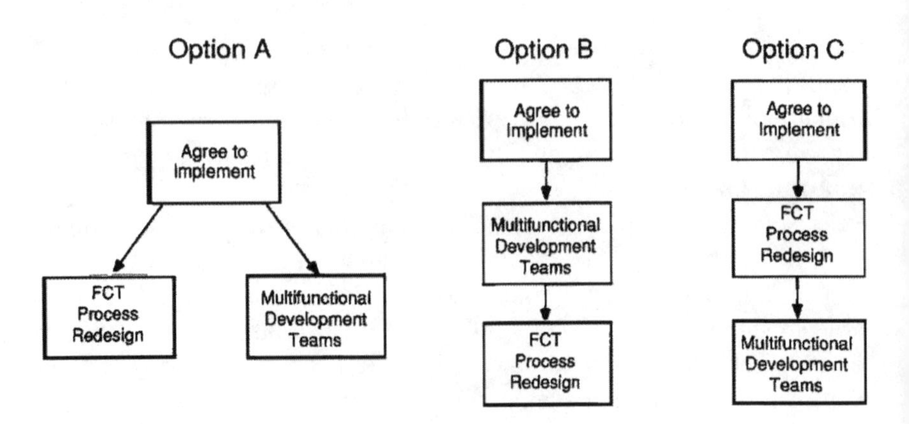


**EXHIBIT 9.5**

velopment process to know that multifunctional development teams are required. Many firms are able to define who needs to be on the teams to get started effectively without reviewing their development process. Option C generates the most pull within the organization, because changes are driven by FCT process redesign rather than by management mandate.

For any option chosen, the FCT redesign teams and the multifunctional development teams need to be designed and the people selected and trained. Although both sets of teams have representation from multiple functions, their scope and timing are significantly different. Because it is easy to get confused, remember that the FCT process redesign teams have a multifunctional composition but operate as a task force that exists only for the time it takes to conduct and implement the FCT process redesign. Multifunctional development teams, as we have described them, are permanent work structures that augment or replace the current functional organization. Multifunctional development teams are responsible for product development or run business units.

### *Define an Implementation Strategy and Structure*

All too often, organizations design a major change but do not put a structure in place that has the responsibility and authority to manage the change effort. *Failure to manage the ongoing change is the primary differentiator between significant success and failure.* As noted above, the task falls to senior management, collectively or through a steering committee.

The implementation planning is facilitated by using the same implementation map format one uses for to plan the FCT process redesign implementation, illustrated in Exhibit 6.8. By defining the stakeholders who need to be involved in the change along the left and the key implemen-

| | *Advantages* | *Disadvantages* | *Comments* |
|---|---|---|---|
| Option A | Highest reward<br>Synergy between development teams and process analysis<br>Strongest signal to organization | Highest risk<br>Largest resource & management burden<br>Training requirement high | Requires management commitment and follow through<br>Can limit development teams and processes to manage risk |
| Option B | Immediate impact on product development<br>Provides lead time to define and implement co-location<br>Attacks functional silos | May delay identifying key opportunities<br>Requires a management push to start | Preferred route in product development |
| Option C | Generates pull and facilitates acceptance<br>Can provide detail for multifunctional development team architecture | Delays immediate impact in product development | Easiest to scale to the organization's readiness |

**EXHIBIT 9.6**

tation phases along the top, one can quickly create a plan that is comprehensive and graphic. Exhibit 9.7 is an example of this.

Implementation issues that should be addressed in the implementation map include the following:

1. Education
    - General FCT education
        - Introduction for all employees
        - Managers program
    - FCT process redesign skills
    - Multifunctional team development
2. Change management structure
    - Composition; executive staff versus steering committee
    - Charter and meeting frequency
    - Link to executive management

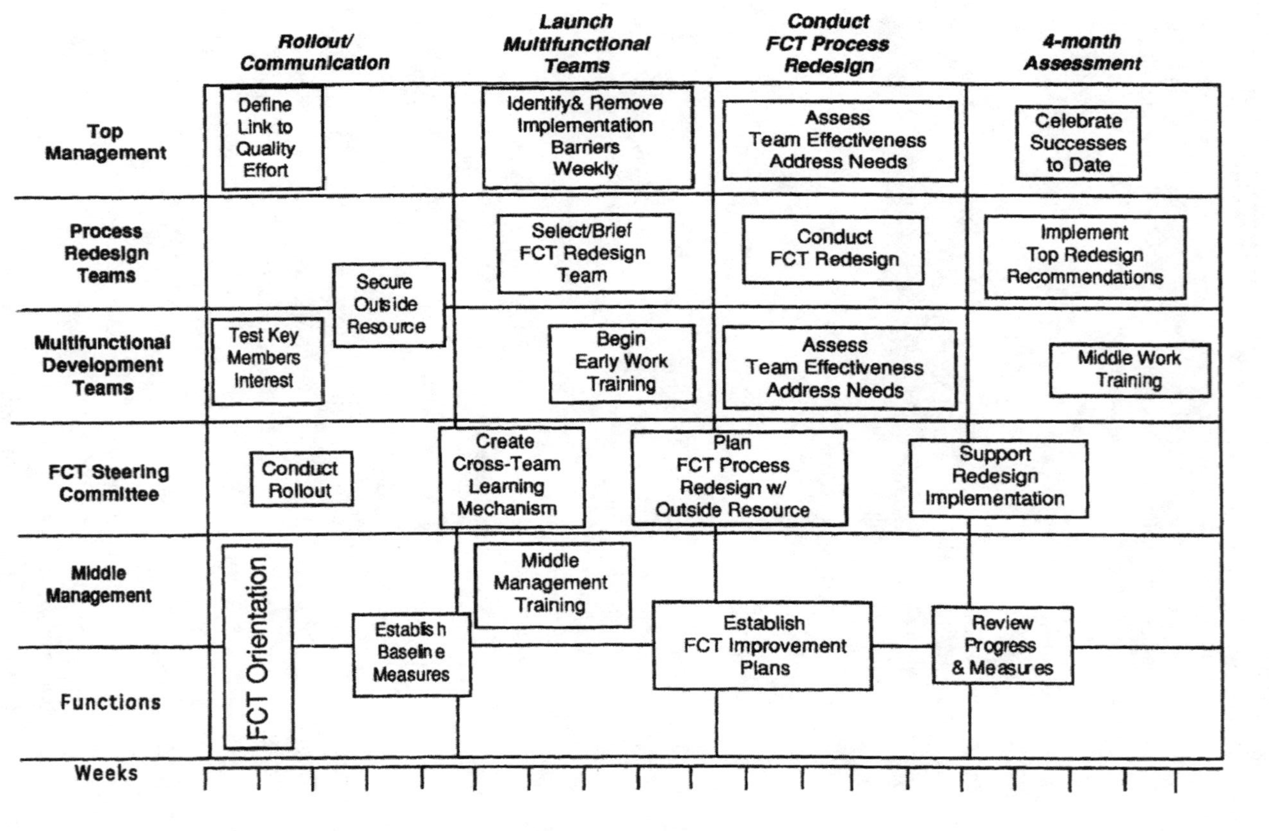
Rollout/ Communication
Launch Multifunctional Teams
Conduct FCT Process Redesign
4-month Assessment
Top Management
Define Link to Quality Effort
Identify& Remove Implementation Barriers Weekly
Assess Team Effectiveness Address Needs
Celebrate Successes to Date
Process Redesign Teams
Secure Outside Resource
Select/Brief FCT Redesign Team
Conduct FCT Redesign
Implement Top Redesign Recommendations
Multifunctional Development Teams
Test Key Members Interest
Begin Early Work Training
Assess Team Effectiveness Address Needs
Middle Work Training
FCT Steering Committee
Conduct Rollout
Create Cross-Team Learning Mechanism
Plan FCT Process Redesign w/ Outside Resource
Support Redesign Implementation
Middle Management
FCT Orientation
Middle Management Training
Establish Baseline Measures
Establish FCT Improvement Plans
Review Progress & Measures
Functions
Weeks

**EXHIBIT 9.7**

3. Measurement definition
   - Cycle definitions
   - Defect measures
   - Overall measures
4. Links to other initiatives
   - Quality
   - Functional priorities
5. Multifunctional team architecture and implementation (see Chapter 5)
6. FCT process redesign target implementation (see Chapter 6)

The planning at this stage is characterized by a combination of strategic thinking and common sense. On the strategic side, one spends time identifying groups and individuals that one expects to be particularly supportive of or resistant to the change. Implementation planning should leverage and respond to each respectively. The ongoing question is, what are the potential obstacles to FCT implementation, and what should we do about them? Every obstacle that is unknown or avoided inhibits implementation. A good implementation is characterized by short cycle times from obstacle identified to obstacle removed.

Particular attention should be paid to middle management. Just as Gorbachev discovered in the former Soviet Union, one can gain the hearts and minds of the leaders, but if the people who run the towns and villages in the provinces don't understand the change, implementation falters. Middle management is a large group that has suffered during the organizational downsizing of recent years. FCT reinforces the trend away from hierarchical organizations; this means there will be fewer traditional leadership positions available and more people contending for them. Middle management *will* sign up readily for the need for local real-time decision making, although it will test senior management's commitment regularly in the early days.

### *Redefine the Organization's Performance Measurement System*

A key element for accelerating implementation is shifting the firm's performance measures to monitor cycle time. Because measures send such a strong signal to employees regarding what management considers important, the faster one can change the measurement process, the better. *Be sure to keep cycle time measures to the critical few.* The change should begin at the top and include measures of business cycle time as well as top team performance (such as decision cycle time). When the rest of the organization sees top management assessing its own process cycle time, the message is unequivocal.

The first measures required are cycle definitions for the chosen value delivery processes. Until the start and finish points of each value delivery process are defined, it is impossible to measure them historically or in the future. There are no industry standards for establishing the start and finish of value delivery cycles such as product development; each firm has to establish these end points itself. One should keep in mind that the points selected are totally arbitrary. Involve others and use common sense, but do not expect unanimous agreement.

Selecting end points for upstream processes is more difficult, because they are not clearly visible. If one asked development team members a year after a product was complete when that development began and when it ended, one could get as many answers as people asked. Exhibit 9.8 illustrates the different approaches Hewlett-Packard (H-P) and Quantum Corporation used to begin their product development FCT efforts.[1] H-P took an approach that closely follows our FCT definition: from latest customer need to delivered, paid-for product. The cycle ends for H-P when the profits from the product equal the development investment. Although "correct" with regard to our definition, its measure is more difficult to use, because the end points are vague and not highly visible. Trying to get a large number of people to understand when applicable technology exists or when the product breaks even is not easy.

Quantum took a different approach. It grappled with a broader definition such as H-P's, but felt that the vagueness at either end would hamper its adoption. It elected to begin with a measure that did not *initially* fit our definition of FCT but was simple to understand and had tangible end points. Quantum uses messy meetings, which makes specification agreement very visible. Their product maturity test is an industry test that has a clear pass/fail indication. The Quantum definition was easily understood by all, as was evidenced by the uproar it generated. When the Quantum engineering community first saw the definition, engineers cried foul. They appropriately claimed that if FCT includes identifying and satisfying customer needs, why should those in the development commu-

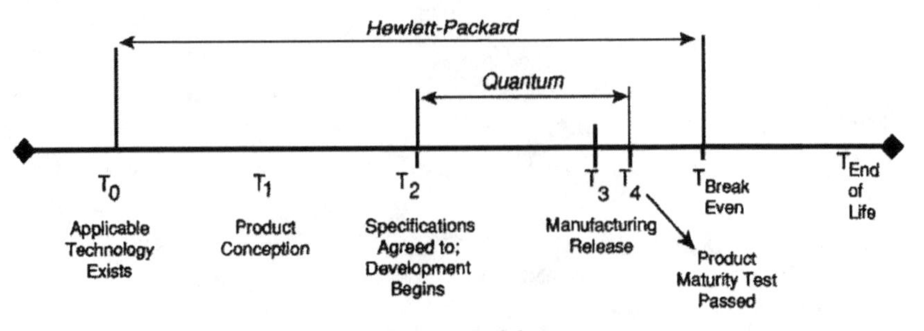


**EXHIBIT 9.8**

nity be the only ones measured? The FCT steering committee listened and struggled with alternatives but decided to start with this definition and improve it as they learned more.

At this point, let's remind ourselves that the purpose of performance measures is to change behavior. Let us now continue and examine Quantum's definition in this light. The engineers were not happy, but they quickly met with their marketing colleagues. They made it clear that since the cycle started with agreed specifications, they would scream loudly if marketing tried to change the specification, because that always caused delays. Notice how Quantum's people were paying attention to exactly the right issues, such as floating specifications.

A month after the metric was established, Quantum conducted its first FCT process redesign. During the Is mapping, it became very clear that floating specifications were a major FCT impediment. The redesign team established a one-month window for developing product specifications and a business plan. Marketing people quickly recognized that if they were to complete a business plan in one month, the company's product planning needed to be current before they started the business plan. This caused the company to examine the frequency and discipline it applied to product planning. It was decided to revisit the product plan every six months.

On the back end of the process, Quantum learned by using this metric that the product maturity test was a good test, but it was not consistently used. As a supplier to computer manufacturers, successfully passing major customer qualification requirements was a more useful and accurate end point that every product went through and had good visibility. Exhibit 9.9 captures what Quantum did. By starting with clear but imperfect end points, it quickly got people's attention. As everyone learned more about FCT and the subprocesses involved, it added elements to the definition, to the point that it now nearly equals H-P's.

Quantum's approach was elegant in that it tapped the process of de-

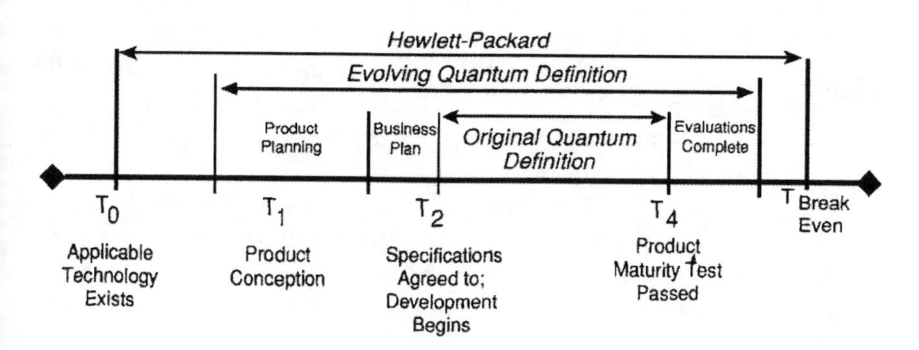


**EXHIBIT 9.9**

veloping the metric as a way to stimulate understanding and energy behind its FCT implementation. Quantum's approach incorporated several key principles:

1. Use the metric definition process itself to begin the change process
2. Gain broad understanding of the goal by using highly tangible end points
3. Use learning to improve the metric continually
4. Modeled FCT learning

An issue that surfaces regularly regards the use of this or any other FCT measure. In particular, engineering organizations like certainty and have a bias for absolute measures. Because cycle time improvement is incremental, the focus should be on relative performance improvement. Certainly people want to know if they have reached their goal, but the fact of the matter is that as soon as we get close, we reset it anyway. Additionally, people often forget that most cycle time visions establish a high reduction target over several years. For example, the H-P and Quantum measures have served both organizations well in that they have provided a yardstick to compare past and successive product developments.

*Additional Measures*

Of all the product development cycle time measures, Hewlett-Packard's break-even time (BET) metric has received the most attention.[2] Illustrated in Exhibit 9.10, the BET metric is used for planning and tracking development efforts. It was created by H-P to support its own FCT efforts and has met with mixed receptions in and out of H-P.

In planning a product, the BET metric is used to compare development opportunities and strategies. For example, two or three products can be compared. One product might be examined using short lead time components that are more expensive versus standard lead time parts that cost less. The metric does not contain any information that one could not put together in a time series of return-on-investment analyses. One could produce a spreadsheet analysis using alternate assumptions based on different introduction dates; however, the BET metric is graphical and makes time much more visible.

During project execution, an actual-cost line is added to the chart, and the break-even time is adjusted based on how the development proceeds. If the effort runs into trouble, break-even time may move out. If a competitor surprises you with a similar product, it might also move, even if the project is on time.

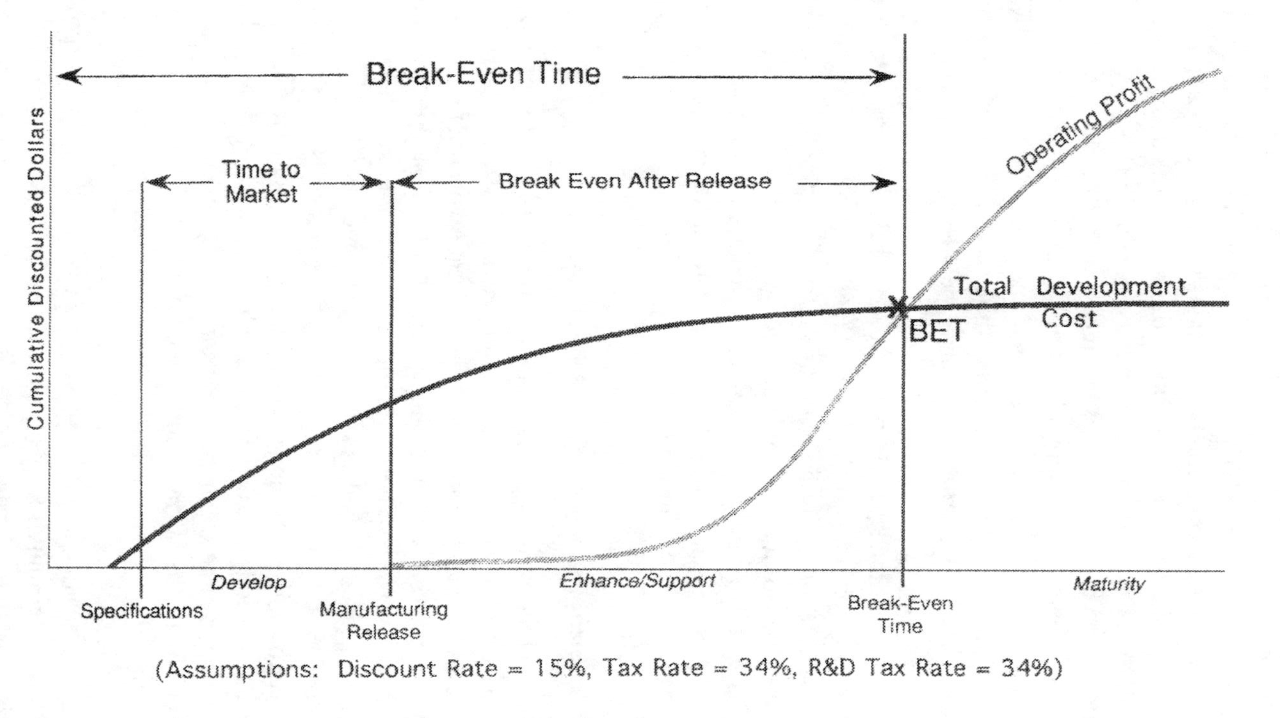


(Assumptions: Discount Rate = 15%, Tax Rate = 34%, R&D Tax Rate = 34%)

**EXHIBIT 9.10**

Because the metric uses profit as a central variable, one has to be able to isolate a product's revenues and costs. Many companies continue to use periodic accounting systems that do not easily produce that information. Furthermore, a product for a brand-new manufacturing facility has to carry more depreciation costs than the same product in an older plant. The metric is easier to use on H-P's more discrete products, such as test equipment, than it is on the more integrated computer products.

The metric can create a bias toward only selecting products that take less time to develop. Development of new platforms or operating systems may be required for competitive reasons but show a longer BET. The goal of reducing development cycle time should apply to large and small projects. The BET metric can drive people to only select small projects.

We conducted a small experiment and used the BET metric to test the McKinsey study's findings that a 50% development cost overrun would only cause a 3.5% loss in profits over the lifetime of a product. The metric confirmed the study's findings, with the qualification that the money had to be invested in regular intervals over the course of the project. Simply throwing money at a project that was two-thirds completed, but stalled, did not produce the same results.

### *Phase 3: Launch*

FCT should be launched quickly. The most powerful way to communicate that cycle time is important is to minimize the time between the first mention of FCT to an employee and their direct involvement in the effort. Not doing so sends an invisible message that speaks louder than any of management's words. Therefore, the definition of complete strategy development is whether one can launch quickly and smoothly.

With this in mind, the first component of the launch is companywide communication and orientation to FCT. This should begin with why FCT is important and how your firm is going to implement it. Without a clear understanding, people will mistakenly think of FCT as "work speed up." Specifically define the business advantage for the company, the major elements of the strategy, how individuals can contribute, and what support will be provided.

The communication should cascade from the top down and purposefully extend the common language developed by organization's leaders during their strategy development. Establishing a common language greatly facilitates people understanding what is meant by terms such as *cycle time, value added,* and *defects.* As much as possible, the initial communication should be conducted by senior management. By using its time for this task, it underlines FCT's importance.

After the orientation, different populations will require more detailed education and training. In addition to the orientation, anyone who serves on a redesign effort should be briefed in the purpose and mechanics of that process. This is best done as just-in-time training during the first FCT redesign rather than as a separate effort. In the same fashion, anyone who serves on a multifunctional development team should take part in an early work development workshop with their team.

Most find it important to conduct a more detailed FCT workshop for middle management. This group is critical to establishing long-term "pull" for FCT in contrast to the initial implementation stage, which is biased toward management "push." Providing a learning forum that describes the plan in greater depth and provides measurement tools increases middle managers' understanding and helps them begin unlearning their old behaviors.

Training people in the process of FCT redesign is much faster and easier to do after they have been through a redesign project. Use outside resources initially to conduct the first FCT process redesigns to demonstrate the mapping mechanics, how to examine a process, and how to identify non-value-added work. Typically one initially trains a cadre of internal people, such as the FCT steering committee, to support the redesign efforts. Not everyone needs to have this detailed training.

If the team architecture was not completed during the strategy development, it should be the first thing attacked now. Once completed, the multifunctional development teams can be launched. They will need immediate support, because the first six months of a team's life are the most critical. Those leading the FCT effort should ensure that the early work component of team training is ready for launch within a month of establishing the teams. The sponsor and team leader should plan on being especially busy during this period and avoid additional assignments. Assuming one has chosen to conduct FCT process redesign and implement multifunctional design teams in parallel, one can expect to encounter the issues shown in Exhibit 9.11.

### *Measurements*

Measurements play a major role in the launch phase. By establishing cycle time metrics, people across the organization take the first step toward integrating FCT into their daily work. Measures should be established for each value delivery process selected. Executive management should

| | Issues | Suggestions |
|---|---|---|
| FCT Process Redesign | Cycle time definition takes longer to set than expected | • Go with what makes sense and don't aim for perfection |
| | Redesign process drags out | • Start only what you can finish crisply |
| | People get bogged down arguing about the maps instead of the process | • Use outsiders to help with the mapping and to keep the group moving |
| | Obstacles are identified, but changes don't get implemented | • Establish new measures quickly<br>• Executive management must identify obstacles to implementation and remove<br>• Use outsiders as change agents |
| | Removing obstacles requires changes not currently possible due to customer or other issues | • Ask, if not now, when? Test what *portion* of change can be made today<br>• Commit to clear change plan and *stick to it* |
| | First successes are smaller than goals established | • Celebrate any success visibly and reiterate long-term goals |
| Multi-functional Development Teams | Functional/team conflict is rife | • Expect it during the first six months<br>• Executive management works from top down and team leaders/sponsors work from bottom up<br>• CEO must work with functional leaders if resistance persists |
| | Obstacles and issues arise that were not foreseen and don't get addressed | • Resolve quickly through team leaders and sponsors<br>• If impasse, elevate quickly to executives for resolution<br>• Empower teams to raise obstacles as high as necessary |
| | Some team members start to fail in new role | • Support where possible; otherwise change<br>• Re-examine selection criteria |
| | A team begins to fail | • Make top issue for sponsor and involve executives<br>• Do what it takes to help team win without doing job for them<br>• Diagnose and check other teams for how they handle issue |
| | Functions/support groups express displeasure over team's role | • Specify concerns and identify as resistance or issues to be addressed<br>• Respond to both directly |
| | Learning doesn't move from team to team | • Use FCT steering committee to facilitate |

**EXHIBIT 9.11**

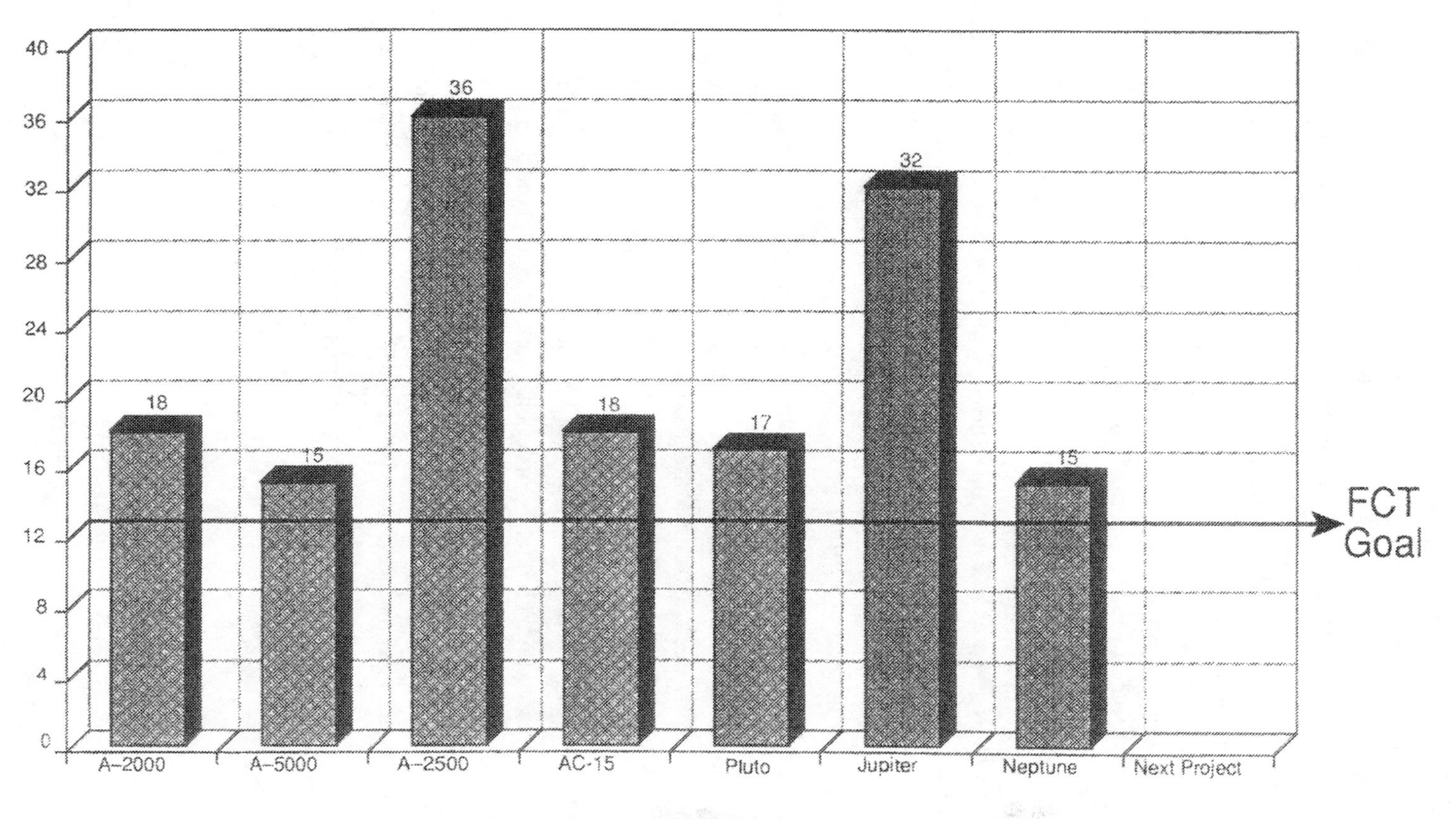
40
36
32
28
24
20
16
12
8
4
0
18
15
36
18
17
32
15
FCT Goal
A–2000
A–5000
A–2500
AC-15
Pluto
Jupiter
Neptune
Next Project

**EXHIBIT 9.12**

model the use of these measures as part of their normal business management and request others do the same.

The baselines can also be used as a first-level diagnostic by operating units. In Exhibit 9.12, the firm's product development cycle time goal is contrasted to past efforts. The chart invites conversation about why one project was quick, followed by a very slow one and then another quick one. The discussion is important, for it raises sensitivity to design strategies and processes.

Additionally, organizational units should begin using measures that support their work. The examples below contain measures that we have found to be extremely effective for supporting FCT implementation. The specific measures you choose should be based on the behaviors that are most important to change in order to improve cycle time and reduce defects. Use the measures as diagnostics and involve those whose behavior you want to change in creating and maintaining the measures. Although each is not illustrated, all of these should be produced as graphics.

### *Engineering Change Orders*

Engineering change orders (Exhibit 9.13) are a very good indication of cycle time problems. Traditional product development has a large number, and they peak at mass production; FCT companies have fewer, and these usually occur earlier. Mass production increases the number, but not as dramatically.

### *Engineering Change Order Cycle Time*

The velocity at which change orders are closed is as critical as the number of them. Because change orders vary in complexity, it is impossible to establish a generic standard. Baseline the current average change order cycle time for all change orders originating during the month and track on an ongoing basis, showing the average, longest, and shortest.

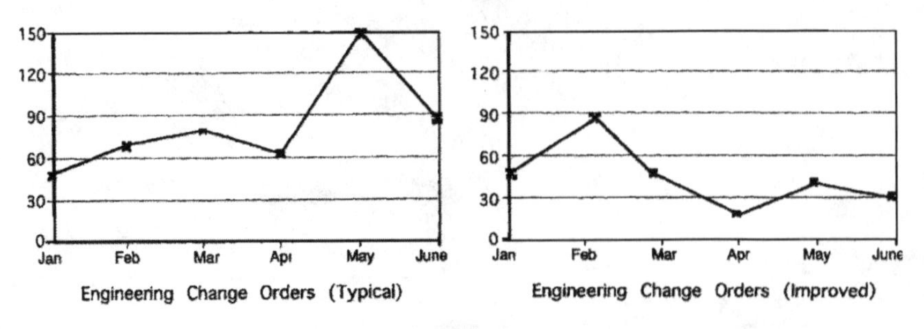


**EXHIBIT 9.13**

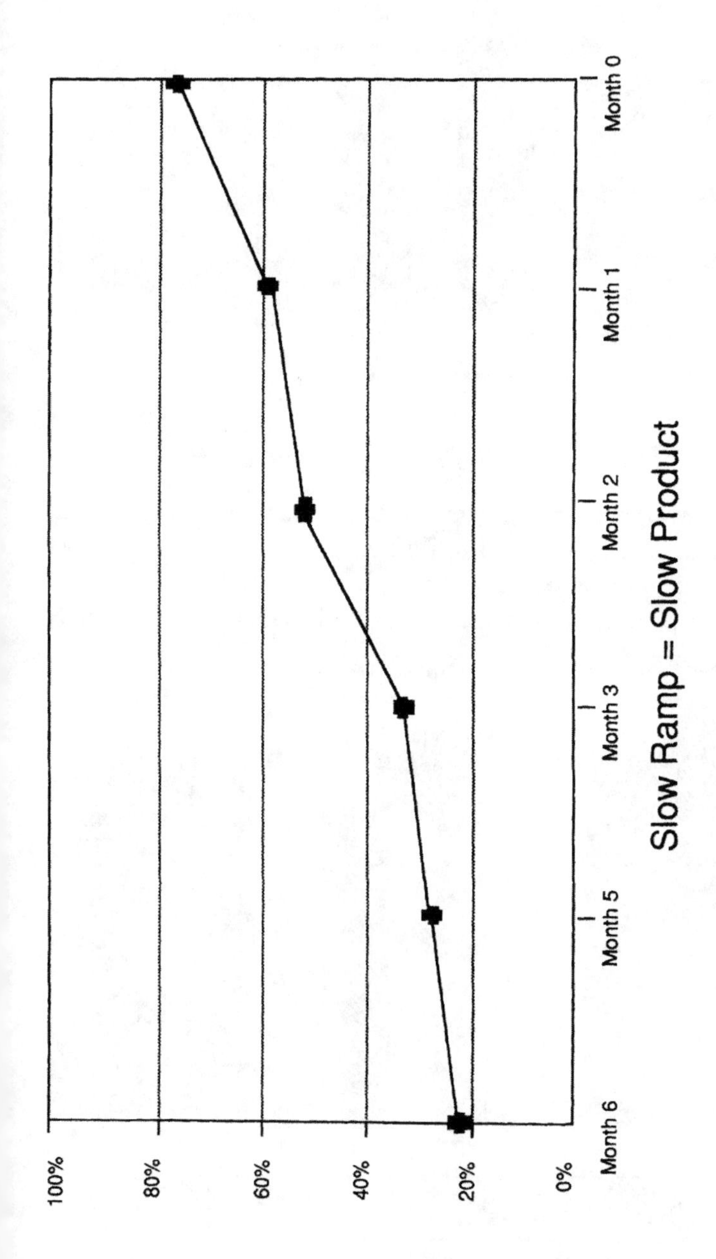


Slow Ramp = Slow Product

**EXHIBIT 9.14**

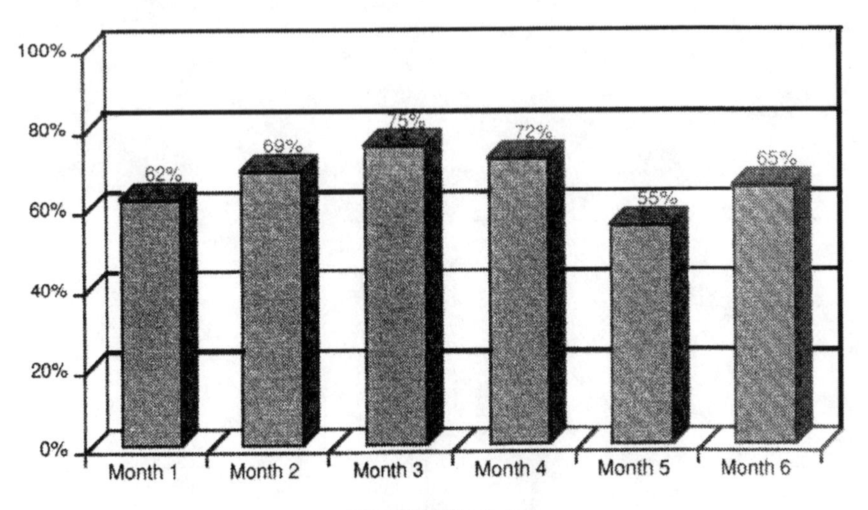


**EXHIBIT 9.15**

*Time Allocated to Development Prior to Mass Production*

This can be a powerful measure when getting critical mass on a development is a major issue because of roll-off or trying to multiplex people between several projects at once. One can also measure time from project approval to approved staffing levels. Slow ramps mean slow products (Exhibit 9.14).

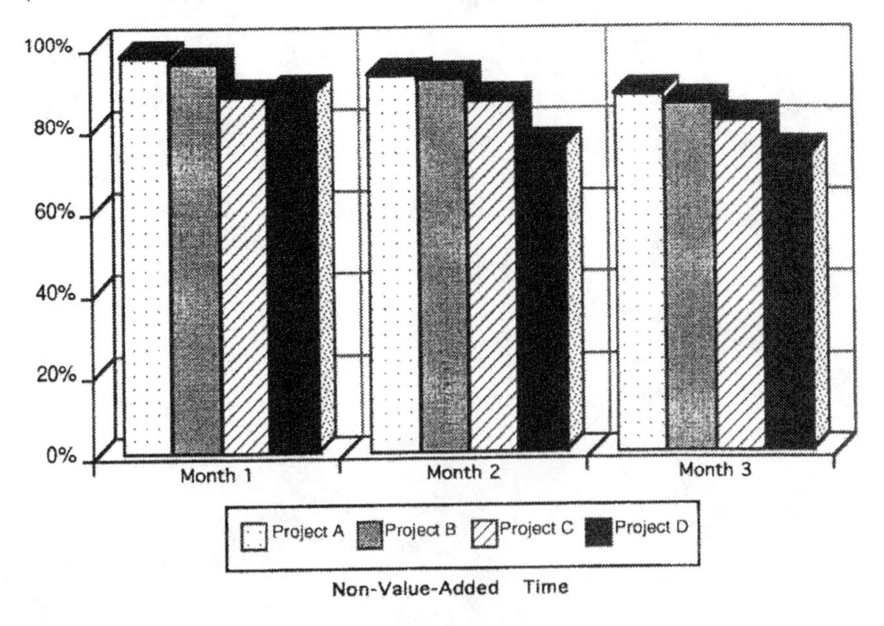


**EXHIBIT 9.16**

*Percentage Completed on Time*

One can also track the number of tasks per month that are completed on time (Exhibit 9.15). It is very important when using this measure to use it diagnostically rather than punitively. The focus is to understand what is causing the slips, whether from technology development or unresolved strategic issues. The goal is to learn, not blame. If people do their own measuring and control the initial learning discussions, they will be less likely to consider the measurements punitive.

*Percentage of Value-Added or Non-Value-Added Time*

This measure can be attacked two ways. One can show value added time, which will yield small indicators, or non-value-added time, which has big indicators (Exhibit 9.16). The measure requires a clear definition of value-added work. This measure is very effective and easy to use in operations and a bit more difficult in development, because there will initially be some controversy about what is value added.

*Design Defect Tracking*

This metric is used widely in the software industry to track bugs. The graph (Exhibit 9.17) is cumulative and separates defects into five categories: unknown, understood, designed fix, implemented fix, and verified fix. It is used to speed up learning and ensure that work is thorough. The last bar is not completed because the product life cycle may end before all fixes can be verified.

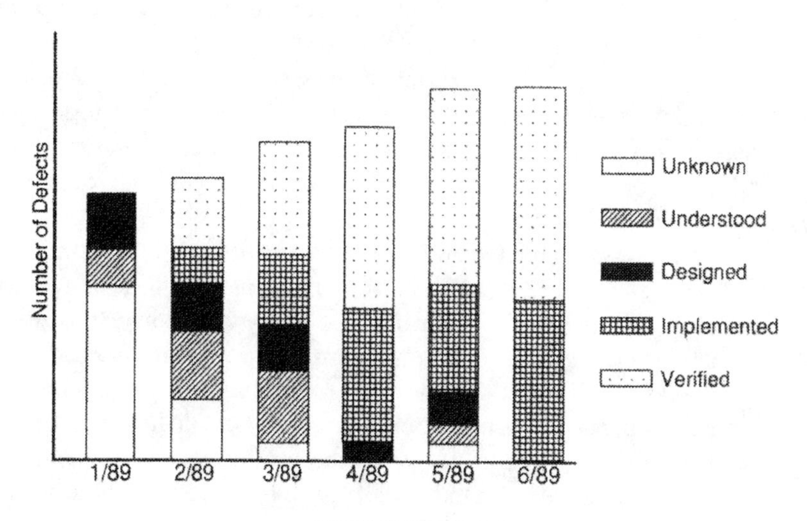


**EXHIBIT 9.17**

***Phase 4: Ongoing Change Management***

A key ingredient for FCT implementation is ongoing executive attention and management. Senior management cannot delegate FCT to another group, because it is the way the business is managed. It remains responsible for the overall architecture and must assess how it is working on an ongoing basis. As the organization catches its rhythm, this role will shift from a constant monitoring to a periodic check-in. During the first year or two, it will be a constant subject of conversation.

One can expect that as the firm peels away the initial cycle time barriers, new obstacles will emerge that require different solutions. For example, many companies find that it takes about a year to make substantial progress on the obstacles identified in the first FCT redesign. One organization discovered that its product concept work was not completed until about a month before it finished the first prototypes. The second prototypes often looked nothing like the first and reflected much wasted effort due to the late product definition. After a year and a half, it had resolved this problem, and in doing so revealed that its supply base was so conditioned to responding to the firm's need for turning prototype parts rapidly that it had lost much of its capability to supply volume production parts. The supply base became the next issue to address.

Business changes will also require adjustments. As customer needs change and markets redefine themselves, the team management structure will have to be realigned to new products and markets. Personnel changes will also require reconfiguring teams. Products will finish development, and people will be assigned to other developments.

Equally important are the tensions one should expect. By definition, the change will cause some instability in the organization. One cannot have change without it, but one should also be sensitive to protecting key accounts and people. For example, safety procedures are often identified as a cycle time barrier. Gaining cycle time at the expense of safety is not acceptable, but neither is exempting safety from cycle time improvement. Extra caution must be taken here.

Crutches such as quality inspections, inventory buffers, and testing will be exposed. As slack resources and buffers disappear, the total system interdependency increases. Everyone has to learn how to manage processes as part of a large system. In the process, some jobs will be redundant once key bottlenecks are resolved. For example, there are many forms of expediting in organizations, from account managers who do little more than push sales orders through the system to the production floor expediter. Executives will have to stay out ahead of these issues as they emerge.

Overall management is more intensive in an FCT company. Communication requirements with large groups such as teams or groups of teams increase. Problems are much more open, as is conflict. It is critical that senior management lead in developing a tenacious attitude toward data and a compassion for the people involved; otherwise, implementation will start to drift. Executives should be thoughtful about the message they send with their public behavior. The more their behavior is in alignment with what they are asking of others, the more likely it is that implementation will flow smoothly.

Management should take the lead in focusing the organization by eliminating options from discussion. For example, there always seems to be a product derivative that is found midway through a development effort. In the disk-drive industry, someone might suggest taking a platter of the drive and quickly making two capacities for the price of one design. Those who have experience know it is rarely as simple as that, yet to the team working on the project, it appears to be. The team is not stupid; it just hasn't run into the problems yet. It takes senior management to say no and stay the course.

*Use of External Change Agents*

Consultants can play a powerful role in FCT strategy development and implementation. The challenge is to use them for their fresh ideas and experience without becoming dependent on them. The most effective define their own success by how much the firm improves *and* makes critical the behavioral changes required to sustain that improvement rate. To do this, the consultants must transfer their skills to the client organization. External change agents also provide anecdotes and experience that help people take the first steps. No matter what any book says, until a person has actually achieved a significant success, 50% cycle time improvement opportunities are not readily apparent.

The most effective change agents understand what it takes to change human systems and all the complexities that these entail. As we will see shortly when we return to Core Products, no FCT implementation follows a clean line. Some things happen that are unexpected, and other things happen that are expected but not at the time they actually occur.

## Core Products, Inc.—Implementation

During the strategic alignment planning process in late 1988, Core Products first sensed that the performance gap between itself and its prime competitor had grown to alarming proportions. Its traditional reputation for performance and quality was no longer as compelling for its customers as it historically had been. Its competitor was a younger but faster-growing company that produced new products faster than CP. CP believed its competitor's products had serious quality problems that would constrain its growth but three straight years of success made this more a wish than a reality. The competitor was compensating by shrinking the size of its product so that the computer manufacturers could do likewise. Even though it had unresolved quality issues, computer companies were buying its products instead of CP's products. CP was finding itself too frequently in the position of having to unseat the competition to make a sale.

With the performance gap clear, CP executives began to educate themselves about FCT through internal and external benchmarking, a site visit to a company that was using multifunctional development teams, and support from an external change agent. The problem recognition period took about four months. CP's CEO, Brad Worster, was itching to get started but used the time to convince his team this was the right thing to do. The site visit conducted in May, combined with the completion of the strategic alignment planning process, pushed Brad over the edge.

CP chose to begin by implementing multifunctional teams. Rather than limiting the team's charter to product development, it segmented its business by product lines and established teams for each. Two of these teams were development teams, but with the expectation that they would be responsible for managing their products through the end of the products' life. One product was already in production, and that team focused on operations.

In retrospect, the choice to implement multifunctional teams before FCT process redesign was based on three reasons. First, CP could clearly see that its functional chimneys were a major obstacle to decision and development speed. Too many decisions ended up in the executive staff's lap simply because lower-level functional managers could not agree. The lack of agreement at the lower levels was only a reflection of how the functional leaders worked within Worster's own staff. Second, the executive staff felt confident that it could design an effective team-based structure without extensive study. The members understood the development process sufficiently to know who should be in the development team's core leadership group. CP bet that starting teams would get FCT gains just by having the right people in real-time contact. Third, Worster had confidence that between CP and the external resource, they would figure out how to make it work even if it was not designed perfectly from the beginning.

In June 1989, CP executives spent two days crafting the team architecture. The teams were started by July 1, and by September, each had completed early work and was performing well. Of the three teams, two performed quite well from the start, whereas one struggled. During this time, team leaders reported on their business weekly to Worster's staff. Worster's staff members placed "team management implementation" as a standing item on their agenda during this period and had the external resource join them for the team reports and implementation discussion.

In September, Worster, the team leaders, the sponsors, and the external resource met to discuss the growing team–function conflicts. They agreed to meet as often as necessary to work on the issue as a subgroup that became nicknamed the "lunch club." The lunch club had all the players who were deeply involved, and though it was not a formal decision-making group, it provided a forum for airing and resolving issues. At one point, the club decided to hold a meeting with all the core group members from each team to discuss many of these issues. The value of the meeting lay more in that it demonstrated management's commitment to making the team management structure work more than in the invention of new answers to the problem.

By the end of 1989, two of the teams were functioning so smoothly that people were asking why CP had not done this earlier. The third team continued to have serious problems and went through many changes during the fall. First, the team leader was changed, and the sponsor was asked to take a stronger role in working with the new team leader. Then the second team leader failed, and the sponsor became the temporary acting leader of the team. This helped the team go forward, but it was not a team as initially conceived anymore; people did what the VP sponsor told them to do. Then the VP sponsor left the organization, a new team leader was appointed, and a *trio* of executives asked to be sponsors for this one team. One had to ask, what was going on here?

This team was responsible for expanding CP's product line into a new, higher-performance market. It developed and managed a set of products that were vital to CP's continued growth but were losing money. Since birth, this team had struggled, and as most organizations do, each failure met with adding more support to the team. In retrospect, everything one could think of was eventually tried. Team leaders, sponsors, and core group members were all changed at one point or another.

The root cause of the problems was twofold. First, the core leadership group was not the same strength as the other two teams. To establish three teams, CP had stretched to the limits of its resource capabilities, and it showed. More importantly, the functional strength behind the core group was sorely lacking for these products. The team's troubles were a reflection of the lack of capability in engineering, operations, and marketing as much as among themselves. CP began to come to grips with this and, beginning in 1990, started on the long road to develop the capabilities throughout the organization to compete effectively in this market. It saw that the team's problems were symptomatic of a much deeper issue.

By late fall, the teams no longer required constant attention from the executives, and they began to discuss what was their next FCT step. Based on the competitor's time-to-market capability, it started by focusing on one value delivery process—new product development. During the first months of 1990, it analyzed this process and identified several major improvement targets, including the need to develop a crisp process for launching products, reducing the amount of invention per product through common architecture, and increasing the leverage of software across products.

Using an FCT steering committee approach, CP developed a new product development handbook that contained the Should map developed during the FCT process redesign and tips on how to make it a reality. The steering committee began circulating a "what works" log that captured successes and techniques from each of the development teams. The steering committee also created baseline measures for the development cycle and general education program.

During 1990, CP implemented what it had learned in the FCT redesign process. The year was one of enormous change but not dominated by any one action. The company established its first co-located team, redefined the role of advanced technology development, educated everyone in the corporation on FCT, developed a plan (through the strategic alignment process) for acquiring technology earlier in the development process, and more. At the end of 1990, the steering committee assessed its successes and disappointments and established a plan for the coming year.

At the end of the first quarter of 1991, the products launched since CP began its FCT program were due. As one might have predicted, two teams were highly successful, and the third still struggled. The two successful products beat the competition to the market. In one case, the success was initially muted by a soft market; this caused dismay, for people felt that if they were first, victory would be theirs. Although they were first this time, they had to unseat their competitor, who was the incumbent because of its prior success. By midyear, however, the market firmed, and CP's product took off and doubled the business plan's revenue projection. The other successful product was a screaming success from the beginning. The demand was so strong that the rest of CP's organization was not prepared to handle it. CP's FCT success was muted by its inability to capitalize on the demand created by its FCT product development process. In late 1991, CP began a second FCT process redesign effort in product development. With so much changed, it was time to take a new look at FCT obstacles and opportunities.

CP's leaders credit their FCT efforts as being a major reason the company's revenues and profits grew *four times* above its initial efforts in late 1988. Its executives have exemplified what we mean by ongoing change management through their high degree of ownership and involvement in the overall effort. Their inability to capitalize on their success with FCT in product development had made it clear that now is the time to extend FCT beyond the product development process. As they add the order-to-fulfillment and customer problem resolution processes to their FCT agenda, they continue to attach product development cycle time and defect reduction.

One would have to call CP's success a happy ending, but by no means a perfect one. The faltering high-performance business continues to struggle. The amount of push required from senior management is still more than desired. Some gains in development speed are threatened by the expanding requests for support services as the customer base grows. The bottom line is the race is never over: although FCT has not solved all of CP's problems, it has enabled the firm to achieve remarkable success.

# 10

# Leaders Pave the Road Ahead

In a time of drastic change, it is the learners who inherit the future. The learned find themselves equipped to live in a world that no longer exists.

—Eric Hoffer

In the course of one project, we were asked to help educate our client's executives about what FCT is and how to implement it. While preparing, we learned of a very successful FCT redesign effort that had already taken place within the client's organization. We suggested that perhaps the most powerful statement we could make about leading FCT implementation would be a question-and-answer session with representatives from this effort.

The idea was embraced, and as we observed each session, we noticed a distinct pattern to the series of questions and the answers. People sat quietly until the presenter mentioned a change or result the group achieved that seemed remarkable to the participants within this organization. Once this happened, the intensity of the questioning increased a notch as the executives probed for the "real story." The testing phase continued for about a half hour, until the executives were satisfied that they had the whole story. People were eventually convinced that what they heard was real, but there was still something unbelievable to it. Their questions shifted to a new level that was more thoughtful and less contentious. At one point someone usually asked, "Did you think you'd be this successful from the beginning?"

The answer was always the same. The representatives thought the goals their leader set gave new meaning to the idea of "stretch goals," but at the same time, he clearly *believed* they could do it. During one session, the representative said to the executives, "At some point, you have to get beyond all the analysis and strategy and just do it because you believe you can. Our boss believed it was possible, and soon we did."

In our experience, no matter how much one prepares, there comes a point where one has to say "Let's go" and just do it. The only guarantee we can make regarding implementation is that it will *not* go exactly according to plan. If anyone claims theirs did, we suggest they must have missed a lot of opportunities along the way. Rapidly transforming implementation experience into new learning and action is how leaders lead FCT implementation.

This final chapter describes how to lead the transformation from a traditional company to an FCT competitor. We will begin by applying principles of organization change to FCT implementation and suggest what leaders can do to prepare themselves. We will next share our experience about how people respond to FCT and what you can do to influence them. As part of this, we will discuss how to use the resistance you'll encounter to build readiness for change. We will close with the short list of "musts" that are required to implement a fast cycle time strategy successfully. Throughout, we will try to illuminate some of the wine making that is inseparable from leading change.

The process of implementing FCT can be broken into five phases, as depicted in Exhibit 10.1. During the first phase, the current way of working dominates the workplace. FCT is a discussion item among the firm's leadership and with few exceptions, not operational. The current status and power hierarchy remains intact.[1]

The second phase begins after FCT is formally launched. Selected elements of the organization now begin to use FCT practices. The old ways continue to dominate, but the conflicts with changes initiated by FCT improvement efforts are increasingly visible and challenging. The familiar is under attack by the new way of working; most watch the conflict rather than get directly involved. During this phase, leaders get a taste of where the pockets of support and resistance are the strongest.

The third phase is the most contentious, in that both sets of behaviors coexist at full strength. FCT has critical mass, and every issue seems to be up for grabs. Those who held power under the old way try to stop the erosion that is occurring, while those who lead the new way have a stronger sense of confidence. During this phase, most of the critical obstacles to implementation are flushed out and become highly visible, as those that seek to retain the old ways dig in for battle. To speed implementation, leaders should remove the obstacles as quickly as possible. One ought to measure the cycle time from obstacle identification to removal. This sends a clear message about which approach is backed by management.

Entering the fourth phase, the traditional work system begins to lose strength. Letting go and unlearning become visible among those who were resisting until now. As people become more familiar with the new way of operating, they seek more support and tools. FCT implementation begins to accelerate as the erosion of the traditional practices begins. This culminates in phase five, where traditional methods are for all intents and purposes history, and FCT becomes the new operating methodology.

As the model illustrates, FCT implementation is a process that occurs over time. At its peak in phase three, the experience for many is similar to the sensation a trapeze artist has when he or she lets go of the first trapeze and has yet to grab the second. To many, this period is terribly unsettling, because one doesn't know which rules apply. For change leaders, this is potentially the most exciting time, because everything is unfrozen and real change is possible. Change can be made if the leaders have a clear and consistent FCT vision that they are trying to forge into reality.

Research in human cognition shows that people process information visually. A FCT vision is a picture of the future you are trying to create. The more one can paint what life will be like in the organization after the implementation of FCT, the more compelling the change becomes. A strong and clear vision not only helps people get started, but it provides inspiration during phases two and three when the road turns decidedly

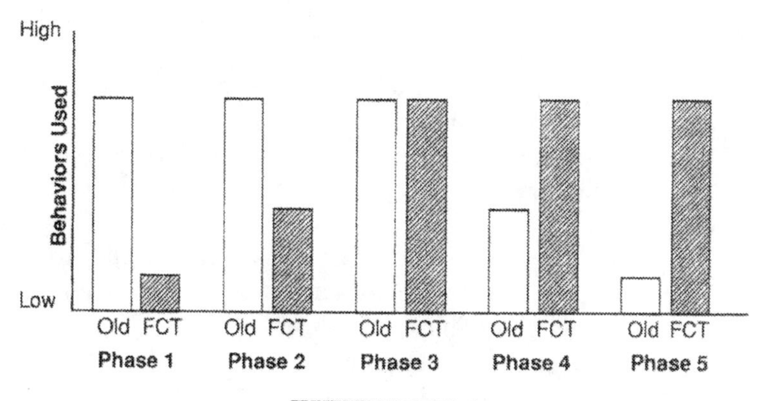


**EXHIBIT 10.1**

uphill. Change is not easy, and common sense suggests that unless people personally identify with the better future, they will lack the stamina and persistence to make it through the turmoil of phase three. The leader's job is to repaint this picture of the future continuously to keep it alive during the transformation process.

A powerful vision has three characteristics.[2] Above all else, it must excite you. If it does not generate your excitement, then you cannot generate excitement in others. Second, it must be challenging and push beyond today's capabilities. Third, it must be achievable so that it invites involvement. Items two and three are always the greatest challenge, because 50% cycle time reductions are indeed achievable, but they do not appear so at the beginning. Case studies, site visits, and simulations can overcome this.

Making it "over the hill" of phase three is dependent on more than the vision. To crest the hill, one has to build momentum. FCT implementation dynamics are like passing someone going uphill while driving an underpowered car. In order to pass safely, one must build up momentum and time the pass carefully. If you try to pass before having momentum, you won't be able to and will actually have to slide back down the hill and start all over again. Sometimes in their zealousness, executives unrealistically try to "fast cycle" implementation and push before the momentum is present. Momentum builds as one person after another understands the change, supports it, and ultimately changes his or her behavior.

When the FCT strategy is first introduced, people typically want to know what is in it for them personally. Depending on how well leaders respond, their personal assessment falls into one of four categories, each with its own consequence:

1. *Destructive.* These people will openly challenge and resist at first. In many respects, these are your best friends, because most of what they say is also bothering others who are unwilling to speak up. This group defines the objections and obstacles your team must have answers for.
2. *Threatened.* This group has many of the same feelings as the first group, but they are often more covert. Rather than standing up, they will gather after meetings and in hallways. In the worst cases, they will openly express their support in public forums but do their utmost to protect the status quo in their own jobs.
3. *Neutral.* This is where the vast majority of people fall. They will listen attentively and participate when asked, but without the commitment that you ultimately want. Their participation and enthusiasm will grow with success, but for now, they support you from the sidelines more than on the field.

4. *Positive.* This is the small group of early adopters. They are enthusiastic, supportive, and often model the behaviors that you are trying to get others to adapt. They are the seed corn of success.

Only the last category is immediately supportive. The secret to building momentum with the others is by involving them in the change process as early as possible. Involvement is essential, because it provides the digestion and unlearning process that allows people to make FCT theirs rather than yours. Until this happens, FCT is management's baby.

As illustrated in Exhibit 10.2, shortcutting the involvement process feels like speeding up implementation, but it actually does not accomplish this.[3] Until people feel positive about FCT through education, tools and understanding, they can comply with management's initiatives, but they cannot initiate themselves. To spread implementation, one needs action from those who are not yet on board. Until they take action to reduce cycle time in their daily work, implementation has not moved forward. The "fast cycle" shortcut underestimates the importance of building momentum.

This does not mean that one should meander one's way to FCT. In fact, one should try to involve people rapidly. The only effective way to do this is to design and cascade the FCT rollout carefully from the top down so that people have the understanding and tools (for example, through FCT process redesign) before they are challenged to implement. Then people can identify the critical processes within their work area, define the be-

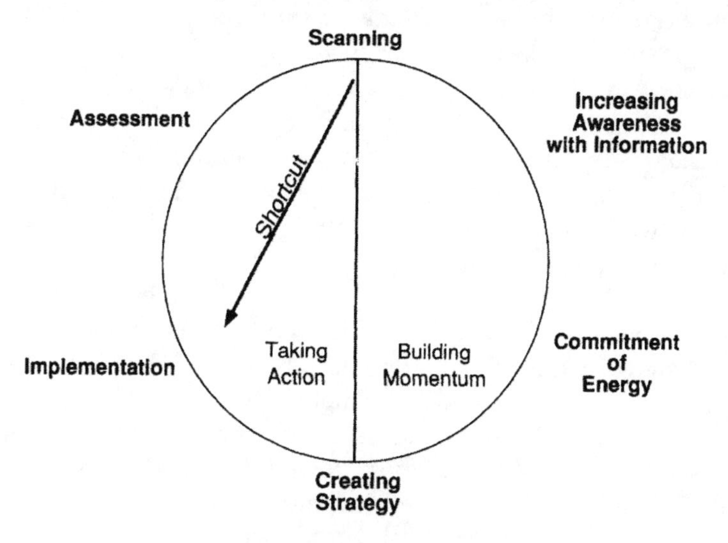


**EXHIBIT 10.2**

ginning and end points for these processes, measure the current cycle time, and begin the FCT redesign process for reducing it.

*Executive management leads by undertaking this same process before it asks others to.* As we have discussed in depth, the highest leverage delays are up and to the left. Executive management is as far up as one can get. By the very nature of his or her position, the executive's time horizon should be longer than that of most others in the company. When executives actively model implementation by identifying the processes that are critical at their level, measuring the current cycle time and establishing improvement plans via FCT process redesign, they "walk their talk," and this speaks loudly to others.

For example, a ripe and highly leveraged area for executive improvement is decision cycle time. Executives should consider identifying processes where their decision is required for the rest of the organization to move forward, baseline their current decision cycle time, study the process, and define an improvement strategy. These measures and improvement goals should be integrated into their normal management process.

The value of identifying and improving executive processes is much greater than just providing a good example for others. By involving themselves in the FCT implementation process, executives personalize the change for themselves. They learn what one gains and loses personally when they do it themselves. As large and impersonal as organizations can be, organizational change is a very personal process that happens one person at a time; this includes executives. Until you personally have struggled to identify the key processes that add value in your job, there is a limit to how much contact and trust you can generate with others you ask to do the same thing. People do not change because it is good for the organization. They change because they care and trust those who are asking for the change. If you as leader have not rolled up your sleeves and done the work, your ability to make the human contact that generates trust is missing.

The active leadership and commitment of the chief executive officer is the essential prerequisite for achieving the executive involvement described above. If the CEO does not lead by example and push the other executives when required, FCT will not get out of the starting blocks. By definition, if the CEO makes FCT implementation a personal objective, the rest of the executives will do so as well. The most successful implementations we witness occur when there is no question that the CEO views implementation of fast cycle time as a personal priority.

Despite all one's efforts, some critical people may still resist. How do you deal with them? The first step is not to take the resistance personally. Resistance is usually expressed personally, but its roots are not. When people resist, they are scared about losing something. And when people are scared, their language and expressions are emotionally contagious. Show compassion for their feelings, but avoiding getting hooked into as the antagonist role.

Second, held broaden people's awareness of the change by helping others see what they will gain, while also openly discussing what they will lose. When scared, people tend to lock in on one or two negative elements of the change and artificially inflate the consequences. Co-location can shift from the reality of being located with others on the project to permanent banishment from the function, which then leads to never being considered for a promotion again! Acknowledge people's primary fears, and then help them see other issues and opportunities. Obviously, for someone to commit rather than just comply with the change, they have to see more positives than negatives. Make sure these are visible, but don't be Pollyanna. People will be much more likely to commit when they know both sides of the story.

Third, never forget to listen closely to the concerns expressed. Most resistance is not irrational by any means; people will certainly identify issues that you and your team have overlooked and need to address. One should not try to bowl over every objection but rather understand what the root problem is; in many cases, you will be thankful you did. Involve those with objections in creating alternatives that enable FCT without causing the problems they foresee.

Fourth, keep a spirit of openness. Get the concerns out on the table and work through them. Creating an environment where those that resist feel they must go underground is deadly. If people feel it is unsafe to go public, it will be very difficult to win them over. Make it attractive to learn FCT.

Last, despite all the above, you will possibly encounter some people for whom operating in an FCT organization just does not fit. If one gets to the point where separation seems to be the only solution, one must be prepared to do so. Without question, this group is in the minority, but it does occur.

## The Short List of Musts

FCT is a way of managing that almost screams the word *focus* at every turn. In that spirit, our closing comments are the short list of what one must do to become a successful FCT competitor.

1. Manage and constantly improve the work processes that add value to the end customer(s)
2. Know the needs of your end customer(s) at every job and level within the organization
3. Redesign your organization so that it is flat and multifunctional-team based, with blurred boundaries inside and out
4. Pursue process development as avidly as product or service development
5. Establish cycle time measures, set "stretch" goals, and publicly measure progress as part of your ongoing management system.
6. Create an environment that stimulates and rewards continuous learning and action

Without question, if you make significant progress on each of the above, you will be well on the road to becoming a fast cycle time competitor. Does it take hard work? Of course; based on our experience, though, you will also find it one of the most exhilarating transformations that you have ever seen.

## Closing Comments

Let us leave with one final thought. FCT is, above all else, a way to manage. Every management concept has a premise through which it seeks to steer the organization. What excites us about FCT is that the premise of managing process cycle time generates a competitive advantage and provides a simple methodology for managers and employees at all levels to work by.

First, anyone with a watch can measure cycle time. Second, by measuring cycle time, we immediately turn people's attention to the processes that generate results and errors. Although process management has been discussed for years by the quality movement, until FCT we lacked a clear method for spreading it across the entire organization. And by doing so we improve quality, because one cannot make mistakes and be fast. Third, speed demands empowerment and involvement. The most insightful and knowledgeable leader will eventually run out of time to lead others directly. FCT establishes the minimum constraints that enable people to break down the functional silos and lead together, without the overhead of daily supervision and management that functional organizations require.

Last, people thrive on accomplishment. When you manage through fast cycle time, you accomplish more.

# Notes

## *Chapter 1: Implementing Fast Cycle Time*

1. George Stalk, Jr., and Thomas M. Hout, *Competing Against Time* (New York: Free Press, 1990).

## *Chapter 2: Be Fast or Be Last*

1. An excellent review of the limitations of technology-based leadership can be found in Kim Clark, "What Strategy Can Do for Technology," *Harvard Business Review*, November–December 1989, p. 9.
2. For further information on the auto industry, see Kim Clark and Takahiro Fujimoto, *Product Development Performance* (Boston: Harvard Business School Press, 1991) and James P. Womack, Daniel T. Jones, and Daniel Roos, *The Machine That Changed the World* (New York: Rawson Associates, 1990).
3. There are several terms used in addition to fast cycle time. "Time-based competition" is favored by George Stalk, Jr., and Thomas M. Hout in *Competing Against Time* (New York: Free Press, 1990), whereas "total cycle time" is used by Philip R. Thomas, *Competitiveness Through Total Cycle Time* (New York: McGraw Hill, 1990). Other works in the field include Joseph D. Blackburn, *Time-Based Competition* (Homewood, IL: Business One Irwin, 1991) and Preston G. Smith and Donald G. Reinertsen, *Developing Products in Half the Time* (New York: Van Nostrand Reinhold, 1991).

4. Christopher Meyer, "Reducing Cycle Time for Sustained Competitive Advantage," *Strategic Alignment Group Monograph,* The Strategic Alignment Group, Portola Valley, CA, 1989.
5. See Joseph D. Blackburn, "Just-in-Time: The Genesis of Time Compression," in Joseph D. Blackburn, *Time-Based Competition* (Homewood, IL: Business One Irwin, 1991), p. 24.
6. For further information on new methodologies in product development, see Stephen C. Wheelwright and Kim B. Clark, *Revolutionizing Product Development* (New York: Free Press, 1992).
7. Steven C. Wheelwright and Kim B. Clark, *Revolutionizing Product Development* (New York: Free Press, 1992).
8. "Lotus Fights to Regain Share with Discounts," *Wall Street Journal,* September 5, 1991, p. B4.
9. Michael L. Dertouzoset et al., *Made in America* (Cambridge, MA: The MIT Press, 1989).

*Chapter 3: Fast Cycle Time: The Basics*

1. See Preston G. Smith and Donald G. Reinertsen, *Developing Products in Half the Time* (New York: Von Nostrand Reinhold, 1991), p. 49.
2. Adapted from Christopher Meyer, "Six to Becoming a Fast Cycle Time Competitor," *Strategic Alignment Group Monograph,* The Strategic Alignment Group, Portola Valley, CA, 1990.
3. My initial contact with the terminology "value delivery system" was in a draft for a McKinsey & Company, Inc. *Staff* paper by Michael J. Lanning and Edward G. Michaels, "A Business Is A Value Delivery System," 1987.
4. Joseph B. White and Melinda Grenier Guiles, "GM's Plan for Saturn," *Wall Street Journal,* January 1, 1990, p. 1.
5. Jim Swartz, *Design of World Class Operations* (Kokomo, IN: Competitive Action, Inc., 1989).
6. Learning loops are also called Cycles of Learning in Philip R. Thomas, *Competitiveness Through Total Cycle Time* (New York: McGraw Hill, 1990).
7. Jeffrey Rothfeder, Jim Bartimo, Lois Therrien, and Richard Brandt, "How Software Is Making Food Sales a Piece of Cake," *Business Week,* July 2, 1990, pp. 54–55, and Jeremy Main, "Frito-Lay Shortens Its Business Cycle," *Fortune,* January 15, 1990, p. 11.
8. The concept of destiny is adapted from Stanley M. Davis, *Future Perfect* (Reading, MA: Addison Wesley, 1987), p. 69.
9. Ikujiro Nanoka, "Redundant, Overlapping Organization: A Japanese Approach to Managing the Innovation Process," *California Management Review,* Summer, 1990.
10. Experts in the field of socio-technical systems design have long advocated this position. See William A. Pasmore, *Designing Effective Organizations* (New York: John Wiley & Sons, 1988).

11. Much has been written about the role of vision in organizations yet without clear agreement. The most powerful influences on my thinking include the work of Innovation Associations, Framingham, MA; Rick Ross, Ross Partners, Encinitas, CA; Peter Block, *The Empowered Manager* (San Francisco, Jossey-Bass, 1987); Dick Richards and Sarah Engel, "After the Vision," in John D. Adams, editor, *Transforming Leadership* (Alexandria, VA: Miles River Press, 1986), and Peter M. Senge, *Fifth Discipline* (New York: Doubleday, 1990).
12. The concept of strategic alignment is an expansion of alignment as discussed in Charles F. Kiefer and Peter Stroh, "A New Paradigm for Developing Organizations," in John D. Adams, *Transforming Work* (Alexandria, VA: Miles River Press, 1984, p. 171). Further discussion on organizational and strategic alignment can be found in a paper by Peter M. Senge, "Systems Dynamics and Leadership," Institute of Electrical and Electronics Engineers, International Conference on Cybernetics and Society, 1980, and Charles Stubbart, "Why We Need a Revolution in Strategic Planning," *Long Range Planning*, Vol. 18, No. 6 (1985), p. 72.
13. The interest in organizational learning has blossomed in recent years. See Donald Schön, *The Reflective Practitioner* (New York: Basic Books, 1983); Peter M. Senge, *The Fifth Discipline* (New York: Doubleday, 1990); and Chris Argyris, *Strategy, Change and Defensive Routines* (Marshfield, MA: Pitman, 1985).
14. Robert H. Hayes, Steven C. Wheelwright, and Kim B. Clark, *Dynamic Manufacturing* (New York: Free Press, 1988), p. 314.
15. Joseph T. Vesey, "The New Competitors: They Think in Terms of 'Speed-to-Market,'" *Academy of Management Executive*, Vol. 5, No. 2 (1991), p. 25.
16. The socio-technical school of organization design has focused on co-location long before cycle time advocates suggested it. See Fritz Steele, *Physical Settings and Organization Development* (Reading, MA: Addison Wesley, 1973).

## *Chapter 4: Systems and Organizational Learning*

1. My initial contact with systems thinking was as an undergraduate at the University of Pennsylvania with Russell Ackoff. See Russell L. Ackoff, *A Concept of Corporate Planning* (New York: John Wiley, 1970); also, by the same author, *Redesigning the Future* (New York: John Wiley, 1974), and *The Art of Problem Solving* (New York: John Wiley, 1978). The term "systems thinking" as used here refers to the work of Jay W. Forrester, Massachusetts Institute of Technology, in systems dynamics. Barry Richmond of High Performing Systems, Inc., Lyme, NH, was my personal mentor in this regard. See Barry Richmond, Peter Vescuso, and Steven Peterson, *Stella*™ *For Business: Users Guide* (Lyme, NH: High Performing Systems, 1987), and Barry Richmond, Steve Peterson, and Peter Vescuso, *An Academic User's Guide to Stella*™ (Lyme, NH: High Performing Systems, 1987). In

addition, my conversations with Mike Goodman of Innovative Associates, Framingham, MA; Rick Ross of Ross Partners, Encinitas, CA; and Peter M. Senge of Center for Organizational Learning, Massachusetts Institute of Technology furthered my knowledge. See Peter M. Senge, Fifth Discipline (New York: Doubleday, 1990); and, by the same author, a paper entitled "Systems Dynamics as an Artifact for the Systems Age," International Systems Dynamics Conference, 1983. A useful newsletter on systems thinking is The Systems Thinker, Pegasus Communications, Cambridge, MA. For application to organization process improvement, see Geary A. Rummler and Alan P. Brache, Improving Performance (San Francisco: Jossey-Bass, 1990), and Christopher Meyer, "Honoring Complexity: Applying Systems Thinking," Vision/Action (San Francisco: California, December, 1988).

2. Organization learning was first introduced to me, during my doctoral work, by Neely Gardner, University of Southern California, and Herbert Shepard, Case Western Reserve, as a central factor in organization design. Additional sources used in this synthesis include Thomas S. Kuhn, *The Structure of Scientific Revolutions* (Chicago: University of Chicago Press, 1962, 1970); Robert H. Hayes, Steven C. Wheelwright, and Kim B. Clark, *Dynamic Manufacturing* (New York: Free Press, 1988); Arie de Geus, "Planning as Learning," *Harvard Business Review* (March–April, 1988); Peter M. Senge, "The Leader's New Work: Building Learning Organizations," *Sloan Management Review* (Fall 1990); Ray Stata, "Organizational Learning—The Key to Management Innovation," *Sloan Management Review* (Spring 1989); Shoshana Zuboff, *In the Age of the Smart Machine* (New York: Basic Books, 1988), and C. K. Prahalad and Gary Hamel, "The Core Competence of the Corporation," *Harvard Business Review* (May–June, 1990).
3. Barry Richmond, High Performing Systems, Inc., Lyme, NH.
4. George Stalk, Jr., "Time—The Next Source of Competitive Advantage," *Harvard Business Review*, July–August, 1988.
5. Personal conversations with Rick Ross of Ross Partners, Encinitas, CA; Barry Richmond of High Performing Systems, Inc., Lyme, NH; and Mike Goodman of Innovation Associates, Framingham, MA.
6. Described to me by Mark Paich of High Performing Systems, Inc., Lyme, NH.
7. Business Week, May 8, 1989, p. 54.
8. Adapted from a detailed discussion found in Peter M. Senge, *The Fifth Discipline* (New York: Doubleday, 1990), p. 115.
9. For further discussion of value delivery, see George Stalk, Jr., and Thomas M. Hout in *Competing Against Time* (New York: Free Press, 1990), p. 61–67.
10. Illustration adapted from Geary A. Rummler and Alan P. Brache, *Improving Performance* (San Francisco: Jossey-Bass, 1990).
11. George Stalk, Jr., and Thomas M. Hout, *Competing Against Time* (New York: Free Press, 1990), p. 76.

12. Stanley M. Davis, *Future Perfect* (Reading, MA: Addison Wesley, 1987), p. 14–15.
13. *Bay Area Computer Currents,* February 13, 1990, p. 63.
14. Ralph E. Gomory, "From the 'Ladder of Science' to the Product Development Cycle," *Harvard Business Review*, November–December, 1989, p. 99.
15. Donald Schön, *The Reflective Practitioner* (New York: Basic Books, 1983). For further information see Peter M. Senge, *The Fifth Discipline* (New York: Doubleday, 1990), and Chris Argyris and Donald Schön, *Organizational Learning: A Theory of Action Perspective* (Reading, MA: Addison-Wesley, 1978).
16. Russell Ackoff, *Management in Small Doses* (New York: John Wiley, 1986), p. 173.
17. This definition was based on a daylong discussion with Rick Ross of Ross Partners, Encinitas, CA, and Bill Isaacs of Center for Organizational Learning, Massachusetts Institute of Technology, Cambridge, MA.
18. *Fortune,* March 2, 1989, p. 100.
19. Rick Ross, Ross Partners, Encinitas, CA.
20. The concept of unlearning was first introduced to me by Robert Tannenbaum in his NTL Workshop entitled "Holding On, Letting Go," and is based on Kurt Lewin's notion of unfreezing.
21. The concept of organizational learning forums is also being explored by Barry Richmond of High Performing Systems, Inc., Lyme, NH, and Peter M. Senge of Center for Organizational Learning, Massachusetts Institute of Technology, Cambridge, MA. Richmond uses the term "strategic forums" and Senge uses "learning laboratories." Their focus is modeling the dynamic behavior of the organization to drive learning by using systems dynamics.
22. Chris Argyris, *Strategy, Change and Defensive Routines* (Marshfield, MA: Pitman, 1985).
23. "King Customer," *Business Week*, March 12, 1990, p. 91.

## *Chapter 5: Strategic Alignment: Up and to the Left*

1. Peter M. Senge, *The Fifth Discipline* (New York: Doubleday, 1990), p. 17, introduces the notion of learning disabilities. Our usage is broader than learning.
2. This model is a synthesis of several influences. See also Henry Mintzberg, "Five P's of Strategy," *California Management Review*, Fall 1987; Bruce D. Henderson, *Henderson on Corporate Strategy* (Cambridge, MA: Abt Books, 1979); Bruce D. Henderson, "The Origin of Strategy," *Harvard Business Review* (November–December, 1989); Rosabeth Moss Kanter, "The New Managerial Work," *Harvard Business Review*, November–December, 1989); Charles Stubbart, "Why We Need a Revolution in Strategic Planning," *Long Range Planning*, Vol. 18, No. 6; Kevin P. Coyne, "Sustainable Competitive Advantage—What It Is, What It Isn't," *Business Horizons*,

January–February, 1986; R. T. Lenz, "Managing the Evolution of the Strategic Planning Process," *Business Horizons*, January–February 1987; and Gary Hamel and C. K. Prahalad, "Strategic Intent," *Harvard Business Review*, May–June 1989.

3. Arie de Geus, "Planning as Learning," *Harvard Business Review*, March–April, 1988.
4. George Gendron and Stephen D. Solomon, "The Art of Loving," *INC Magazine*, May 1989.

*Chapter 6: Structuring for Speed*

1. Ikujiro Nonaka, "Redundant, Overlapping Organization: A Japanese Approach to Managing the Innovation Process," *California Management Review*, Summer 1990, pp. 28, 35.
2. I am indebted to Jack Sherwood of Organizational Consultants, Inc., San Francisco, for helping me understand the role of power and politics in shifting to a team-based organization.
3. Robert H. Hayes, Steven C. Wheelwright, and Kim B. Clark, *Dynamic Manufacturing* (New York: The Free Press), p. 320. Used with permission.
4. The accepted use of structured multifunctional teams in knowledge work is relatively new. For further information, see Homa Bahrami and Stuart Evans, "Stratocracy in High-Technology Firms," *California Management Review*, Fall 1987; Donald C. Hambrick, "The Top Management Team," *California Management Review*, Fall 1987; William A. Pasmore, *Designing Effective Organizations* (New York: John Wiley & Sons, 1988); Steven Buchholz and Thomas Roth, *Creating the High Performance Team* (New York: John Wiley, 1987); Rosabeth Moss Kanter, "The New Managerial Work," *Harvard Business Review*, November–December, 1989; J. Richard Hackman and Greg R. Oldham, *Work Redesign* (Reading, MA: Addison-Wesley, 1980); and Warren G. Bennis, Kenneth D. Benne, and Robert Chin, *The Planning of Change* (New York: Holt, Rinehart and Winston, 1961, 1969).
5. Harold J. Leavitt, *Corporate Pathfinders* (New York: Penguin Books, 1986).
6. The concepts of early work, middle work, and ongoing work are based on *Team\Work*, a complete program for multifunctional team development available from Strategic Alignment Group, Inc., Portola Valley, CA, and Ross Partners, Encinitas, CA. For further information on team development, see Neely D. Gardner, *Group Leadership* (Washington, D.C.: National Training and Development Service Press, 1974) and W. R. Bion, *Experiences in Groups* (New York: Ballantine Books, 1959).

*Chapter 7: FCT Process Redesign*

1. "Picking Japan's Research Brains," *Fortune*, March 25, 1991, p. 88.
2. For further information on process mapping, see Geary A. Rummler and Alan P. Brache, *Improving Performance* (San Francisco: Jossey-Bass, 1990).

3. Ibid. Rummler describes maps of this type as "relationship" maps.
4. George Stalk, Jr., and Thomas M. Hout in *Competing Against Time* (New York: Free Press, 1990), p. 76.

## *Chapter 8: Tools and Tactics to Speed Product Development*

1. Bill Moon of Quantum Corporation created DFAT, based on the traditional "design, build, test" sequence, to "defat" product development.
2. Kim Clark, "What Strategy Can Do for Technology," *Harvard Business Review*, November–December 1989, p. 94.
3. R. Balachandra, Presentation at Case Western Reserve, 1989.
4. Carrie Gottlieb, "Intel's Plan for Staying on Top," *Fortune*, March 27, 1989, p. 99.
5. Alex Taylor III, "Why Toyota Keeps Getting Better and Better and Better," *Fortune*, November 19, 1990, p. 66.
6. James J. Mitchell, "Breakthroughs Alone Won't Do It," *San Jose Mercury News*, September 17, 1989, p. D1. For further information, see Ralph E. Gomory, "From the 'Ladder of Science' to the Product Development Cycle," *Harvard Business Review*, November–December, 1989.
7. Donald G. Reinertsen and Preston G. Smith, *Developing Products in Half the Time* (New York: Von Nostrand Reinhold, 1991), p. 43.
8. For further information on Quality Function Deployment, see John R. Hauser and Don Clausing, "The House of Quality," *Harvard Business Review*, May–June, 1988.
9. Kathleen M. Eisenhardt, "Speed and Strategic Choice: How Managers Accelerate Decision Making," *California Management Review*, Spring 1990, p. 41.
10. Donald G. Reinertsen and Preston G. Smith, *Developing Products in Half the Time* (New York: Von Nostrand Reinhold, 1991, p. 104).
11. For a broader discussion of prototyping, see Wheelwright and Clark, *Revolutionizing Product Development* (New York: Free Press, 1992).
12. Stereo lithography can produce small 3D objects in plastic based on a 3D computer model. It's a "printer" for small objects.
13. Wheelwright and Clark, *Revolutionizing Product Development*, p. 260.
14. *Fortune*, September 21, 1992, p. 103.
15. James P. Womack, Daniel T. Jones, and Daniel Roos, *The Machine That Changed the World* (New York: Rawson Associates, 1990).

## *Chapter 9: Implementation Dynamics and Measures*

1. Hewlett-Packard's model was presented by Marvin Patterson at the California Institute of Technology, 1989, and Quantum Corporation's was provided by Bill Moon.

2. For a detailed description, see Charles H. House and Raymond L. Price, "The Return Map: Tracking Product Teams," *Harvard Business Review*, January–February 1991, p. 92.

*Chapter 10: Leaders Pave the Road Ahead*

1. For further information on paradigm change, see Thomas S. Kuhn, *The Structure of Scientific Revolutions* (Chicago: University of Chicago Press, 1962, 1970).
2. Peter Senge, "Systems Dynamics and Leadership," International Electrical and Electronics Engineers 1980 International Conference on Cybernetics and Society, 1980, p. 4.
3. The basic change model was created by the staff of the Gestalt Institute of Cleveland, Organization and System Development Program, Cleveland, OH.

# Index

9 781416 57624